CW00821409

THE AGE OF
PANDEMICS

CHINMAY TUMBE

THE AGE OF
PANDEMICS
1817–1920

HOW THEY SHAPED
INDIA AND THE WORLD

HarperCollins *Publishers* India

First published in hardback in India by
HarperCollins *Publishers* in 2020
A-75, Sector 57, Noida, Uttar Pradesh 201301, India
www.harpercollins.co.in

2 4 6 8 10 9 7 5 3 1

Copyright © Chinmay Tumbe 2020

P-ISBN: 978-93-5357-945-6
E-ISBN: 978-93-5357-946-3

Typeset in 11.5/15.3 Dante MT Std at
Manipal Technologies Limited, Manipal

Printed and bound at
Replika Press Pvt. Ltd.

Contents

'Were there pandemics in the past as well?' asked Siddhartha, my eight-year-old son.

I paused nervously, registering the fact that the word 'pandemic' had entered his vocabulary at such a young age.

'Well, there was something known as influenza …,' I began. But before I could complete, he pulled out *Tintin and the Picaros* from his prized collection and opened page sixteen of the Egmont edition. Sure enough, a villainous army officer on that page laments the cancellation of Tintin's trip due to influenza in Europe.

Taken aback by the effortlessness with which he had spotted a word that I had assumed he would never know, I said nothing further, until he pressed on, and asked me, 'Go on, tell me more.'

A Timeline of the Age of Pandemics, 1817–1920

1817

Onset of Cholera Pandemic

1866

Third International Sanitary Conference held in Constantinople
(Istanbul)
(First two conferences were held in Paris in 1851 and 1859)

1894

Third Plague Pandemic
(Onset of first two being the sixth century CE and the
fourteenth century CE)

1918

Influenza Pandemic
(Milder prior outbreak in 1889)

Death toll estimates in millions

Pandemics	Period	World	India
Cholera	1817–1920	19	8
Plague	1894–1920	13	12
Influenza	1918–1920	40	20
Total	1817–1920	72	40

1

Pandemics of the Past

'Our dead are never dead to us until we have forgotten them'
– Mary Evans/George Eliot[1]

Once upon a time, we barely lived before we died. We would celebrate on average only twenty-five birthdays in our lifetimes and we rarely grew old enough to see our grandchildren. Mass mortality through war, famine, natural disasters and epidemics was a way of life. We began to live longer only when we fought fewer wars, understood how to prevent famines, grew resilient to natural disasters, and learnt how to control the spread of disease.

Different parts of the world began their journeys out of mass mortality at different times. In India, this journey began in 1920.[2] Between 1920 and 2020, death rates in India fell consistently from forty-five deaths per thousand people to seven deaths per thousand people. At birth, Indians can now expect to celebrate on average nearly seventy birthdays instead of only twenty-five, the norm before 1920.[3] It is an incredible achievement that stands in stark contrast to the remarkable century that preceded it.

Between 1817 and 1920, over 70 million people in the world died from pandemics, a figure far greater than the number of people killed by wars.[4] These pandemics were principally of three diseases—cholera, the plague and influenza—and India was at the epicentre of this mortality crisis, where over 40 million people perished.[5] Never heard about this? Perhaps it is because we had collectively forgotten about pandemics till the words 'COVID-19', 'lockdown' and 'social distancing' came into our consciousness.

Epidemics and Pandemics

One of the fundamental laws of mortality in the past century has been that over time, and especially as we get richer, we tend to die in smaller proportions from 'communicable' diseases.[6] In the US, the share of such diseases has fallen to under 10 per cent today and in India, it has fallen to less than 30 per cent.[7] The list of such communicable diseases is long and even seasoned medical practitioners routinely consult their books for diagnosis.

Malaria has been the deadliest communicable disease in history, transmitted to humankind through female *Anopheles* mosquitoes, for several millennia.[8] Those mosquito bites that you feel on your hands, those desperate claps to kill the buzzing irritation you hear, those stagnant water pools you see and smell with great dismay, provide a fulsome sensory experience even before getting the disease. I have vivid memories of open-air musical performances in my boarding school held in the evenings, less for the music and more for the organized mosquito-killing sprees we conducted through whispers and silent claps, with the sole objective of saving our hands and legs. We spared no singer, male or female, young or old, Hindustani or Carnatic; our attention was unabashedly directed towards the mosquitoes because the music, evidently, did not kill them.

If those mosquitoes successfully inject malaria-causing *Plasmodium* parasites into your bloodstream, then, depending on the level of your immunity, you could expect the first symptoms, common to many diseases—fevers, chills and headaches. Death by malaria was exceedingly common until the early twentieth century in much of the tropical world, and in places like India it formed the single most common cause of death. However, medical developments in the twentieth century drastically curtailed fatality rates. Today, around half the world is still at risk of getting malaria, around 230 million cases occur every year, but there are only 500,000 deaths worldwide, which is equivalent to what a small province of India would suffer annually in the nineteenth century.[9]

The medical knowledge of malaria and its transmission evolved over centuries, and several malarial *epidemics* have been noted at various times, but few would consider malaria to be a *pandemic*, even though it has affected many countries at the same time. What then distinguishes a disease from an epidemic, and an epidemic from a pandemic, or equivalently, for animals, an epizootic from a panzootic?

For a disease to become an epidemic, it must suddenly affect many members of a community at the same time. Time, that is, simultaneity, matters more than space, or geographic coverage. Simultaneity is often matched with seasonality, as many of us realize during our visits to the doctor's clinic when the seasons change. When that happens periodically and is localized, those diseases are considered to be *endemic* to the region. An endemic disease may or may not turn epidemic in a given year depending on the rate of transmission between human beings or that between vectors, like mosquitoes, and humans. Thus, while malaria is endemic in many parts of the world, it can quickly turn into an epidemic if disturbed environmental conditions in a year or in a particular time period lead to stagnant pools of water suitable for mosquito breeding.

But for an epidemic to become a *pandemic*, both time and space are equally important, that is, the disease has to spread across a sufficiently wide geographical region to be declared a pandemic. What constitutes as 'wide' has typically been a judgement call involving either countries or continents as the regional units. The use of the word 'pandemic' picked up only in the twentieth century; major outbreaks of diseases in the nineteenth century were routinely referred to as epidemics by observers of that time even though historians have now classified them as pandemics. An English-language dictionary in 1775 defined 'pandemic' as an adjective derived from Greek that meant 'incident to a whole people'.[10] The word was rarely used in the way it is used today, and 'pandemic love' was a phrase used to describe forms of vulgar love.[11] The corresponding word for pandemic in parts of north India, *mahamaari*, was used in the nineteenth century, though the word *maari* (referring to epidemics) was more in vogue.[12]

An early reference to the English word 'pandemic' in the medical sense was used, ironically, to disprove the existence of one in the context of an attack on quarantines and lockdowns. Benjamin Moseley (1742–1819), a physician and the author of *A Treatise on Tropical Diseases*, wrote the following in a chapter on the plague in a treatise on sugar in 1800:

'I never could discover that fevers are propagated by contagion. Were it possible so to be, I should have been long since dead. Quarantine, always expensive to commerce, and often ruinous to individuals, is a reflexion on the good sense of countries. No pestilential, or *pandemic* fever, was ever imported, or exported; and I have always considered the fumigating ship-letters, and shutting up the crews and passengers of vessels, on their arrival from foreign places, several weeks, for fear they should give diseases to others, which they have not themselves- as an ignorant, barbarous custom.'[13] (Emphasis added)

Many economists today would concur with this rare economic assessment undertaken by an epidemiologist but they would also disagree with his sense of epidemiology. It is worth pointing out that when Moseley wrote his book in 1800, it was possible to deny the existence of contagious diseases and abuse quarantines. Moseley would have found it hard to maintain such a position a century later.

This is because the transmission of diseases across wide areas intensified in the nineteenth and twentieth centuries through revolutions in the means of transport and communication, making the word 'pandemic' more frequent in medical circles. A recent dictionary of epidemiology defines it as 'an epidemic occurring worldwide, or over a very wide area, crossing international boundaries and usually affecting a large number of people'.[14] The key theme is 'simultaneous worldwide transmission', not severity, and pandemics are declared by the World Health Organization (WHO) in *anticipation* of severity.[15]

Malaria, therefore, is unlikely to become a pandemic, even though it affects many people in many countries, because there is little evidence of transmission of the disease from one place to another and the affected regions are usually those where malaria is endemic. Unsurprisingly, diseases that can be transmitted directly from one human to another tend to spread more rapidly than vector-borne diseases such as malaria and are more likely to become pandemics. Influenza, better known as the 'flu', is the classic contagious disease that exhibits seasonality but can also easily turn into a pandemic.

Dropping severity from the definition, however, puts the spotlight on WHO when pandemics are declared. In 2009, the H1N1 influenza pandemic was declared as such by WHO, but eventually it turned out to be as mild as the seasonal flu.[16] The declaration of the pandemic was then questioned, as were the links between WHO advisors and pharmaceutical industries which stood to benefit from vaccination orders.[17] Whether to declare a pandemic or not is therefore not as simple as it may appear, as it is closely tied with international relations, trade and business.

From a historical viewpoint, though, pandemics are inextricably linked with the notion of severity because in the absence of global data collection systems, mild pandemics would never be recorded. What we observe across the centuries are instances in which one or two or several continents were simultaneously affected by the same disease through some means of transmission, due to which mortality increased substantially. Before the late fifteenth century, 'worldwide' disease transmission was almost impossible to establish as the knowledge of the American worlds was practically unknown to the others and vice versa. Our consideration of pandemics in history therefore uses the simple definition of at least two continents being affected by mass mortality through the simultaneous transmission of a disease. Those pandemics left their marks not necessarily in statistical registries, but in literature, art and culture, on tombstones and even *inside* the occasional tomb.

Pandemics before 1817

If one looks hard enough, one can find the concern with disease and epidemics expressed in numerous texts, medical doctrines and holy scriptures from the ancient world. To quote one example, here are translated extracts from different sections of Kautilya's *Arthashastra*, an ancient Indian treatise on statecraft compiled at least eighteen centuries ago:

> Calamities due to acts of God are fire, floods, diseases and epidemics and famine.
>
> Other calamities of divine origin are rats, wild animals, snakes and evil spirits. It is the duty of the king to protect the people from all these calamities.

Whenever danger threatens, the king shall protect all those afflicted like a father and shall organize continuous prayers with oblations.[18]

But in ancient texts and holy scriptures, including in the *Arthashastra*, epidemics tended to receive less attention than war, natural disasters and famines, the other reasons for mass mortality. One explanation for this relative inattention could be a lack of dramatic impact. Death in epidemics often came silently, without the destruction of buildings, the plundering of cities, the devastation of earthquakes, the havoc of floods or the tragic desiccation of fields due to lack of rain. Epidemics might have been under-reported in history simply because they were not glamourous enough to be noted; those which were reported were epidemics that left clearly identifiable marks on the body.

Among the few known epidemics that grew to become pandemics on account of affecting at least two continents simultaneously, one disease stands out prominently—the plague. If malaria and the mosquito are the historical torchbearers for epidemics, the plague and rats are those for pandemics. Historians have identified three clearly discernible episodes of pandemic plagues that started in the sixth, fourteenth and nineteenth centuries, respectively. The evidence so far suggests that Europe was most affected in the first two plague pandemics while Asia was affected more in the third.[19] All three are generally considered to be plagues of the bubonic variety, referring to the bubo or swollen lymph node caused by the disease, typically around the groin or armpits. This striking visual element of the disease has been useful for historians in identifying it, compared to other types of plague that can be septicaemic (involving blood clotting) or pneumonic (involving lung infections).

Since the discovery of the plague-causing bacterium in 1894, medical knowledge about the plague has grown tremendously. We now know that it is caused by the bacterium *Yersinia pestis*, named after Alexandre Yersin (1863–1943), a Swiss physician who made the discovery in Hong Kong, a key city affected in the third plague pandemic. The plague bacterium could well have been named *Kitasato pestis* as Yersin and Kitasato Shibasaburo (1853–1931), a Japanese physician, competed in a 'rat race', as it were, to discover the root cause of the plague. Yersin's analysis was found to be more comprehensive, though Kitasato had published the results first.[20]

A theory soon developed of plague transmission from rats to rat fleas to humans via flea bites, though research has also suggested other rodents and animals as vectors, and that rodents themselves are not necessary for the transmission. While bubonic and septicaemic plagues generally spread through the rat-flea-human transmission path, pneumonic plague can spread through human-to-human transmission via infection-laden droplets.

The first plague pandemic

The first plague pandemic, recorded in the sixth century, is referred to as the 'Justinianic' plague. It occurred during the reign of Emperor Justinian I of the Byzantine Empire around 540–550 CE.[21] The descriptions of the disease in those times suggest that it was bubonic. Procopius, a historian of that period, identified the trading centre of Pelusium in Egypt as the point of origin from where the disease spread to Alexandria, and further on to Palestine. A traveller's record of that time mentions the depletion of the population of a town 'with (only) seven men and one little boy ten years old remaining in it'.[22] By 542 CE, the plague reached the capital city of Constantinople, and by one account, even managed to infect the emperor. The plague then moved to Italy and Spain, reaching as far as the British Isles.

The demographic devastation in the Mediterranean world was stark, with records in multiple languages describing how thousands of people died in a single day or how, as per one traveller, corpses were 'lying in the fields and along the roadside, and cattle wandering untended into the hills'.[23] Here is Procopius on the inability to keep pace in digging new burial sites, a common theme in all lethal pandemics:

> [T]hose who were making these trenches, no longer able to keep up with the number of dying, mounted the towers of the fortifications in Sycae (Galata) and tearing off the roofs, threw the bodies in there in complete disorder.[24]

The plague did not immediately lead to the fall of the Byzantine Empire but the depopulation of rural and urban areas and the desertification of farmland is said to have created a fiscal crisis, with the emperor also lamenting the high wage expectations of the diminished workforce.[25] A few decades later, there would be mutiny against a cut in military expenditure, a civil war and a Persian invasion.

The global population in the sixth century has been placed at around 250 million and the largest mortality estimates of the first plague pandemic, hazy as they are, run into a few tens of millions, mostly in Europe.[26] Thus, this pandemic may have killed around 10 per cent of human beings in the world at that time, though this figure would be higher for Europe, ranging from 25 to 50 per cent. Its impact on Asia, home to around 70 per cent of the global population at that time, is largely unknown. It is quite plausible, based on current evidence, that the impact was marginal.

The second plague pandemic

The plague reappeared sporadically over the next few centuries but came back with a vengeance in the fourteenth century. Between 1346 and 1353 CE, the second plague pandemic ravaged Europe, northern

Africa and West Asia—an episode dubbed 'Black Death'. The colour in this title refers to the colour of the bubo that the plague causes, though given the high mortality rate in Europe, 'White Death' would have been equally appropriate. It was also called the 'Great Mortality', 'Great Pestilence' and 'Universal Plague' by contemporaries.[27] This plague pandemic has been better studied than the first and is said to have had consequences that are open to debate, such as laying the foundation for the rise of Europe, the Renaissance movement, the Protestant Reformation and even accelerating anti-Semitism. Not surprisingly, the history of pandemics has focussed disproportionately on this particular episode given its Eurocentricity and purported long-term consequences. Curiously enough, the source of this plague is attributed to East Asia, despite little evidence to that effect.

In a classic study titled 'Plagues and Peoples' in 1976, William McNeill had argued that plague reservoirs in wild rodents existed in three key locations of the world: the Himalayan foothills between India and China, a region near the Great Lakes in central Africa and the Eurasian steppe region from central Asia to China.[28] The second plague pandemic arose, in McNeill's reconstruction, when the Mongols' expansionist empire connected north-eastern China, where an epidemic broke out in 1331 CE, all the way to Europe via the shores of the Black Sea. However, evidence of the plague occurring in China or India in the fourteenth century has recently been shown to be very weak. Thus, the exact origins of the second plague pandemic are still unclear.[29]

The plague appeared in Crimea in 1346–47 and reached Constantinople soon after. From there, it surged through the Mediterranean world and by 1348, reached Spain, France and southern England.[30] In 1349–50, it devastated northern France, the British Isles, Germany and the Scandinavian region. It then crept up to Russia, touching Moscow in 1353. It moved like a wave, spreading

over an average of five to six months in one place. Winters were
generally safer as the bubonic plague then seems to have flourished
in warmer climates. The pandemic affected both rural and urban
areas, killed people across classes though more among the poor, and
spread throughout Europe in a very short time. This characteristic
and the apparent absence of rodent-related observations have led to
speculation over the exact mechanism of transmission.

Port towns seemed to receive the disease first, suggesting that
it travelled faster by sea than by land; some remote areas in the
Balkans were spared entirely. Infected rodents on ships could have
transported the disease but fleas could survive even without rodents
and be transported in clothing. Incidents of pneumonic plague
in pockets also suggest airborne transmission. Overall, death in
Europe was widespread, and the impact, seen as a share of the
population, was possibly higher than in the first plague pandemic.
Up to 50 million people could have died, representing 35 to 60 per
cent of Europe and the Mediterranean world, and 10 to 20 per cent
of the global population at the time.[31]

The experience of the pandemic was unprecedented for those
who lived through it, since the last recorded plague had occurred
in the eighth century. Instant flight to relatively safer zones was
the most common reaction. Christian and Islamic religious leaders
organized events to pray for the pandemic to end, and some
marked it as an apocalypse.[32] Jews emerged as scapegoats in Aragon,
Provence, Catalonia, Switzerland, Rhineland and southern Germany,
accused by Christians of spreading the plague by poisoning wells, as
the exact cause of the plague was not known at that time. Despite
the Pope's intervention, violence ensued and property was destroyed
or confiscated.

The medical fraternity tried in vain to provide cures. Steeped in
the medical traditions of Hippocrates and Galen and the 'miasma'
theory of diseases, which attributed causes to impure air, corpse

decay and even astrological events, it found the plague to be a formidable disease to fight against in the fourteenth century. Large-scale public health measures were taken more readily in parts of Europe than in the Middle East, with Italy taking the lead in passing sanitation and burial legislations and travel and cloth-trade regulations. Public assemblies were also curtailed, and at least one city, Milan, which forcefully implemented these measures, rode the plague wave better than others.[33] Economic compulsions of keeping infection rates low and trading channels open drove several of these efforts in Italy. These measures in the fourteenth century were critical in shaping European public health organizations in later centuries.

The short-term effects of the pandemic were costly in human lives, in economic damage through trade disruption, in the psychological impact on survivors, and in the resources expended to contain it. Solidarity and trust also suffered. As observed and fictionalized by the Italian writer Boccaccio during the pandemic, 'One citizen fled after another, and one neighbour had not any care of another. Parents nor kindred never visiting them, but utterly they were forsaken on all sides.'[34]

The legacies of the second plague pandemic also varied across regions. In relatively underpopulated Spain and in eastern Europe, the pandemic may have further worsened the position of labour as the smaller workforce could not make the most of existing natural resources.[35] In Italy, wealth inequality declined in the aftermath as real wages rose due to substantial labour scarcity. In northern Europe, the labour shortage may have led more women to join the labour market and thus fundamentally change demographic behaviour.

The second plague pandemic was at the peak of its severity between 1346 and 1353 CE but also covered a wider cycle of localized plague outbreaks that stretched on into the early nineteenth century. Many cities in France and Italy were affected from 1628 to 1631 and London was severely affected in 1665–66, first by the plague and then by a fire. The plague in Marseilles in 1720 was the last major plague outbreak in western Europe. Mortality rates in these subsequent outbreaks were lower than in the fourteenth century and disproportionately affected the poor since they lived in densely populated, unsanitary areas and had limited access to treatment. The selection of victims meant that the plague also began to be seen as a way to check population growth. As one seventeenth-century friar battling the plague in Genoa in 1656–57 noted,

> What would the world be, if God did not sometimes touch it with plague? How could he feed so many people? ... Contagion is the effect of divine providence, for the good governance of the universe.[36]

Pandemics from new encounters

When Christopher Columbus sailed to the Caribbean islands in 1492 CE and inaugurated a 'New World' for Europe to discover and exploit, he inadvertently set in motion a remarkable pandemic. Known as the 'Columbian Exchange', the European colonization of the American world carried new goods and animals across the Atlantic Ocean but also circulated new diseases.[37] Syphilis, the sexually transmitted disease, is likely to have entered Europe from the American world and travelled from Europe to Asia and Africa, tormenting many generations. But more devastatingly, the Americas began to grapple with diseases from Europe, Asia and Africa, against which the native population had little immunity.

Among such diseases brought to the Americas, smallpox was the deadliest. Today's generation may not remember smallpox, as the last infectious case was registered in the 1970s. The virus (*Variola major* and *Variola minor*) has been successfully eradicated from general circulation and is now preserved only in laboratories. Transmitted through airborne droplets, it had an incubation period of around twelve days, after which the body would show symptoms like high fever, body aches and rashes, followed by pimples turning into pustules.[38] For survivors, those pustules would erupt, dry and crust and the scabs would fall off three or four weeks after the onset of the disease, leaving marks on the skin. In fact, perhaps the earliest evidence of smallpox comes from marks preserved on the body of the mummy of the ancient Egyptian Pharaoh Ramses V, who reigned during the twelfth century BCE.[39] Blindness and male infertility were only some of the potential side effects of smallpox. But if you did not die from it, you did get lasting immunity against it. That is why an old saying in India, common in the nineteenth century, was that children were not counted as permanent members of the family until they had encountered smallpox once and survived.[40]

Smallpox was widely prevalent in the non-American world. It broke out as an epidemic at least once, if not twice, in the first millennium CE and wreaked havoc in the Roman Empire. A ninth-century treatise, *The Treatise on Smallpox and Measles*, by a Baghdadi physician named Rhazes, outlined the disease's characteristics in great detail.[41] In India, Goddess Sitala came to be revered for her power to spark or curtail smallpox, and the disease was well-known in China as well. Between the sixteenth and eighteenth centuries, it affected Europe substantially, with records indicating that the disease was responsible for 10 to 15 per cent of all deaths annually in a few countries in the eighteenth century, the victims being mostly children under the age of ten.[42] It is in this period, roughly after 1519 CE, that the disease landed in the Americas.

Tribe after tribe, society after society, whether in the West Indies or in Mexico or further south in the Incan Empire or north towards Canada, perished in staggering numbers. While researchers have found it difficult to distinguish between mortality by war and mortality by disease, the native American experience was nothing short of a demographic catastrophe. Because the disease was transmitted from Europe and because it was raging simultaneously in Europe and the American world for much of the sixteenth and seventeenth centuries, this episode may be categorized as a pandemic. By some estimates, the population of the American world shrank by 80 to 90 per cent—a far greater impact than what Europe suffered during the second plague pandemic.[43] This mortality was around 2 per cent of the global population of that time. In the late eighteenth century, a similar wipeout took place in Australia and other Oceanic regions when Europeans reached those shores, though on a much smaller population base than in the Americas.

An early form of vaccination, known as inoculation or variolation, involved some measures to protect oneself against smallpox. These practices had long been known in Asia and Africa and were eventually also adopted in Europe and by non-native American folk in the eighteenth century. This included rubbing a part of the scab into one's skin or blowing it up the nose so as to contract a mild infection that granted lasting immunity.[44] Edward Jenner (1749–1823), an English variolator, perfected a vaccination procedure using cowpox matter (*vacca* means cow in Latin) in the 1790s that proved to be a superior technique and was adopted around the world in the nineteenth century, but not without controversy. Hindus in India, who worship the cow, were hostile to the idea of using bovine material in vaccination and the arm-based injection method was also unpopular.[45] However, the initial hostility decreased, presumably after seeing the effects, and smallpox-related mortality started to fall rapidly.

To sum up, based on the evidence available today, the first and second plague pandemics and the pandemic from the new encounters barely touched Asia, in relative terms. This historical asymmetry was to change in the nineteenth and early twentieth centuries, when pandemics corresponding to three different diseases would ravage many parts of Asia and other territories. These pandemics had one thing in common and that is the country with the highest mortality. Good luck would finally run out in the land of karmic beliefs, and it would be India's turn to be affected in a new century of pandemics.

The Age of Pandemics, 1817–1920: Cholera, the Plague and Influenza

The Age of Pandemics saw cholera break out in recurring bouts and on a wider scale from 1817 onwards, the plague wreak havoc from the end of the nineteenth century, and reached its crescendo with the influenza pandemic of 1918–20. Cholera was endemic in India but a new strain seems to have appeared in 1817 that gradually moved out of the country and overwhelmed the world. In western Europe and the Americas, the impact was felt acutely between the 1830s and 1860s, but in Russia and Egypt the impact was felt throughout the nineteenth century. Around 20 million died worldwide in the cholera pandemic until 1920. Its impact was lesser after 1920 because techniques on both, prevention and cure, improved dramatically in the twentieth century.

The third plague pandemic in history began in China in the late nineteenth century. It broke out in Hong Kong in 1894 and arrived in Bombay in 1896, most likely via ships, before becoming endemic in many parts of western and northern India. It also circulated across leading ports and some hinterlands of the world. The plague had tapered out by 1920, though it continued to break out in a few places for a while afterwards. Until 1920, it had claimed around 13 million lives, 12 million in India alone. Unlike cholera and the plague, the influenza pandemic was far more global in distribution. It was also shorter-lived, lasting for only a few months in most countries, with the peak occurring between September and December 1918. The influenza pandemic of 1918–20 is considered to be the deadliest pandemic in history, wiping out over 40 million people.[46] Again, the

Indian subcontinent was affected most severely as 20 million people died in the span of a few months, making it the worst demographic disaster ever to fall upon a region in such a short period of time.[47]

This book is about these pandemics between 1817 and 1920, which are unique for their wide geographical coverage and high mortality impact, especially in places previously unaffected by other major pandemics. The book is centred on India because India was at the epicentre of mass mortality in all these episodes. In contrast to the several volumes written on pandemics before 1817, this period has so far attracted scant attention outside the limited world of medical historians. The reason for this neglect is not surprising: this period overlaps with a period of tremendous significance in history, known in Eric Hobsbawm's classic series as the 'Age of Revolution, 1789–1848', the 'Age of Capital, 1848–1875', the 'Age of Empire, 1875–1914', and in Christopher Bayly's seminal work as 'The Birth of the Modern World, 1780–1914'.[48]

In economic history, this is a period of the 'Great Divergence', when western Europe and North America marched ahead of China, India and the rest of the world in economic terms.[49] This is also a period of globalization and mass migration, both of which picked up pace in the late nineteenth century and peaked at the onset of World War I in 1914. And yet, chronicles of empire, economic advancement and globalization tend to downplay or omit the significance of pandemics in this period, presumably because Europe was not as adversely affected as in the past.[50]

To put it simply, it would be impossible to write the global history of the fourteenth century without mentioning the plague or, for that matter, to write the history of the twentieth century without mentioning the two world wars. And yet, the Age of Pandemics that this book describes has curiously been forgotten, even though the pandemics of this period collectively killed an equivalent number of people or more.

Together, the pandemics claimed over 70 million lives (40 million in India) between 1817 and 1920, which is about the same as the battle casualties of the two world wars of the twentieth century.[51] And because these deaths were concentrated in Asia, it contributed to the stunning decline in Asia's share in global population from 65 per cent around 1817 to close to 50 per cent in 1920. This is important to note because the vast literature on the 'Great Divergence' shows that in the same period Asia's contribution to global economic output fell from over 50 per cent to close to 20 per cent on account of the 'rise of the west'.[52] And yet, Asia's falling share in global population has not attracted equal attention. The unequal geographical distribution of mortality in the Age of Pandemics was certainly one factor which caused this phenomenon.

After 1920, the world rarely witnessed severe pandemics. The influenza pandemics of 1957–58 and 1968 killed less than 3 million, mostly in Asia, while the 2009–10 H1N1 influenza pandemic killed even fewer. The SARS (Severe Acute Respiratory Syndrome) 2002–04 outbreak caused a major scare, especially in Hong Kong and China but the number of infected people ran into only a few thousands. A similar case is observed for the Ebola virus in west Africa in recent years. The deadliest pandemic since 1920 has been that of HIV–AIDS (Human Immunodeficiency Virus–Acquired Immunodeficiency Syndrome), moving slowly through populations to claim over 30 million lives since it was first recorded in the 1980s. The HIV pandemic spread widely but had its biggest impact on sub-Saharan Africa.

Between 1920 and 2019, around 40 million deaths can be attributed to pandemics but in the same period the population of the world has also grown enormously, from under 2 billion to over 7 billion. Pandemic deaths of the past century, therefore, comprised around 1 or 2 per cent of the global population in this period. In contrast, this figure was over 5 per cent for the Age of Pandemics between 1817 and 1920. And this figure was never so high for any other century in recorded history, barring perhaps the sixth and the fourteenth.

The historical amnesia about the Age of Pandemics in Europe and North America is understandable as mortality rates were relatively lower there, though COVID-19 is reviving interest in the events of 1918–20, the most recent lethal pandemic to affect those regions. The memory loss in Asia is harder to understand, more so in India, the country most affected by the pandemic age. This was brought home to me starkly at the beginning of the COVID-19 outbreak in early 2020, when social media was rife with misinformation, attacking China as the source of all pandemics in history, applauding the wholesome diets and vegetarianism in India as a traditional bulwark against pandemics and more generally lauding the nation for never having been the originator of pandemics.

In early March 2020, there were articles written on how Indians were not affected in recent influenza pandemics and that there was no need to overreact to COVID-19. Public conversation was filled with boasts about the special nature of Indian immunity against diseases contracted from growing up in unclean environments, and that the West was susceptible to pandemics *because* they did not develop immunity due to childhoods spent in clean environments!

It was as if the Age of Pandemics that devastated India for a century had been wiped clean from people's collective memory. The nineteenth and early twentieth centuries in Indian history are known for the rise and fall of British colonial rule, not for pandemics. This book hopes to change this narrative. And, as we will see, these pandemics were important events that served as springboards for the resistance towards colonial rule and therefore had a significant impact on the history of India.

But the Age of Pandemics did not shape only India. It also shaped the world. The quest to control the pandemics transformed medical science. Public health systems were revolutionized, cutting down mortality in some parts of the world and laying the foundations for it to happen after 1920 in the other parts. The health surveillance system that started with a series of conferences to control pandemics from 1851 ultimately led to the formation of the WHO in 1948. And as each of the chapters of this book will attest to, the Age of Pandemics had social, economic and political ramifications.

2

Cholera

'Bahut bade doctor miya Haiza ki soorat dekhte hain to unki rooh
kaanp uthti hai'
(Even distinguished doctors tremble with fear when they see Cholera
[haiza])

– Hakim Saiyad Amaldar Hussain in India, 1883[1]

A walk around the graves at the South Park Street Cemetery in
Kolkata makes for an offbeat outing in a city with multiple
tourist attractions. Established in 1767 and known as 'The Great
Cemetery', it is today a charming place with distinctive tombstones
and obelisks, curious epitaphs, thick foliage and lovers seeking
privacy in one of the most densely populated cities in the world. It
is also immortalized as the site of the action in *Gorosthaney Sabdhan*
(The Secret of the Cemetery) from Satyajit Ray's detective series
featuring Feluda.

The identities of those buried here are, of course, no secret. They
were mostly Europeans living in the late eighteenth and nineteenth
centuries in what was then Calcutta, at a time when the English East

India Company, and later the British government, administered the city. A glance at the epitaphs discloses professions such as 'surgeon', 'translator' and 'schoolteacher', even 'breeder of cattle', but the real secrets of the cemetery unfold through a statistical analysis of the burial records, available as a slim book at the entrance counter.[2] This shows that the median age of the 2,000-plus who are buried here was only twenty-nine. Of them, 40 per cent were female and 20 per cent under the age of ten, a feature less easily recognizable while walking around the graves. It also shows that in a particular year, burials that had averaged twenty every year for decades suddenly doubled to over forty and stayed similarly high for the next few decades as well.[3]

The year that marked this tragic shift was 1817, the beginning of a great cholera pandemic that would sweep the world in the nineteenth and early twentieth centuries. The cholera pandemic would reshape commerce and pilgrimage through quarantine regulations, spark global cooperative efforts in the form of periodic sanitation conferences, trigger riots and revolts, generate legendary medical controversies and scientific breakthroughs, haunt cities such as Calcutta, Cairo, London and New York, dampen the euphoric mood of western Europe's industrial revolution and even, mysteriously, become associated with the circulation of chapatis. By the late nineteenth century, the cholera pandemic was so widespread that it could be identified as a defining period, inspiring the novelist Gabriel García Márquez in 1985 to title his book, set in the South American past, as *El amor en los tiempos del cólera* or *Love in the Time of Cholera*.

Cholera Strikes, 1817–1823

The year 1817 was otherwise a relatively ordinary one in global history. There were around 1 billion human beings on the planet, nearly two-thirds of whom lived in Asia—around 200 million in

India and close to 400 million in China.[4] In Europe, the Napoleonic Wars had just ended two years before, by which time Britain had emerged as the undisputed supreme naval power in the world.[5] Much of Africa had not yet been colonized by European nations. Slave trade persisted in certain pockets, despite mounting pressure from those seeking to abolish the system. The Russian Empire under Tsar Alexander I had just scored a famous victory against Napoleon in 1812; the long-running Ottoman Empire was struggling to hold on to its territories; Muhammad Ali Pasha was earning respect for his military accomplishments in Egypt. The Qing dynasty ruled in China, the Saud dynasty in Arabia and the Qajar dynasty in Persia.

The English East India Company ruled less than a third of the land mass of the Indian subcontinent, and was mostly confined to the east and the south. It had lost its monopoly over trade with India in 1813 but had profited vastly from the opium trade with China in return for tea. The cities of Calcutta, Bombay and Madras were key sites of commerce and the Company also raised land revenue from the places it governed directly in the hinterland. The Maratha Empire administered large tracts of India and the Nizam-ruled Hyderabad state was another formidable power in the south. On the other side of the planet, the clarion call for freedom reverberated in South America. The United States was in its forty-first year of independence and had a small population of 10 million, a figure smaller than the population of Kolkata today.[6] (That year, two brothers in the US started a publishing house, Harper Brothers, whose later avatar would publish a book on pandemics in 2020.)

The most important event of 1817, then, in hindsight, would not be related to business or politics, but to the outbreak of a disease—also what 2020 is likely to be remembered for in the future. The cholera outbreak began in Bengal in eastern India, owing to a likely mutation of certain bacteria, much later named *Cholerae vibrio*. Its key disease-causing symptoms—a diarrhoea with rice-water stool, vomiting, dehydration, sunken eyes and changes in the colour of the skin, often to blue—had almost certainly been noted before 1817 in India and in other parts of the world. [7] Historically, since bile was a common humoral element in the Hippocratic tradition of medicine in Europe and in Ayurvedic practice based on the texts of Sushruta and Charaka in ancient India, various interpretations have been drawn on the existence of cholera in the world. [8] *Vishuchika*, in Ayurvedic traditions, is now considered to mean 'cholera-like' while Arabic references used *haiza* or similar sounding words to describe the disease, which stuck on in Unani medicinal practices in India. [9]

A clearer reference to an epidemic known as *moryxy*, marked by crippling stomach pains and mass mortality with cholera-like symptoms, emerges in 1543 CE in Portuguese-ruled Goa. [10] Every burial was accompanied by the ringing of the church bell but as the death count increased, this practice had to be banned by the governor, Martim Afonso de Sousa, to calm the citizens. When patients died in hospital, the orders were to open up the corpse for examination, but all they found were shrunken stomachs. Steeped in Hippocratic and Christian traditions of that time, climatic factors and demons were held responsible for the epidemic. A few decades later, the physician Garcia da Orta added eating disorders and excessive 'conversation with women' to this list of causes. [11]

More mentions of cholera-like diseases followed and by the eighteenth century the French in India were referring to the disease as *mort-de-chien* (dog's death), a corruption of *mordexim*, used by the Portuguese, which in turn is likely to have been derived from the Konkani verb *moixi*, which means to fall. [12] Military and pilgrim sites were noted to be worst affected by the disease, and would later emerge as major centres in the nineteenth century. For instance, a reference appears to cholera affecting the invading army of Ahmad

Shah Durrani, the ruler of Afghanistan, in 1757, close to the holy
city of Vrindavan in north India.[13] The army was forced to retreat
due to the epidemic.

In 1783, the pilgrimage centre of Haridwar on the banks of the
Ganga in north India, which attracted crowds in the hundreds
of thousands, if not millions, suffered a cholera outbreak that
killed around 20,000 people.[14] Then, in 1813, James Johnson, a
physician, devoted an entire chapter in his book on diseases in
tropical climates to *Cholera Morbus*, as it was then being called by
the British.[15] He argued that the bile secretions should not be seen
as the cause but as a symptom of the disease and that the cure
should focus on 'the early restoration of balance in the circulation',
which was remarkably prophetic for that time.[16] The greatest cure
for cholera, and indeed, against other diarrhoeic diseases, would
be invented only in the middle of the twentieth century as Oral
Rehydration Therapy (ORT), and involve salts, sugars and fluids
to restore balance in circulation. Johnson's recommendations for
therapy, instead, focussed on the prevailing practice of a dosage
of opium and calomel (mercurous chloride) to allay 'the orgasm
of the stomach and bowels'.[17]

The British medical system at this stage did not confer substantial
advantages over what was being offered by the vaids and hakims
practising Ayurvedic and Unani medical traditions, respectively. In
fact, the British themselves had it as tough as the Indians when it
came to surviving diseases in India. According to the historian David
Gilmour, in his book *The British in India*:

> In 1805 one visitor reported that he had twice lunched with men
> whose burials he had been invited to attend before supper that
> same day. When an epidemic arrived at a station, people began
> measuring their lives in hours: they went to the Club 'each

evening apprehensive to know who was missing from the night
before'. Death was so familiar to the British in India, so quick and
so frequent, that there hardly seemed room for prolonged grief.
If an officer died on campaign, his belongings were auctioned as
soon as the funeral was over: horses, clothes, revolver, even his
cooking-pot and his water-bottle.[18]

Leonard Roger's sketch of the cholera outbreak in India, 1817–1819

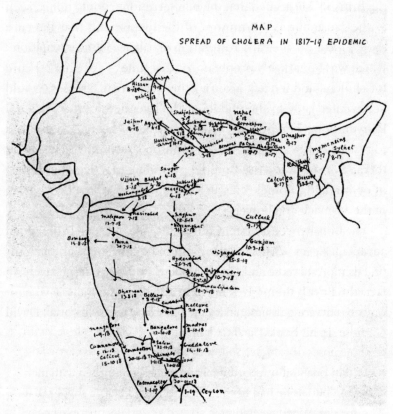

Numbers marked on the map refer to the dates of cholera outbreak.
Source: Leonard Rogers, 'The Forecasting and Control of Cholera
Epidemics in India', *Journal of the Royal Society of Arts*, 75 (3874) (1927): 323.

The cholera of 1817 came amid this background of high mortality caused by other infectious diseases such as malaria, and was still noted for its lethality and virulence. The official report of the Medical Board of Bengal in 1820 pointed out that the disease was 'quite new' when it appeared in 1817.[19] While the officials blamed it on fluctuations of weather in 1816 and 1817, this was most likely a new strain of cholera, just as another strain was identified in the late twentieth century, which quickly became the dominant strain in the world, albeit with a milder impact than the one before it.[20]

Much of what we now know about cholera in the nineteenth century is due to detailed medical reports prepared by numerous physicians and government officials, especially in India and Europe.[21] Despite their many scientific errors, as later research would show, those reports were valuable in identifying outbreaks and understanding how officials responded to medical crises. An early announcement of the first of many explosive cholera outbreaks came by way of a letter dated 23 August 1817 from Dr Tytler, a civil surgeon at Jessore in Bengal, who wrote the following to the district judge:

> An epidemic has broken out in the bazaar, the disorder commencing with pain or uneasiness in different parts of the body, presently succeeded by giddiness of the head, sickness, vomiting, griping in the belly, and frequent stools. The countenance exhibits anxiety, the body becomes emaciated, the pulse rapidly shrinks, and the patient, if not speedily relieved with large doses of calomel, followed by one of opium, is carried off within four and twenty hours.[22]

The first reaction in Jessore (a centre of indigo processing), as in other towns of the region, was a mass exodus as people fled in panic.[23] By September, reports of a major cholera outbreak were pouring in from various parts of the Bengal province, a region comprising much of modern-day Bangladesh, West Bengal, Bihar, Jharkhand and coastal Odisha. The epidemic struck during the prelude to the Third Anglo-Maratha War and caught the English forces unawares. The governor general, Francis Rawdon-Hastings (1754–1826), was camping in Bundelkhand in November 1817 in a bid to oust the Pindaris, powerful mercenaries operating in central India under Maratha patronage. Cholera ripped through his camp, killing hundreds by the week. Hastings's diary entry for 14 November reads as follows:

> Ninety-seven deaths are reported to me as having occurred during yesterday forenoon. There is an opinion that the water of the tanks, the only water which we have at this place, may be unwholesome and add to the disease; therefore I march to-morrow, so as to make the Pohooj river, though I must provide carriage for above 1,000 sick.[24]

The association of cholera with water stood him in good stead as he survived the ordeal, won the war, obtained a greater part of western India and continued as governor general till 1823. In 1817–18, cholera devasted the countryside of Bundelkhand and hit most parts of the subcontinent, claiming many more lives than the war. Cholera reportedly killed 10,000 in Allahabad in March 1818, though curiously, not one of the 700 prisoners in that city suffered from the disease.[25] In Calcutta, it was not just the South Park Street Cemetery that reported a spike in deaths. The number of deaths attributed to 'Cholera Morbus' recorded at the Kashee Mittens Ghat crematory ground for Hindus rose from a couple of hundred in 1815 and 1816 to over 1,000 in 1817 and nearly 3,000 in 1818, before dropping to a little under 1,000 in 1819.[26] In 1818, over half of all deaths at the Ghat were attributed to cholera.

Epidemics provoked desperate prayers and the reigning deity for cholera in Bengal was Ola Bibi, just as Sitala was for smallpox. Temples to the goddess had been springing up even before 1817, but the events of that year led to a huge demand for the worship of Ola Bibi, much to the dismay of priests at other temples.[27] A publicity drive by the priests of the Kali temple at Kalighat, emphasizing the protection provided to all those who came to that temple, was met enthusiastically with the theatrics of Ola Bibi devotees.[28] In Bundelkhand, Hurdoul Lala became the cholera deity; the disease was blamed on Hastings's British soldiers who sinned when they killed cows to feed themselves in the sacred grove of Lala, a former king's son.[29] While Hurdoul Lala was worshipped earlier for different reasons, the connection with cholera after 1817 led to his soaring popularity extending, by some accounts, from Calcutta to Lahore.[30]

In villages, religious processions were common to ward off the evil spirit of cholera, though as one traveller observed in the Narmada Valley in central India, there could be fights between those who wanted a silent procession and those who preferred noise.[31] One Sanskrit scholar from that region mused that there were three types of disease in the world—for sins committed in past lives, for sins of the current life and for accidental sins—and that an epidemic like cholera came under the second category.[32] In the Konkan region on the west coast, 'witches' and 'sorcerers' were blamed for cholera and attacked by the villagers.[33]

Despite these views, the native physicians, vaids and hakims, did command respect and were enlisted by the British in relief efforts. The cures offered could be a mixture of various medical traditions.[34] The vaids prescribed black pepper, ginger, cloves and that most beloved Indian ingredient, *heeng* or asafoetida.[35] In Madras in south India, physicians practising Ayurveda, Unani and Siddha (native to the region) assisted the government.[36] And where the cures seemed to be effective, it won the appreciation of the locals, irrespective of who the ruling class was, the British or the local royals.[37] Raja Serfoji II of Tanjore even established a *chattram* or charitable institution, with a public hospital for men and another for women built in 1802–03 along the Rameswaram pilgrimage route in south India, which saved numerous travellers during the cholera epidemic.[38]

Quarantines were rarely employed against cholera at this stage since the disease was not seen to be contagious and was instead attributed to poverty, filth, lack of ventilation, bad sanitation and environmental factors. In Calcutta, the worsening of congestion was noted and led to proposals of urban reform.[39] A Lottery Committee was set up in 1817 to generate funds from public lotteries, and after the cholera outbreak, public health became its central focus. In this, the memory of London freeing itself from the plague in the seventeenth century provided the inspiration that it was indeed possible to combat epidemic diseases.[40] Despite their efforts to clean up the city, cholera would continue to ravage Calcutta for four more decades until the introduction of piped drinking water, since cholera was mainly a water-borne disease.

The exact means of cholera transmission, including the water-borne theory, was a hotly debated topic during the nineteenth century and shall be discussed in greater detail in a later section. For now, it is worth noting that the cholera outbreak of 1817 is likely to have been transmitted across the subcontinent by soldiers, pilgrims and traders. The means of transport and communication were still slow and the disease moved from station to station in weeks, so it may not have been registered as a unified event. It took about sixteen months to overwhelm the Indian subcontinent; the epidemic nature of cholera receded only around 1821.[41] Nepal in the north and Punjab in the north-west were not spared either, though the epidemic appeared late in those places.[42]

Cholera death rates were 21 per 1,000 among European troops and 10 per 1,000 among the native troops serving in the Madras army, and would have been much higher in north India.[43] The statistics on deaths among the general population are unclear and from the scattered records of towns and villages, the historian David Arnold estimates that 1–2 million died in this cholera outbreak in the subcontinent.[44] Such large demographic losses were commonplace since India's fragile monsoon-dependent economy had caused a number of famines throughout history whenever the rains failed. The Bengal famines of the late eighteenth century were particularly devastating. And yet, for non-famine years, the loss of lives in the cholera outbreak of 1817 was perhaps unprecedented for that time.

However, what distinguished the 1817 cholera outbreak from all records of preceding ones was its rapid spread to places as far away as Japan in the east and the borders of the Russian Empire in the west. In boats and caravans and in deserts and plateaus, people watched in horror the passing of rice-water stools and the subsequent deaths. As in India, prayers, calomel and opium were resorted to as possible remedies in many places.

Ceylon (modern-day Sri Lanka) and Burma (modern-day Myanmar) had also reported cholera before 1817 and were affected in due course in 1818–19. Outside the Indian subcontinent, Singapore and Penang (in Malaysia) were vulnerable as they were ruled by the government of Bengal, and commanded by troops of the Bengal Native Infantry, and were thus exposed to constant troop movement from Bengal.[45] Their position at the crossroads of east–west traffic provided trading benefits but also brought with it the risk of epidemic. Cholera appeared in Penang in October 1819, by when medical orders on the disease had already arrived from Bengal. Mortality was light in Penang and non-existent on the island of Singapore, which had ship-quarantine systems in place.[46] However, from Penang, it spread inland through the Malay states, and from there to Siam or Thailand, where, reportedly, over 100,000 people died. The king of Siam conducted a religious ceremony in 1820 to ward off cholera but 7,000 died in the event.[47]

Around the same time, the Dutch-ruled island of Java in the Indonesian archipelago was also devastated, with some 17,000 dying in Batavia (now Jakarta) alone.[48] Next on cholera's path of destruction was China, where it perhaps first reached the busy port of Canton, and then other ports all the way up to Peking or Beijing. By one account, it also crossed the Great Wall, and then, on a caravan route, reached the borders of the Russian Empire.[49] It touched Manila in the Philippines in 1820 and Nagasaki in Japan in 1822, most likely from a ship that sailed from Java, and spread to Osaka and other places, taking a considerable toll.[50]

Going west, cholera hit the Arabian and Persian worlds quite hard. A British expeditionary force from India took cholera to Oman in 1821. From there, it went up the shores of the Persian Gulf all the way to Persia or Iran. In Basra, over 15,000 people died within three weeks. Further north, cholera affected a war being fought between Turkey and Persia over an alleged insult of Persian pilgrims travelling to Mecca.[51] A prince of Persia's Qajar dynasty, Mohammad Ali Mirza Dawlatshah (1789–1821), who had previously won battles against the Ottomans and besieged Baghdad in 1821, was finally humbled by cholera and his forces had to retreat after his death. The disease proceeded further to Astrakhan on the border of the Russian Empire and to Aleppo in Syria in 1822, but there are no records of cholera outbreaks beyond those points. It appeared in Port Louis, Mauritius, imported from a ship that sailed from either Ceylon or India in 1819; that outbreak killed 6,000 people, mostly slaves working in plantations. From there, it proceeded to Reunion Island, and later was also observed in Zanzibar in coastal Africa in 1820–21.

Between 1817 and 1823, cholera had ripped through India and other parts of Asia, touched Africa and reached the frontiers of Europe. After a brief pause, it began a longer march and would regularly be called 'epidemic cholera', 'Indian cholera' or 'Asiatic cholera' for its apparent origin.

A Hundred Years of Intestinal Melancholy

In the century that followed 1817, momentous changes took place in the world. In the realm of politics, European imperial powers overcame brief internal revolts and grew from strength to strength, with a unified Italy and a unified Germany joining France, Britain and Russia in the race to colonize the independent regions of Africa and Asia. Japan's imperial ambitions also rose after the Meiji restoration in 1868. Wars and famines weakened China, the Ottoman and Persian empires waned in relative terms, and the British consolidated their hold over India, with Company rule transforming into Crown rule in 1858 after a major uprising.

In business and economics, the cotton textiles–based first industrial revolution, which had begun in Britain in the late eighteenth century, was followed by a second industrial revolution towards the end of the nineteenth century. This one was led by advancements in chemicals, electricity, steel and petroleum. Scientific knowledge grew exponentially in various fields and at the turn of the twentieth century, bacteriology was fast replacing millennia-old notions of diseases based on miasma. In the realm of transport and communication, the concept of distance and time was fundamentally altered by the introduction of the railways, steamships and telegraphs. A wave of globalization, driven by the movement of goods and people and the trans-Atlantic boom of the late nineteenth century, led to a demographic reordering in the Americas. The population of the US rose ten-fold to around 100 million by 1920, raising its share in the global population from about 1 per cent in 1817 to nearly 6 per cent in 1920.[52] Urbanization took place unevenly in the world in this period but the population of the largest cities ran into hundreds of thousands, if not millions, across continents, with greater congestion and more slums. By 1920, nationalism and capitalism were widely entrenched, though the euphoria of the latter was punctured by World War I (1914–18) and the Russian Revolution of 1917.

Amidst all these developments, cholera lurked in the background, bursting forth with great ferocity in certain places and times, leading to panic and protests. It was the nature of the disease, with its clear symptoms of watery excrements, that shocked societies. Cholera remained a mystery almost throughout this period, spurring endless unresolved debates on its causes and means of transmission, but always provoking actions and reactions in the form of quarantines and treatments. Based on a variety of statistical records, I estimate that cholera killed around 50 million people worldwide between 1817 and 1920.[53] Of this, over 10 million people died outside the Indian subcontinent, some 3 million in Russia alone. Egypt experienced arguably the worst loss, relative to a country's population, anywhere in the world. Another 10 million people died in the Indian subcontinent during the raging epidemics; around 30 million died because of cholera's endemicity in India.[54] Pandemic cholera thus killed about 20 million in this period. Table 1 at the end of this chapter provides a brief global distribution.

This is not an exceptionally large figure by pandemic standards and we will see later how influenza killed 20 million people in India alone in a matter of a few months in 1918–19. Cholera's significance is to be understood more in terms of how it captured the popular discourse rather than in the number of its victims. It was undoubtedly the most talked about among the four big diseases of the nineteenth century, the others being the plague, smallpox and typhus. Malaria was far deadlier but unlike cholera, it did not sweep across the world in the form of a pandemic.

Since the late nineteenth century, cholera researchers have attempted to characterize pandemic cholera in distinct waves that began and ended in particular years, the first being 1817–1823.[55] Robert Pollitzer wrote a monumental book on cholera in 1959 for the WHO, outlining six cholera pandemics beginning in 1817, 1829, 1852, 1863, 1881 and 1899.[56] The implicit assumption then was that all the cholera pandemics originated in India, a position that is difficult to defend today given the recent research on the nature of the disease.[57] This is because the bacteria that cause cholera have been found to live in certain maritime systems and the disease can become endemic in certain regions over time. Thus, one possibility is that the new and virulent strain of cholera, which probably emerged in 1817, spread initially and settled in certain water bodies, causing frequent outbreaks and spreading outwards from those locations. Seen in this light, the six pandemics could be considered as being nested within one large pandemic extending over a century.[58] While Bengal in India could well have been the origin in 1817, it was unlikely to have been the source of all the observed outbreaks over time. It is therefore more useful to understand pandemic cholera in geographic rather than in sequential terms.

The Indian Subcontinent

Cholera was endemic in eastern India and parts of the south and the west and hurt the poor disproportionately, but in epidemic form it haunted all alike, especially the British rulers.[59] Prominent members of the ruling elite killed by cholera in India in the nineteenth century included Commander-in-Chief General Anson, on his journey to Delhi during the 1857 uprising, and General Barnard, his successor, while he was attacking the city; Olive Fergusson, the wife of the presidency's governor, in 1882 in Bombay; Thomas Munro in 1827 and George Ward in 1860, both governors of Madras.[60] Nearly 9,000 British soldiers fell prey to cholera between 1818 and 1854, and in the decade that followed nearly a third of all deaths among them were attributed to the disease.[61]

There were several cholera epidemics in India after 1817, but the severe epidemic of 1856–57 is of some political significance because it coincided with a major revolt against British rule that began in the first half of 1857. Indian soldiers in some garrisons in north India mutinied because of rumours of animal fat being used in gun cartridges, which had to be bitten off before being loaded into the gun; eating the meat of certain animals was prohibited in both Islam and Hinduism. These mutinies soon sparked a full-blown violent confrontation between several princely states and the British, which the latter eventually won. What is less widely known about this saga is the circulation of chapatis and cholera.

In early 1857, district officials observed a mysterious circulation of chapatis, the staple unleavened wheat bread of north India, which were being prepared and passed on from one village headman to another.[62] This was taken to be sign of protest by ruling officials but some historians have interpreted it to be a way of passing communication about the arrival of cholera. As one study has shown, regiments that observed this circulation were likelier to mutiny because fear of the disease inflated their prejudice against ethnic outgroups (the British) that were rumoured to be interfering with their religion.[63] Chapatis and cholera also appear in J.G. Farrel's novel *The Siege of Krishnapur* (1973), which is set against the backdrop of the 1857 revolt.[64]

Whether or not the practice of warning by chapatis persisted over time we do not know, but cholera certainly did. Alarmed by the devastating cholera epidemics of 1856–57 and 1860–61, the British instituted a death registration system, first for the military and then for the general population. It is from this point onwards that we obtain a clearer understanding of cholera. Using these statistics and scattered sources for previous decades, I estimate that around 40 million Indians died due to cholera between 1817 and 1920.[65] This works out to around 300,000 gut-wrenching deaths every year, comprising around 5 per cent of all deaths in the Indian subcontinent in this period.

What the death statistics also show is that cholera death rates were *increasing* in India in the late nineteenth century, even as they were receding in most parts of the world. A major factor in this was the series of devastating famines in the late 1870s and 1890s as India experienced record shortfalls in rain.[66] Famines led people to congregate in relief centres where the water quality could be unpredictable, spurring large outbreaks, and they also weakened people's bodies, making them susceptible to infectious diseases. In 1900, the year cholera mortality in India peaked, around 1 million cholera-related deaths were reported, closely associated with a famine. From 1919, cholera began to recede—in impact because of better treatment methods and in incidence because major famines in peacetime conditions had ceased to occur.[67] It briefly resurfaced in the 1940s during the Bengal famine and at the time of the Partition of 1947 but never displayed its past ferocity again.

In the nineteenth century, there emerged several popular ideas to beat cholera, all based on the assumption that it was transmitted by air. The residential segregation in urban settlements was intensified to keep infectious diseases away from British quarters.[68] In the military, 'cholera-dodging' was considered to be effective: troops would break up into smaller groups and move to higher grounds.[69] Hill stations were one popular way to beat the Indian heat and diseases. Cholera, it was observed by the British in the nineteenth century, had ravaged the plains for forty years but touched Nepal only twice and had barely ever touched Darjeeling.[70]

The means of communication improved with the telegraph system in the late nineteenth century and information of cholera outbreaks began to be relayed in real time to the public. The mobility of people within and emigration from India both rose in the nineteenth century, widening the arc of the cholera epidemics.

The semi-permanent, male-dominated, remittance-based Great Indian Migration Wave that took off in the late nineteenth century provided the ideal transmitter of infectious diseases: the circulatory migrant labourer.[71]

All throughout this period, Bengal was undoubtedly the worst affected region, registering the highest cholera death rate of nearly 3 per 1,000 before 1920.[72] This was followed by the Madras Presidency in the south, where cholera was endemic in some places, and then by parts of central and north India. Punjab in the north-west was the least affected and when epidemics did occur there, they were traced to Hindu pilgrimage routes connected with the famous Kumbha Melas in Haridwar and Allahabad, discussed in greater detail later.[73] The regional variation in endemicity almost certainly reflected the survival prospects of *Cholerae vibrio* in different water systems.

We know less about how cholera affected India's princely states even though they comprised close to 40 per cent of the subcontinent's land mass during British Crown rule. The Nizam-ruled Hyderabad state was certainly affected. One account shows that cholera was known there as *gattara*, and that it was remembered as a painful episode of the early twentieth century.[74] In his memoirs about his family, published in 2011, Dr Y.B. Satyanarayana noted the devastating impact of a cholera outbreak in a region close to Karimnagar. His grandfather, Narsiah, had to carry the dead bodies of his parents and bury them with his own hands; soon afterwards, his wife would also die of cholera at a very young age. He describes the taboos around cholera in the first decades of the twentieth century as follows:

In those days, infectious diseases were widespread in villages, particularly in untouchable dwellings. Cholera was one such disease. Each house had at least a couple of deaths due to cholera. People called this dreadful disease gattara and were even afraid of touching the dead body of a person who had died of the disease. Only the inmates of the house could carry the dead body for cremation.[75]

Such taboos persisted till the middle of the twentieth century, by when the impact of cholera had greatly reduced. Dr B.R. Ambedkar (1891–1956), a key architect of independent India's Constitution, recounted the following incident that occurred in 1943 and was reminiscent of the attacks on 'witches' during the early nineteenth century:

> It was reported from Nasik on 1st September that the Hindus of a village attacked an Achchut [Untouchable] family; tied the hands and feet of an elderly woman, placed her on a pile of wood which was subsequently set on fire. All this because they thought she was the cause of the Cholera in the village.[76]

Such cholera deaths or retributions evoked horror but the deaths themselves, when sufficiently large in number, could have unexpected economic consequences. From the viewpoint of factors of production, an important distinction between epidemics, and wars and natural calamities, is that epidemics usually destroy only labour while the others potentially destroy land, labour and capital. The consequence of this is the possibility that people who survive epidemics can work with more land and capital and that there could be changes in the bargaining positions of different sections of society. The evidence for this occurring due to the cholera epidemics of India is limited, though very early on, the Bengali social reformer Ram Mohan Roy (1772–1833) did note the following to the House of Commons in 1831:

The vast number carried of late years, by cholera morbus, having greatly relieved the pressure of surplus population, the condition of the labourers has since much improved in comparison with what it was before the people were thinned by that melancholy scourge.[77]

On the other hand, cholera reduced workdays in the year and could slow economic activity. It could also cut short budding talent, as it did with Henry Louis Vivian Derozio (1809–1831), whose grave lies in the South Park Street Cemetery. Born in Calcutta, the Anglo-Portuguese Derozio was a gifted poet who accomplished a lot in his twenty-two short years.[78] In a poem titled 'To India–My Native Land', he lamented the advent of colonial rule in India and longed for a brighter past, one without colonialism—presumably, also a past without epidemic cholera. It was a fitting tribute to him that the landmark discovery that resolved much of the mystery of cholera was made by a team of Indian scientists in independent India, and only a few kilometres away from his grave.

Europe

The first major cholera outbreak had stopped at the borders of the Russian Empire in 1823. This was not by chance. Due to the recommendation of one German physician serving Tsar Alexander I, the government had set up a board for all medical-administrative matters, which worked towards stopping cholera from entering Russia.[79] This seemed to work until 1829, when cholera finally made inroads and worked itself westwards slowly across the Russian rivers, reaching Moscow in 1830 and England in 1831–32. Troop movements due to the Polish–Russian war of 1830–31 hastened cholera's transmission from Russia to western Europe and were criticized by the French, who pointed out that it was 'historically known that it first appeared and was propagated in India by Lord Hastings' army'.[80]

Cholera broke out in Europe repeatedly until the 1860s, after which it abated in most places. Military movement, markets and fairs, inland and overseas water transport, railways and the roads were cited as key reasons for disease dispersion. Like in India, deprivation and famines pushed countless people from the countryside to the towns in central Europe, where many eventually succumbed to the disease.[81] Cholera's impact in Europe was significant because it challenged the notion of material progress. According to the historian Richard Evans, cholera 'challenged common assumptions of European cultural and biological superiority by demonstrating the vulnerability of even the most civilised people to a disease associated mainly with oriental backwardness'.[82]

Cholera's disproportionate impact on the urban poor also exacerbated social tensions and exposed the weaknesses of urban infrastructure. London, for instance, was not very different from Calcutta in terms of sanitation in the early nineteenth century. The novelist Charles Dickens (1812–1870), whose son's epitaph lies in the South Park Street Cemetery in Calcutta, eloquently described the inequality and abysmal living conditions of the urban working poor in the England of those times. In 1849 and 1853–54, poorer London districts like Rotherhithe and Bermondsey experienced cholera mortality rates nearly eight times higher than those in Kensington or Westminster.[83] Among the poor, the seeming immunity of the rich led to perceptions of exploitation and deliberate action taken against them. To make matters worse, the anatomy departments of medical schools required corpses to examine, leading to the suspicion that doctors were gravediggers. In such settings, 'cholera riots' took place in many corners of Europe and outbreaks of the disease coincided with Europe's revolutionary year of 1848, the Crimean War in the 1850s, the overthrow of the German Confederation in 1866, the end of France's Second Empire in 1871, and the skirmishes in Russian Poland in 1892.[84] However, the pandemic was usually a consequence rather than a cause of those political upheavals, although it was one that could claim more lives than the upheaval itself.

Russia had it the toughest, connected as it was with west and south Asia by road networks in many directions, and it is likely that cholera became endemic there to some extent. Nearly 500,000 cases were reported in 1831, nearly 2 million in 1848, and nearly 1 million in 1892, with several other years in between with hundreds of thousands of cases. Case fatality rates, that is the death rate among those infected, when reported, hovered around 50 per cent and the death toll for 1817–1920 is estimated to be around 3 million.[85] The famous Russian music composer Pyotr Ilyich Tchaikovsky (1840–1893), shortly after composing his Sixth Symphony, died due to cholera (a glass of unboiled water in a restaurant being the likely culprit), just like his mother had years before.[86]

Prizes were offered in the early days of the pandemic to anyone who could develop an effective cure for cholera. Those prizes remained unawarded but based on a Russian doctor's recommendation, steam baths became a fad as a way to treat cholera.[87] The first instances of intravenous treatment of cholera occurred in Russia but the method would be perfected only in the early twentieth century in India. However, at that time, injections were treated with great suspicion, as in 1910, when one Dr Pantchenko was accused of being a 'hitman' and injecting cholera bacteria into his 'victims'.[88]

In England, cholera first arrived in 1831–32 on ships that sailed from the Baltic region, and quickly claimed over 5,000 lives.[89] A London medical journal observed in 1832, 'In Asia the fiend was contemplated by us with curiosity—in the wilds of Russia, with suspicion—in Germany, with alarm—but on English soil, with TERROR!'[90] The experience of tackling cholera in India from

1817 to 1821 came in handy and those measures were imported to England.[91] During the 1848 outbreak, measures to combat the epidemic included 'cholera belts', flannel or woollen belts to be worn around the belly, as per an army manual. Called 'kummerbunds' in India, these were widely worn by military folk in the late nineteenth century to prevent abdominal chills supposedly associated with cholera.[92] In 1854, a year of high cholera mortality, a public debate focussed on the question 'Which Is Worse – War or Cholera?'[93] Military deaths during the conflict-ridden years between 1793 and 1815 amounted to around 20,000; in contrast, in 1848–49 alone, cholera killed over 70,000. Expenses on sanitation and war were compared with each other to make an argument for greater expenditure on public health measures. Those efforts arguably did yield results in ending cholera but not before it had claimed close to 200,000 lives in the nineteenth century.[94]

Spain was the worst hit by cholera in western Europe, where the death toll amounted to around 600,000 over four waves, occasionally bringing the reigning monarch to the streets to show solidarity with the suffering public.[95] Cholera claimed around 300,000 lives in France in the nineteenth century. When it first arrived there in 1832, it killed 7,000 in Paris within three weeks. Significantly, it killed two important political leaders, one a supporter of the monarchy and another who opposed it, sparking riots and the June 1832 Rebellion. In Brest, fishermen in 1832 looked at cholera as a punishment from God. Generally, the cholera epidemics led to a religious revival in Catholic Marseilles.[96] It also prompted charity from unexpected quarters. Dwarkanath Tagore (1794–1846), a Calcutta-based Indian businessman and philanthropist, and grandfather of Nobel Prize–winning poet Rabindranath Tagore, donated money to the cause of cholera victims in France, thereby projecting moral parity with the Europeans.[97] Cholera's sweep across Europe was wide, hurting Hungary and Germany extensively. As urban sanitation, water supplies and sewage systems improved, cholera outside Russia receded from the 1870s onwards.[98] Sporadic outbreaks continued, including one in 1892 in Hamburg, Germany, caused by a contaminated water supply, but that only reconfirmed the role of water contamination in spreading the disease.

Cholera's impact on Europe also led to its eventual downfall. Russia would provide the inspiration for the intravenous treatment of cholera, Britain the water-borne transmission theory, France and Germany the bacteriological revolution, and Italy and Spain would discover the vibrio and the vaccine, though both discoveries would be overlooked at the time.

The Americas

Cholera first arrived in the Americas through trans-Atlantic sailing routes in the 1830s. As in Europe, the outbreaks ended in most places around the 1860s.[99] It lingered in Mexico and Cuba until the 1880s and in Brazil, Uruguay and Argentina for even longer. By the end of the nineteenth century, there had been over 500,000 deaths due to cholera in the Americas.

Cases first appeared in Quebec in Canada in 1832, brought on ships carrying cholera-infected immigrants from Britain.[100] While some ships were quarantined, the disease still managed to slip through, and was blamed on the easterly winds blowing in from the infected atmosphere of Europe.[101] Over 1,000 died within a few weeks.[102] After that, across the eastern seaboard of North and South America, trans-Atlantic and coastal traffic would bring cholera to various ports, from where it would make its journey inwards through transport networks, especially waterways.

The US suffered significant nationwide outbreaks in 1832, 1849 and 1866 and even lost a former president, James K. Polk (1795–1849), to the disease only months after he vacated the top post.[103] When cholera first arrived in the US in 1832, a newspaper reported the event as follows, with the headline 'The Destroying Angel Has Reached America':

> It is with feelings of no ordinary nature, that we announce to our readers the alarming fact that the India CHOLERA, that dreadful scourge of Asia & Europe, which has swept off, it is thought, at least *fifty* millions of human beings, has reached the shores of America, and is already carrying death and desolation before it.[104]

The exaggerated death toll in the article notwithstanding, 'India Cholera' (like the 'Chinese virus' in 2020) caused substantial alarm and mass movement in the US. When it hit New York in 1832, the richer folk left the city just as the 'inhabitants of Pompeii fled when the red lava showered down upon their houses', reported one newspaper.[105] Business dried up and according to one painter's description, there was no work to be found barring that done by 'Doctors, Undertakers, Coffinmakers'; the streets had fallen silent.[106] Over 3,500 died in New York, which was around 2 per cent of the city's population. When cholera went southwards to the plantations, it affected the African-American slaves, whose masters blamed the high mortality rates on their habit of not eating during the day but 'eating enormously very late at night'.[107] Such observations were common around the world where the victims were blamed for lack of appropriate behaviour during an epidemic.

Cholera made a dramatic entry in Cuba in 1833, quickly overwhelming the two cemeteries of Havana and spreading further, wiping out over 20,000 or 3 per cent of the Cuban population.[108] Cuba would face an outbreak again in the 1850s, disproportionately affecting its slave population. Plantation owners also suffered as the fields were left desolate. Cholera affected other islands of the Caribbean unevenly as quarantines were implemented with greater vigour; Puerto Rico succeeded in escaping almost entirely, except for an outbreak in 1854–55. A church in San Juan interpreted the event as a punishment from above for 'excesses, vices, and public and private scandals'.[109]

In Mexico, the arrival of cholera in 1833 coincided with civil war (due to which Texas was eventually lost in 1836) and very soon the disease had claimed more lives than the fighting.[110] This was in contrast to Guatemala, which had anticipated the epidemic after it hit the US in 1832 and had imposed a strict quarantine despite opposition from political opponents and merchants, thus saving itself from the outbreak.[111] Mexico reacted late, only after cholera struck Cuba in February 1833, and political uncertainties delayed the action required to contain the epidemic. Civil war broke out in May just as the first cholera cases began appearing via the ports. Soon, town after town suffered from cholera, with those who pushed the 'death carts' wearily making the rounds. One local tale described how a French tailor who lay unconscious on the ground was carted to the burial ground but as per custom, was not buried because he was picked up on the last round of the day.[112] The story said that he was actually alive and eventually walked back to his house, much to the amazement of the townspeople the next day. Such stories were told in Mexico for several decades as cholera entered the common vocabulary.

Brazil felt the effect of the disease only in 1855, leading some to speculate until then that it was cholera-resistant because of equatorial heat or the long distance that separated it from Europe.[113] The illusion was broken when cholera struck the city of Belem, along the equator, initiating 'the blackest page in the medical history of Brazil' as one chronicler in 1873 put it, since over 200,000 died in 1855–56.[114] Belem alone lost 4 per cent of its population. As reported by the British consul based in the city, cholera was 'chiefly confined to the negro, the mixed races, and the Indians'.[115] Public charities received orphaned infants in the havoc, which also claimed the life of the acting governor of the province, who was seen healthy in the morning but was dead by the afternoon. Farms lay desolate as people either died or deserted them, and as one doctor described, 'all was confusion, all was horror'.[116] One of the consequences of the large loss of labour was that the government, which had banned slave imports in 1850, became more open to encouraging European immigration. The great migration from Europe to Brazil that occurred in the late nineteenth century thus had some roots in the crisis created by cholera. This is useful in understanding a central paradox of cholera in the Americas, that is, why it began receding in the late nineteenth century at the same time that mass immigration from Europe picked up. Cholera receded after the 1860s presumably because of a better understanding of the nature of the disease, but its ravages in the prior decades also contributed to a greater demand for European immigrants.

Africa and Asia

Cholera would skim the coasts of Africa, from around Madagascar on the south-eastern end, all the way north and west to Senegal.[117] Traders, troops and pilgrims to Mecca would be seen as the transmitters of the disease that killed around 1 million people in the nineteenth century. The bulk of those victims were in Egypt, where cholera took over 100,000 lives each year in 1831, 1855 and 1865, and many thousands in other years until 1902.[118] Like in Russia, it is likely that cholera became partly endemic in the region. Egypt's unique location, close to the intersection of three continents, and the fact that the seaport, Suez, oversaw traffic between the west and the east through a canal, certainly exposed it to epidemic risks. Along with cholera, Egypt also had to battle the plague in the early nineteenth century. When cholera first appeared in Cairo in 1831, it killed 40,000 people, or over 10 per cent of the city's population, within a month.[119] Panic led to mass flight as camel processions left the city. Enraged, the ruler, Muhammad Ali Pasha, later dismissed the medical officers who had abandoned the city during the crisis. But mass desertions continued to take place in later outbreaks as well.

The cholera pandemic had its greatest impact on the African continent in the 1860s. Tunisia was badly affected and the cholera crisis led to people shunning the ruling elite. Historians have argued that this later contributed to the French annexation of Tunisia in 1881.[120] Senegal, Algeria, Ethiopia and Somalia were also affected by cholera in the 1860s. The outbreak in Zanzibar city and island in 1869–70, among the worst recorded anywhere, wiped out 10–20 per cent of the local population, or some 40,000 people.[121] This outbreak was carefully recorded by a doctor called James Christie who provided important evidence on the east African slave trade that compounded the crisis and also the water-borne nature of the disease.[122]

In Asia, outside India, cholera made its presence felt in the Arabian peninsula, with regular outbreaks in the holy city of Mecca until 1912, after which it became cholera-free.[123] Pilgrims, as will be seen later, were blamed in large part for spreading cholera to different corners and an elaborate quarantine system was implemented in response. In Iran, public baths or hammams, among other reasons, were blamed for the cholera crises.[124] East Asia suffered sporadically all through but had its worst moments in the last two decades of the nineteenth century. China, Japan, Korea, the Philippines, Indonesia, Thailand and Burma all had their periods of sorrow, and it is likely that cholera had become endemic in some of those regions. One 2019 study argues that cholera was endemic in Japan in the late nineteenth century and that the country did not suffer repeated outbreaks brought from outside, as has long been argued, but from within.[125]

From 1817 onwards, cholera affected humans across most continents, touching the whole world at some point or the other, barring perhaps south-west Africa and Oceania. But what exactly caused cholera and which factors led to its transmission? It would be the ultimate medical whodunit of the nineteenth century that would play itself out in the high stakes of imperial scientific competition. In many ways, though, it is also a question that has not been fully answered yet.

Sanitation versus Contagion

In the late 1830s, a young English woman, Julia Charlotte Maitland (1808–1864), travelled across south India and wrote letters describing her new surroundings in great detail. She described a particular cholera outbreak raging near Rajahmundry, twenty days after 100,000 people had assembled there for a grand festival that was held once in twelve years, as follows:

> When I arrived in the town I was fast asleep in my palanquin, and was literally awakened by the horrible stench … There is little fear of cholera among Europeans, except in travelling. It is caused among the poor natives by bad feeding, dirt, and exposure to the climate … The poor natives go on beating their tom-toms, or drums, all night, in hope of driving it away; and the want of rest weakens them, and makes them still more liable to catch it.[126]

Her observation summarizes the prevailing view of that time: that cholera was synonymous with poverty and that climatic factors and insanitary conditions were the *cause* of cholera. Since climatic factors were outside one's control, better sanitation was seen as the best way to prevent cholera. The corollary was that the disease was not passed through humans, and the most obvious implication was that quarantines were ineffective. This was what Benjamin Moseley had in mind in 1800, as seen in the previous chapter.

There were three clearly discernible positions on cholera held before 1860, described by the historian Christopher Hamlin as 'contagionism', 'positivist anti-contagionism' and 'miasmatist anti-contagionism'.[127] On the question of whether the disease was internal, the positivists maintained that diet was an important factor whereas the other two maintained it was caused by an external factor. On the origins, the contagionists were unsure but the miasmatists maintained that climatic factors were of paramount importance. On transmission, the miasmatists argued that the disease moved due to the changing conditions of the atmosphere or soil while the contagionists insisted on human carriers.

Finally, there was an important question that contagionists were always asked: why did the disease attack some and not all in places where cholera appeared? Surely, contagious diseases should have been passed on to doctors, but that was rarely the case. In one incident in Russia, a few villagers abducted two doctors on duty who espoused quarantine, tied them to cholera corpses and placed them in a pit.[128] Their survival would be proof against contagion. In that particular case, they did survive and were eventually pulled out of the pit. The contagionists argued that survival depended on how exposed one was to the disease while the miasmatists argued that people differed in their predisposition to the disease.

The evidence in favour of the contagionists was that outbreaks were often noted after the arrival of a person infected with the disease, a fact that the miasmatists found hard to explain with their pet theory of a change in climate. As for other diseases, contagionism was widely accepted as an explanation for smallpox but the history of the plague over centuries had also led to debates similar to those over cholera. Scientific developments in the late nineteenth century convincingly turned the tide towards contagionism, albeit with a lot of resistance and theatrics. Cholera provided this spark as the leading minds of the day wanted to decipher the disease.

In 1849, John Snow (1813–1858), a doctor from Yorkshire in England who had seen the cholera visitations of the 1830s, published a short pamphlet titled *On the Mode of Communication of Cholera*.[129] The pamphlet started with an assertion of cholera being contagious and also noted that 'many eminent men hold an opposite opinion'. Ruling out transmission via blood poisoning, he likened the disease to those caused by 'intestinal worms' in acting directly on the alimentary canal and in the significance of the excretions.[130] One of the mysteries of cholera was how the disease could affect people in quarters distant from those who were sick. Snow posited a faecal-oral transmission theory with a simple example, explaining how those attending the sick could have picked up the patient's 'ejections' from soiled bedding or clothes, and proceeded to prepare the food for their families back home without washing their hands.[131] This way, faecal matter could be transported and ingested elsewhere. A more systematic method of transmission, he argued, was when sewers emptied out into the 'drinking water of the community'.[132] He provided examples from the 1830s cholera outbreaks, pointing out that they appeared to be more severe when the sources of drinking water were mixed with sewage more frequently. Other examples were also provided to support a water-borne faecal-oral transmission theory of cholera.

The same year that Snow's pamphlet was published, two microscopists, Frederick Brittan and J.G. Swayne, and separately, an epidemiologist, William Budd, argued that there were 'living organisms in the rice-water evacuations of cholera'.[133] Later, in 1856, Filippo Pacini, an Italian anatomist, discovered a vibrio linked with cholera in Florence, whose significance was realized by the medical community several decades later and the cholera-causing bacillus was then retrospectively named *Cholerae vibrio* in his honour.[134]

While these discoveries were being made at the microscopic level, Snow worked harder on observing cholera outbreaks carefully in London in 1853–54 to test his water-borne transmission theory. He studied the distribution systems of companies supplying water to inhabitants and found that there were fewer cholera outbreaks in the areas served by Lambeth, which used a relatively purer source upstream, than in Vauxhall and Southwark, whose water source was the sewer-fed Thames.[135] In some areas, neighbouring houses could be served by competing water companies and hence it proved to be an experiment that identified the impact of contaminated water supplies on cholera incidence. But the case study which is famous all around the world today is Snow's identification of the Broad Street water pump as the source of the cholera outbreak in Soho in August 1854, which killed hundreds within a week.[136] Snow depicted the incidence of the disease on a map of the neighbourhood, which was an early example of the power of Geographic Information System (GIS) mapping to substantiate theories in other fields.

At the time, these discoveries were treated with immense scepticism by the miasmatists, who respected Snow's argument but did not consider it to be the only explanation for cholera. As one critic pointed out, 'He has not been able to prove that all were attacked who drank this water, and that none were attacked who did not drink.'[137] Nevertheless, Snow's water-borne transmission theory, coupled with a general thrust towards the provision of clean water, led to reforms in urban water supply in many parts of the world. Even in Calcutta, where cholera incidence was very high and claimed upwards of 3,000 lives annually for decades, the number of cholera deaths seems to have reduced substantially to around 1,000 after the introduction of piped water supply in 1869–70.[138]

Other theories continued to flourish, including one extremely popular one about the inverse relationship between the elevation of the settlement and cholera incidence, that seemed to fit the facts in Europe and India.[139] Soil poisons and wind-based transmission were other contenders. Despite the major scientific discoveries on cholera happening in Britain, policymakers there continued to take anti-contagionist positions to avoid quarantines and serve trading interests. But this was being challenged by a new field: the study of germ-based diseases, which was strengthened by the growing use of microscopes. Scientists such as Louis Pasteur (1822–1895) in France, after whom 'pasteurization' is named, and Robert Koch (1843–1910) in Germany, were its leading proponents.

It was thus a remarkable combination of British denial and Franco-German competition that ultimately uncovered the disease-causing agent of cholera. In 1883, some months before the infamous Berlin conference that led to the eventual 'scramble for Africa' by European colonizers, the cholera pandemic was raging in Egypt. British colonial officials were keen to demonstrate that cholera was endemic to the region and had not come through human traffic in the Suez Canal, in order to avoid demands for quarantine.[140] At the same time, the French and German governments dispatched teams, one picked by Pasteur and the other led by Koch, to the city of Alexandria to understand the cause of the disease, successfully doing which would confer much honour in the high stakes of imperialism and science.[141] In the event, Koch, who had earlier discovered the tuberculosis bacterium (for which he won the Nobel Prize in 1905), found success. But since the cholera epidemic was receding in Egypt, he moved to Calcutta for further investigation between December 1883 and April 1884.[142] A contaminated water tank associated with cholera outbreaks was examined for samples, and this confirmed what he had seen in Egypt: a comma-shaped bacillus, which was also what Pacini had seen decades earlier. But unlike Pacini, Koch could grow cultures and infect other animals with the bacillus, lending greater credibility to his findings.

The discoveries made by Snow and Koch moved the pendulum firmly in the direction of contagionism worldwide, but the sanitarians or anti-contagionists still held forth in some quarters. Florence Nightingale (1820–1910), the renowned English social reformer and pioneer of modern nursing, lived during the Age of Pandemics and wrote extensively on the health issues of India.[143] A lifelong sanitarian, her views on the causes of cholera changed only partly and slowly after Koch's findings and her own peek through a microscope.[144] But Max von Pettenkofer (1818–1901), a German sanitarian, stuck to his soil-poison theory all his life, attempting also to disprove Koch by ingesting cholera-afflicted cultures (and surviving), before finally committing suicide.[145] Remarkably, the place where the impact of this new science was felt least was in the place most ravaged by cholera: India. The Anglo-Indian physicians continued to adhere to the anti-contagionist position because cholera was endemic in India and environmental explanations and local influence appeared to be key.[146] J.M. Cunningham, who was British India's sanitary commissioner between 1868 and 1884, was a staunch anti-contagionist and a disbeliever in quarantines.[147] So was another Cunningham, this time with the initials D.D., who served as a scientific assistant to the government from 1869 to 1897.[148] Despite working in a laboratory in India for decades, he refused to validate Koch's path-breaking findings because of his loyalty to Pettenkofer's view and attempted to maintain a distinct medical tradition in India.[149]

One exception to this 'cunning' stubbornness was M.C. Furnell, who served as the sanitary commissioner of Madras and wrote a book called *Cholera and Water in India* in 1887.[150] The book started with a telling paragraph:

I believe that water is the chief means by which cholera is spread, especially in India, and that it is on account of the peculiar treatment water obtains in that country, that India, the only country in the world, is subject to such frequently recurring and such terrible epidemics of this dread scourge.[151]

The Indian peculiarity he referred to was the practice of washing clothes, bathing and drawing water for domestic use from the same tank, considered to be ripe conditions for a cholera outbreak. He clarified that there could be other means of transmission such as clothes and food, but thirty years of experience in India had convinced him that water was the most important factor and that the provision of 'pure and uncontaminated' drinking water could end cholera in India, as it had done elsewhere.[152] Indeed, while piped water supply was reducing cholera in India's large cities, in the smaller towns and villages it remained a 'pipe' dream. There, access to water was governed by caste segregation and notions of purity, so much so that different caste groups within a village would access different sources of water. In this, the marginalized castes usually had the least access to clean water, and were thus particularly hard-hit by water-borne diseases. In fact, just as the variation of water supplies in London was used by Snow to identify their significance for cholera outbreaks, Furnell did the same using the variation of water supplies by caste within a village. And, inspired by Snow, Furnell used a map (see next page) to show that in one south Indian village, only the 'high castes' had contracted cholera due to their contaminated wells while others had escaped, despite everyone living in close proximity.[153] In this case, the only 'low caste' victim of cholera was the 'washerman of the high-caste people'.[154]

Furnell also pointed out the irony that during ancient times, 'when the inhabitants of England were rude savages, running about naked, or nearly so', the people of India 'were far advanced' and had 'laid down rules regulating the use and conservancy of water'.[155] At the time of his writing, there was little knowledge about the ancient

Furnell's map of cholera in a south Indian village

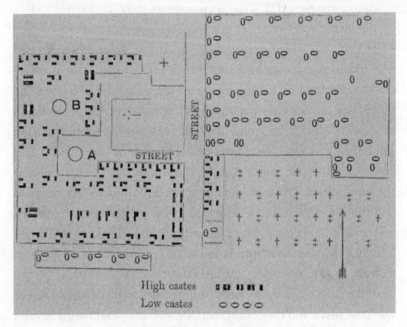

The circles marked 'A' and 'B' on the map represent the
two contaminated wells.

Source: M.C. Furnell, Cholera and Water in India (J. & A. Churchill, 1887), p. 17.

Harappan civilization but historians now claim that there was a
'high degree of social sanitation in Harappa'.[156] Observe again the
clear instructions of Kautilya's *Arthashastra* in ancient India on the
responsibilities of townspeople:

No one shall throw dirt on the streets or let mud and water
collect there. This applies, particularly, to royal highways. No
one shall pass urine or faeces in (or near) a holy place, a water
reservoir, a temple or a royal property, unless it is for unavoidable
reasons like illness, medication or fear. No one shall throw out
dead bodies of animals or human beings inside the city. Corpses
shall be taken out of the city only by the prescribed route and

the gate for corpses and cremation or burial done only at the designated places.[157]

Elsewhere, the ancient text also specifies that fines for contaminating water reservoirs would be double those for spoiling holy places.[158]

The nineteenth-century world that Furnell inhabited was quite different from the one we live in today. None of his insights and recommendations, including one on a cheap mass-produced hand pump, were well-received in officialdom and, by one account, his advocacy even cost him his job.[159] One exception, though, was the 'Maha Rajah of Travancore' from the region now called Kerala in south India, who wrote a letter to Furnell in 1882, describing him as a 'public benefactor', and praised his work on cholera and water after hearing his lecture, which he also had translated into Malayalam and included in the official gazette.[160]

Generally, what came across universally in the debate between the sanitarians and the contagionists was India's exceptionally poor sanitary conditions. In 1866, the *Indian Medical Gazette* wondered who gave Calcutta the name 'City of Palaces' and why, unless it was given in derision, and went on to describe the city's filth in great detail.[161] In the early twentieth century, Leonard Rogers of the Indian Medical Service would report about the unique conditions of a water tank thus:

When inspecting a remote municipality, the Indian chairman showed me a fine tank that had been reserved for drinking purposes. It looked quite suitable until on walking round it, I found that a urinal had been placed on its inner slope draining into the water. An IMS predecessor assured me that at an inspection, he was shown a tank with two notices: one read, 'This end of the tank is reserved for drinking purposes', the other, 'This end of the tank is reserved for washing purposes'.[162]

While the situation has improved since then, Indians in the twenty-first century still struggle, the government's recent Swachh Bharat Abhiyan (Clean India Mission) notwithstanding. But better water supply has undoubtedly reduced the chances of a major cholera outbreak.

Pilgrimages, Conferences and Quarantines

Even the antagonistic contagionists and anti-contagionists usually concurred on the role pilgrimages played in the cholera pandemic. For the contagionists, pilgrims were one of the most important conduits of the disease in Asia and for the anti-contagionists, the pilgrimage sites, routinely described as filthy and insanitary, were the sources of the disease. Internationally, it would be the Muslim pilgrim from India going to Mecca who was under scrutiny, and within India it was the Hindu pilgrim going to places such as Haridwar and Allahabad in the north, Nasik and Pandharpur in the west, Tirupati and Kanchipuram in the south and Puri in the east.

The Jagannath Temple in Puri, Orissa (now Odisha), on the east coast of India, and its attendant pilgrims frustrated British officials, who cried foul about the lack of public hygiene and its role in spreading cholera. While writing on the history of Orissa in 1872, William Wilson Hunter (1840–1900) pointed out that 10,000 people died every year in the pilgrimage.[163] Calling it a 'homicidal enterprise', he argued that the pilgrimage massacred more people than those lost in the wars at Plassey and Waterloo.[164] For him, the implication was clear:

America, Europe, and the greater part of Asia, may justly blame India for all they have suffered from cholera and India can blame Puri for annually subjecting whole provinces to the chance of the epidemic ... Europe has a right to demand the necessary preventive measures at the hands of the Government of India.[165]

Simply put, Puri and many other pilgrimage sites were perceived by Europeans in the nineteenth century in the way many see Chinese wet markets of meat in 2020, that is, as places that generate pandemics. In north India, the situation was worse because the holy sites along the Ganga drew pilgrims to not only pray but also to take a dip in the river and take 'Ganga *jal*' or the holy water back home to distribute to others. This was perfect for the faecal-oral transmission of cholera and as noted by an observer in Lahore in 1884, pilgrimages 'distributed cholera to the devotees like prasad (food offered to devotees)'.[166] One sanitation official, W.A. Roe, analysed the subject in great detail in the 1890s and established a clear relationship between the Haridwar Kumbh Mela, which attracted millions of pilgrims, and cholera in the villages of north India.[167] He showed that 'Ganga jal' was distributed by the pilgrims when they went back to their villages and also thrown into local tanks to, ironically, make them 'holy'. Later studies confirmed this link with systematic data collected over several decades.[168] The British regularly laid the blame on the Indian pilgrims but the Indians saw it differently; they believed that the British themselves were not providing the necessary infrastructure for sanitation that could curb cholera.[169]

Muslim pilgrims had their own practices that inadvertently increased the chances of spreading cholera. Clothes replaced water as the holy objects that could transmit the disease. Pilgrims would often not change clothes and the used clothes would be distributed back home as religious gifts. Many believed that flowing water was always safe and that it could never be polluted.[170] Mecca was hit hard by cholera in 1831 and half the pilgrims there were estimated to have died. Again, in 1846, around 15,000 died and in 1865, 30,000 out of the assembled 90,000 pilgrims died.[171]

By then, Hindu and Muslim pilgrimages were attracting international attention for their possible role in spreading cholera. In 1866, an International Sanitary Conference was convened in Constantinople (now Istanbul), in which Puri and Mecca were blamed for the cholera pandemic.[172] This was the third such conference in a series initiated by France, the previous two editions having been held in Paris in 1851 and 1859. They were attended by mostly European states, who sent diplomats and physicians to deliberate on coordinating a response against epidemics through quarantines.[173] Since the cholera outbreaks of the 1830s, European states had achieved mixed results in preventing cholera by imposing *cordons sanitaires* (localized lockdowns that restricted movement), military cordons and quarantines.[174] Britain was generally against quarantines and, backed by a strong merchant lobby, wanted to maintain the free flow of trade in its empire. The Habsburg monarchy claimed that quarantines and cordons led to 'consequences more mischievous than those resulting from the malady itself', while the Russians relaxed their controls over time.[175] The prevailing belief in anti-contagionism tilted opinion against quarantines. Only France consistently advocated quarantines.

The 1866 conference was a turning point which, according to the historian Mark Harrison, 'ushered in a new concept of disease prevention in which the Middle East would become a kind of sanitary filter, protecting the West from Asiatic diseases'.[176] The Ottoman Empire, in particular, instituted international health boards which would certify whether diseases from the east required quarantines or not. In Egypt, El Tor would emerge as an important quarantine camp on the Mecca pilgrimage route, often proving to be a humiliating experience for the pilgrims. The British were forced to rethink their anti-quarantine stance in light of the emerging evidence of contagionism and increasing pressure from other governments to act on containing cholera within India. But J.M. Cunningham, that committed anti-contagionist sanitary commissioner of India, would have none of it and fought London hard. While he was on leave in 1870, the Indian Quarantine Act was passed by the government of India, on demand from the provincial governments, but upon his return, he continued to press against quarantines.[177] India, in fact, did pass a Contagious Diseases Act in 1868, but that had nothing to do with cholera and everything to do with venereal diseases and regulating prostitution.

In the late nineteenth century, the British in India faced the dilemma of either succumbing to international pressure and imposing quarantines against Indian pilgrims, and earning their ire, or not doing so and facing complaints in Europe.[178] A key issue was religious sentiments, which, after the 1857 uprising, was a sensitive point that the British did not want to raise in India. A large number of Muslim pilgrims who undertook the Hajj to Mecca also lived in the wider British Empire, complicating the geopolitics.[179] As a result, the next six International Sanitary Conferences in Vienna (1874), Washington (1881), Rome (1885), Venice (1892), Dresden (1893) and Paris (1894) involved much hand-wringing and negotiations. But they did have some impact on imposing regulations on movement between Asia and Europe in an attempt to secure borders without incurring economic losses.[180] Ultimately, the conferences, which began with cholera and quarantines in mind in 1851, culminated after nearly a century in the creation of the WHO, which declared the COVID-19 pandemic in 2020.[181] The recent effort of the US to withdraw from the WHO can thus be seen in some aspects as being similar to British stubbornness during the heyday of its empire in the nineteenth century.

Blood and Salts

Treatment procedures for cholera in the Age of Pandemics ranged from the mild to the bizarre or, as one British official commented in 1831, 'as various as incredible'.[182] The real breakthrough in reducing case fatality rates, which otherwise stayed above 50 per cent, came only in the first decades of the twentieth century. Before that, the treatments were described by one reviewer as being 'largely a form of benevolent homicide'.[183] One treatment method widely adopted in the early nineteenth century was 'bleeding', which now appears to be as unwise as restricting the supply of money during an economic recession. The more the bloodletting, it was reasoned, the better the chances of recovery, which was confusing cause with effect. Recovery happened because it was only in the mild cholera attacks, when the blood had not greatly dehydrated, that it could be extracted. In severe cases, little bloodletting was possible. Blood was usually taken from the veins but leeches were also employed for the task, sometimes fifteen of them, placed strategically at the anus.[184] Bloodletting was popularly used by European physicians in India and was emulated in Europe when cholera broke out in the 1830s, but faded away by the 1850s.

Calomel and opium, as prescribed by Johnson in 1813, were regularly recommended across the nineteenth century. Even Pettenkofer, who contracted diarrhoea after deliberately ingesting those vibrio to disprove Koch, was recommended this option.[185] Other medications prescribed for cholera at various times and in different places included ammonia, croton oil, magnesia, laudanum, belladonna, rhubarb and quinine, among others. There was also cauterization, mostly along the spine, and separately, a method of pouring boiling water to raise blisters.[186] Therapies ranged from the severe, such as electric shocks that were documented in St Petersburg and Paris, to the extremely mild, such as the recommendation of baths with either hot or chilled water, based on the particular doctor's pet theory.[187]

While the types of treatment proliferated, the fear of cholera persisted through the nineteenth century because few of them proved to be reliable. In 1832, a Frenchman observed that 'the whole of Europe is nothing but a vast billboard announcing admirable recipes in colossal letters'.[188] Unani accounts of cholera in India also acknowledged the difficulty in curing the disease. As one Lahore-based text of 1892 noted, 'If anyone is ever cured of the disease, this is owing to good fortune rather than medical expertise.'[189] Miasma, described as *fasad-i-ab-o-hawa* (pollution of the climate), was seen as an important generator of cholera.[190] So was improper diet, blamed for disturbing the balance of the body, and recommendations included *doodh ka barf* or milk-ice and rose water as 'cooling foods'.[191]

Vaccinations were also attempted to curb cholera, since they had proven to be such an effective preventive device against smallpox in the nineteenth century. Around the time that cholera hit Spain in 1884–85, a general practitioner there, Jaime Ferrán (1851–1929), began to experiment by injecting weak cholera, first in pigs, then on himself and finally on his comrades in makeshift trials.[192] The results were encouraging but were dismissed by the powerful scientific academies of Europe, suspicious of the primitive setting of his laboratory and his crude medical apparatus. This was less of a handicap for Waldemar Mordechai Haffkine (1860–1930), a young Jewish bacteriologist from Odessa, then a part of the Russian Empire, who joined the famed Pasteur Institute in Paris and developed a vaccine against cholera by 1892.[193] He then visited India to conduct field trials over the next few years and sought to promote compulsory vaccination, with little success, though his tryst with India would turn out to be long-lived and dramatic, as will be seen in the next chapter on the plague.[194] The British officials were sceptical of the effectiveness of Haffkine's vaccine and resisted compulsory vaccination for decades, fearing a backlash from the public. Vaccination was a prickly subject in India, as witnessed in the case of smallpox earlier, with all sorts of notions and rumours in different places. For example, during World War I it was difficult to convince Indian soldiers serving in Mesopotamia to inoculate themselves against cholera because of stories heard from their days in Egypt that it would lead to impotence.[195] While voluntary inoculations began to be practised on a larger scale, compulsory inoculations, like for pilgrims on major pilgrimage routes, began only in the 1930s.[196]

Along with vaccination for prevention, a potential cure for cholera also emerged in the early twentieth century. Since dehydration was acute once a person fell sick with cholera, some felt that adequate rehydration seemed like a good line of research to pursue. The eventual breakthrough that emerged in the early twentieth century was intravenous (IV) infusions of fluids to restore the 'balance in the circulation' that Johnson wrote about in 1813. The roots of this method can be traced back to a time as early as 1830. R. Hermann, a chemist, and Jaehnichen, a physician, were German expatriates working with the Institute of Artificial Waters in Moscow and attempted to inject water into the veins, with limited success.[197] Similar methods were adopted in England and other places but had minimal effect on mortality rates, possibly because of inappropriate instruments or fluids used for the infusion.

The perfection of the IV method is attributed to Leonard Rogers (1868–1962), who, by doing so, also salvaged the reputation of the Indian Medical Service that had earlier stubbornly dismissed Koch's findings on cholera. From 1906, Rogers conducted numerous experiments at the Calcutta Medical College Hospital and managed to bring down the case fatality rate from 60 per cent to 20 per cent.[198] He did this by carefully analysing the composition of the blood and stools by varying the intensity of saline solutions injected into the veins. Decades later, he could state in his memoirs with much pride that he had established 'a scientific basis for the life-saving value of the hypertonic saline treatment'.[199] The success of IV methods opened up new lines of enquiry and in the latter half of the twentieth century, oral rehydration therapy would be established as an even more effective cure, available at a low cost, dramatically cutting case fatality to negligible rates.

In the treatment of cholera during the Age of Pandemics, Western physicians often blamed 'oriental fatalism' for what they thought was the callousness of people in India.[200] In practice, the gap between European medical treatments of cholera and the Indian ones was negligible in the early nineteenth century, and widened only by the end of it. But this was sufficient to drive a religious agenda to win adherents and wean them away from their 'superstitions'. For instance, cholera in India was depicted in a 1923 black-and-white silent film called *The Catechist of Kil-Arni*, made by Thomas Gavan Duffy of the French missionary order, and filmed in locales around Pondicherry in south India. It was a film of Catholic propaganda that showed how a cholera outbreak in a village called Chetpet led to the conversion of a person to Christianity due to the relief offered by the local missionary. While it is unbearable to watch today, both for the tragedy of the disease it depicts and the brazenness of the filmmaker's propaganda, not to mention the excruciating forty-minute screen time of a silent video, it merits attention because it is probably the earliest video ever made on an epidemic's outbreak in India and on a cholera-related theme in the world.

The film begins by depicting people bathing and at the same time others collecting water for their daily chores from the same water body. Then, in the seventh minute of the film, the screen displays a message, 'The tainted water does its work. Cholera has broken out in the village,' followed by a visual of people running around, after which the screen reads, 'Panic'. It then depicts a local superstitious practice of people jumping over a pig that is still alive but buried in the ground up to its neck, followed by a scene of people leaving the village. The screen then reads, 'Heartless desertion of the dead,' soon followed by another which says, 'Father Albert hears of Chetpet stricken with cholera, and, with the missionary Sisters, hurries off to help.' Father Albert is played by Duffy himself, who worked as a missionary in India from 1911 to 1941, the year of his death.[201] Overall, the film contrasts the practice of deserting the sick with that of tending with care to drive home its propaganda. The Age of Pandemics could at times coincide neatly with the 'civilizing' instincts of imperial powers.

It was thus ironic that one of the most significant discoveries that would be made in our understanding of cholera would be by an Indian scientist. In 1959, some seven decades after Koch's discovery, Sambhu Nath De (1915–1985), born in a village close to Calcutta in the region from where the first cholera pandemic is said to have originated in 1817, discovered that *Cholerae vibrio* secreted enterotoxin.[202] Until then, it was believed that the vibrios had only endotoxins, which were released as the bacteria fell to the body's immune system.[203] But as it turned out, that did not produce the symptoms of cholera. De's work on enterotoxins and on the exact action of the vibrios on the membranes of the intestines led to the eventual adoption of oral rehydration therapy and targeted vaccines against the enterotoxins.

Shortly after De's discovery, a new strain of cholera was identified, named the *El Tor* variety after the historic quarantine station at Suez. This led to the *seventh* cholera pandemic, going by the usual convention, which had a mild impact worldwide. Since the 1960s, research on cholera has been so wide-ranging that many assertions of Koch in the 1880s have been found to be inaccurate. It turns out that cholera may not always have been an Indian phenomenon, is not necessarily water-borne, can depend on seasonal and environmental factors just as the sanitarians had so assiduously maintained in the nineteenth century, and that it is caused by unstable organisms whose major home was warm seas rather than bowels.[204] As per one 2013 study, 'V. cholerae is a natural inhabitant of brackish riverine, estuarine, and coastal waters, and only a subset of strains are known to be pathogenic to humans.'[205] The study also argues that 'cholera is a zoonosis with a diverse group of vectors and reservoirs, since a zoonosis is an infectious disease that can be transmitted from animals to humans by a vector'.[206]

The history of cholera shows how incremental scientific knowledge can successfully curb diseases even though that knowledge itself has often had to go full circle, back to once-discarded hypotheses. Many puzzles about nineteenth-century cholera, such as its regional seasonality and recrudescence, still await investigation by curious medical researchers interested in history.[207]

Today, the fear of cholera remains in pockets of Africa and in other places where a war or a refugee crisis breaks out. But its incidence has reduced globally, and especially in India. Indians hear the word 'haiza' only in schools when reading Munshi Premchand's popular Hindi story 'Eidgah'. Set in the early twentieth century, the story's protagonist, Hamid, is said to have lost both his parents at a very young age, his father specifically, to haiza. Or the student of English literature may encounter Rudyard Kipling's (1865–1936) poem, 'Cholera Camp', with lines such as these:

> We've got the cholerer in camp—its' worse than forty fights;
> We're dyin' in the wilderness the same as Isrulites.
> It's before us, an' be'ind us, an' we cannot get away,
> An' the doctor's just reported we've ten more to-day![208]

But over a century ago, cholera commanded fear even among physicians, as reflected in Hakim Saiyad Amaldar Hussain's quote at the beginning of this chapter. The word 'cholera' appeared in nearly 3 per cent of all articles published in a leading Indian English newspaper between the 1840s and 1880s, more than any disease in those decades, despite claiming fewer lives than malaria.[209]

After the 1890s, cholera's significance in the popular discourse decreased gradually. Cholera would be replaced by another dreaded word, mentioned in nearly 5 per cent of all articles for the next few decades, with opinions galore yet again on its causes and spread, and treatments and tragedies. That dreaded word was 'plague'.

Table 1: Estimates of Cholera Pandemic Deaths (1817–1920) Worldwide[210]

Region	Deaths, Millions	% of World Total	Population in 1870 (Millions)	Deaths/ Population in 1870, %
Asia	11.5	61	765	1.5
India (Epidemic)	8.0	42	253	3.2
China	1.0	5	358	0.3
Japan	0.4	2	34	1.2
Thailand	0.4	2		
Burma	0.4	2		
Philippines	0.3	2		
Rest of Asia	1.0	5		
Europe	5.8	30	328	1.8
Russia	3.0	16	88	3.4
Spain	0.6	3	16	3.8
Hungary	0.5	3		
France	0.3	2	38	0.8
Germany	0.2	1	39	0.5
UK	0.15	1	31	0.5
Rest of Europe	1.0	5		
Africa	1.0	5	90	1.1
Egypt	0.6	3	6	10.0
Rest of Africa	0.4	2		
North America	0.2	1	40	0.5
South America	0.5	3	40	1.3
Oceania	-			
World Total	**19.0**	**100**	**1,272**	**1.5**

Endemic deaths in India estimated to be 31 million.

3

Plague

> 'When it was about to break out, a mouse would rush out of its hole
> as if mad, and striking itself against the door and the walls of the
> house, would expire. If, immediately after this signal, the occupants
> left the house and went away to the jungle, their lives were saved; if
> otherwise, the inhabitants of the whole village would be swept away
> by the hand of death.'
>
> – c.1615 CE, Ikbal-nama-i-Jahangiri[1]

From the vantage point of history, it would appear that human beings have had a love–hate relationship with rodents. The hate is perhaps more evident and is best exemplified by humans' panicked squeals upon suddenly encountering rodents in the house. The love is less visible, though the cartoon show *Tom and Jerry* (since the 1940s) and, more recently, movies such as *Stuart Little* (1999) and *Ratatouille* (2007), have done a lot to make these little mammals appear more endearing in popular imagination. In *Ratatouille*, the rat is a star chef who does wonders for a restaurant kitchen in Paris, much to the chagrin of the health inspector and of his own family members, who are depicted as creatures associated with filth.

In China, the twelve-year cycle of zodiac signs begins with the Rat; 2020 happens to be the Year of the Rat. In India, the statue of a mouse (*mushak*) gets pride of place in millions of homes as the vehicle of Ganapati, sitting dutifully beneath the much loved elephant-headed god. The reverence for rodents is taken to astonishing heights at the Karni Mata Temple near Bikaner in Rajasthan, also known as the Temple of Rats, where thousands of rats live peacefully; worshippers consider the food animals have nibbled on to be auspicious.

So it may come as a surprise to those with only a rudimentary understanding of the plague and rats that the plague actually causes more harm to rats than to humans. And that when rats suddenly start dying in large numbers, it is an ominous sign, as described in the quote earlier. Such signs had long been noted in the Indian subcontinent, but became more frequent during the global plague pandemic that began in the late nineteenth century. If, as observed in the first chapter, Europe was the epicentre of death in the pandemic plagues of the sixth and fourteenth centuries, the third pandemic plague revolved mainly around India. It would claim over 13 million lives, 95 per cent of them in the Indian subcontinent alone.

The third plague pandemic also raged in southern China and touched cities across continents—Hong Kong, Sydney, Cape Town, Buenos Aires, Glasgow and San Francisco.[2] Most of the deaths occurred between 1894 and 1918, after which the pandemic gradually lost steam. That it *generated* a lot of steam was without doubt; the containment measures were often unprecedented, leading to showdowns between governments and people, people and rats and, as we will see in a few cases, between rats and cats.

Decoding the Plague: The Rat and the Flea

The exact significance of rodents in outbreaks of the plague and the mechanism of disease transmission would be comprehensively decoded only in the late nineteenth and early twentieth centuries; indeed, many questions about the plague mysteries of the past still remain unanswered.[3] In the history of plague outbreaks in Europe, rats appeared infrequently, leading many to theorize about other forms of transmission or speculate that in certain episodes, the plague was pneumonic rather than bubonic.[4] A classic nursery rhyme from the old plague eras of Europe has no reference to rats, and therefore points to pneumonic plague:

> Ring a ring of roses [skin lesions], a pocket full of posies [nosegays],
> Atischoo atischoo [pneumonic plague], we all fall down [dead].[5]

In stark contrast, rats appear frequently in references to epidemics in Indian history. One of the earliest references to rat-related calamities, as noted in the first chapter, was in Kautilya's *Arthashastra*, compiled at least eighteen centuries ago, in which the rodents were considered to be one of the several calamities of divine origin that the king had to protect his people from. But rats are also mentioned in the same text in a more definite manner:

> In case of danger from rats, locusts, birds or insects, the appropriate animals (e.g., cats or mongooses) shall be let loose and (these predators) protected from being killed or harassed by dogs. Poisoned grain may be strewn around and purificatory rites may be performed by experts. Or, the rat tax (a quota of dead rats to be brought in by each one) may be fixed.[6]

This reference has so far not been documented by medical historians and I would speculate that the 'rat tax' specified here could be related to the plague in those times. We will later see how closely this description matches the plague prevention measures eventually adopted in India in the early twentieth century.

Another historical Indian source on the plague, this time referring to rat mortality and recommended evacuation, is the *Bhagavata Purana*, which appears to have been formalized by roughly the tenth century CE.[7] Many more specific references to the plague start appearing in the seventeenth century CE.[8] Around the year 1615 CE, in the tenth reigning year of the Mughal emperor Jahangir, bubonic plague was documented in north India—in Punjab, Lahore and Agra—by travellers and by none other than the emperor himself in his autobiography.[9] Jahangir recounted a story narrated by the daughter of Asaf Khan, that of a mouse running around distractedly in the courtyard of her house. When it was fed to a cat, the cat dropped it from its mouth showing aversion. Soon, people in the vicinity started dying with buboes marked on them. This episode of the plague lasted several years and reappeared in travellers' records between 1684 and 1702, during Aurangzeb's reign, mostly in western India and in the Deccan.[10] Places like Surat, Ahmedabad, Bombay and Bijapur were affected in this outbreak. The Indian plague outbreaks of the seventeenth century coincided with those documented in Europe and the relative absence of the plague in the eighteenth century also mirrors Europe's experience.

In the late eighteenth and early nineteenth centuries, major plague outbreaks were documented in the Mediterranean world. Egypt was hit especially hard, and between 1798 and 1801, when France and Britain were warring for control over it, the plague was an additional hardship in a time of general distress.[11] Over 2,000 Indian troops of the English East India Company, drawn from across the subcontinent, served in the war effort in 1801 and were devastated by the plague.[12] At this stage, while the causes of the plague were unknown, quarantines were seen to be an effective measure for prevention in Europe. The plague had led to strict quarantine measures in Egypt and European officials began to prepare for the same in India.

When ships carrying those troops returned to India, the men and women were not allowed to disembark the usual way; in Madras, the vessels had to wait for a few weeks at Quarantine Point, north of the Madras city port.[13] In Bombay, the ordeal lasted months as a lazaretto (an isolation facility) was set up on Butcher's Island with strict protocols.[14] The system seems to have worked as no plague outbreak was reported in the period that followed in India. The plague in Egypt in the early nineteenth century and its potential impact on India was a recurring theme, especially in later arguments on opening steam navigation between Britain and India; opponents of the plan argued that it would bring the plague to India by increasing the intensity of contact with Egypt, which was on the shipping route.[15]

A severe plague also affected the Ottoman Empire between 1812 and 1819, coinciding with a plague outbreak in Gujarat in western India that devastated several places. In Ahmedabad, there were first-hand accounts of the plague causing 'swellings' in 'groin and armpits'.[16] The plague later broke out in Pali in western India between 1836 and 1838 and affected the wider region of Marwar, where it was observed that the 'inhabitants of any house instantly quitted it on seeing a dead rat'.[17] Kumaon and Garwhal, in the Himalayas, were also affected by the plague in the nineteenth century; the disease was commonly referred to as *mahamari* here.[18]

The theatre of action quickly moved to central Asia and China, in the second half of the nineteenth century. Most medical historians trace the origin of the world's third plague pandemic to Yunnan in south-western China at this time, or to a subsequent outbreak in Hong Kong in 1894, or an outbreak in Bombay in 1896. It is the geographic switch from Europe, the Mediterranean world or central Asia to south Asia and east Asia in the intensity of plague outbreaks that marks this periodization rather than the emergence of the plague itself, which struck sporadically in different parts of the nineteenth-century world.

Yunnan, a mountainous region bordering Burma, was rife with war, famine and the plague in the 1870s when European explorers documented the events that had taken place there.[19] Major depopulation had occurred due to the strife and all the classic markers of the plague on the human body were noted in great detail, coupled with passing references to 'sickness and mortality among rats'.[20] The disease seemed endemic to this region, with references to it found in the past as well. Throughout the 1870s and 1880s, doctors found plague-related human and rat mortality in various hinterlands of southern China, but it finally attracted international attention in 1894 when it hit the port of Canton, the largest city in that area.[21] Case fatality rates of over 80 per cent caused instant panic and alarm, and about 40,000 perished in the first half of 1894, most of them 'poor, over-crowded and badly-housed'.[22] Those who escaped death tended to reside in the upper storeys of houses or in boats.

People began to flee Canton; Hong Kong, 80 miles away and ruled by the British, was the next major city to fall to the plague in May 1894. Deaths in Hong Kong were far fewer than in Canton, around 3,000, but its position as an important entrepot of Asia meant that it received far greater attention. It was here that the Japanese physician Kitasato discovered a bacillus (rod-shaped bacterium) as the causative agent of plague. His discovery was soon followed by that of Alexandre Yersin, both in the month of June. Kitasato had been a student of Robert Koch and was sent to Hong Kong by the Japanese government to study the disease, while Yersin was working with the Pasteur Institute in Paris and was sent to Hong Kong by his employer and the French government. The root cause of the disease that had ravaged continents in the past had finally been identified, but its transmission still remained a mystery. That puzzle would slowly be unravelled in the Indian subcontinent through numerous research studies after 1896, the year when the plague arrived in the city of Bombay.

The key to the puzzle lay in analysing the strong correlation observed between the plague in rats (*R. rattus* or house rats) and the plague in humans, which would inevitably follow within a week or a fortnight.[23] Further, the mere handling of plague-infected rats did not necessarily infect humans, so there had to be a mechanism for the transfer of the plague bacillus, later referred to as *Yersinia pestis*, from the blood of rats to the blood of humans.

An insect-based theory of transmission would not have sounded all that preposterous at the time. Almora-born Ronald Ross (1857–1932), a member of the Indian Medical Service for nearly twenty-five years, had just proven the link between mosquitoes and malaria in Secunderabad in 1897, a breakthrough for which he was awarded the Nobel Prize for Medicine in 1902. And so, after several studies by researchers in India and outside, it was discovered that the tiny rat flea was the connecting link between rat plague and human plague. Rat fleas do not generally bite humans but when rats are infected by the plague and die in large numbers, rat fleas, hungry for blood, transfer their attention to humans.[24] This explained the lag between rat mortality and human mortality observed during plague outbreaks. Rat fleas also enabled the multiplication of plague bacilli in their stomachs and thus served as good disease transmitters. A particular variety of rat fleas called *X. cheopis* was seen to be the most efficient vector for plague transmission, so regions which had this rat flea would witness larger outbreaks than others.

This opened up a new dilemma: was the plague transmitted to a new region by rats, fleas or humans, or a combination of all of them? It would prove to be a vexing problem, one that in turn would shape the nature of plague prevention policies around the world. For the first years of the pandemic, however, most health officials were clueless about the mode of transmission and thus implemented health measures that were a combination of segregation, isolation and disinfection. These policies triggered a sharp backlash, particularly in the country most affected by the pandemic: India.

Crisis in Western India, 1896–1898

The year 1896–97, like 2020, was not one of the best for India. Some idea of the tragedy of that year can be judged by the provocative title of a book published in 1898 by George Lambert: *India: The Horror-stricken Empire Containing a Full Account of the Famine, Plague and Earthquake of 1896-7.*[25] In the larger scheme of things, it would be the famine, following deficient rainfall in 1896, that would exact the greatest toll—it claimed over 2 million lives.[26] Mortality figures for the plague in India in 1896, 1897 and 1898 were relatively low in comparison: around 3,000, 50,000 and 100,000, respectively, and almost all of it concentrated in the Bombay Presidency in western India. And yet, it would be the plague that would spark off protests, riots and even an assassination as the people of India began to contest the harsh pandemic containment measures initiated by the colonial government.

When the plague was reported in Bombay in 1896, by some accounts after a lapse of nearly 200 years, it was not a well-known disease in the city, despite its presence in other parts of India in the nineteenth century.[27] The first cases appeared near the dockyards in Mandvi in July–August 1896, where, along with rats, people started dying suddenly. B.F. Patell, a teacher at Elphinstone College, would later compose a sixty-page poem, *The Plague of Bombay*, beginning with these memorable lines:

I stand in Mandvi, all around, With cries of woe the streets
  resound.
This quarter, crowded at the best, First falls a victim to the pest.
The 'Jains' and 'Bhatias,' sad to tell, First in alarming numbers
  fell;
In every home a death or two, Meets the bewildered gazer's view.
These sects seemed as picked out to bear alone the burden of
  despair;
The other races, as yet free, Could not the lurking danger see;
Half callous to their neighbours' woes, The plague disturbed
  not their repose;
But soon all undeceived they stand, The Ravager, with scythe
  in hand,
Scours every corner of the land.[28]

The reference to Jain and Bhatia trading communities is significant,
for trade and foodgrain stores, as sites providing nourishment and
shelter to rats, would emerge as an abiding theme of the plague
pandemic in India. A trading link to Hong Kong from the docks
of Mandvi was later traced as, and is still considered, the most
probable source of the plague in Bombay, though later reports
also speculated on a connection with Egypt.[29] The first cases were
mistaken for fever and diphtheria and drew attention as the plague
only on 23 September 1896, after they were diagnosed by Goa-
born Dr Acacio Viegas (1856–1933), a graduate of Grant Medical
College in Bombay.[30] The diagnosis was treated as tentative and few
believed it until it was confirmed on 13 October by W. Haffkine, the
government bacteriologist of cholera inoculation fame.

  The spread of the plague from Mandvi across the city was slow
and irregular but everywhere it was accompanied by significant rat
mortality, prompting Patell to observe in his poem that 'dead rats'
struck fear into people's hearts.[31] Soon, in October 1896, municipal

authorities were granted sweeping powers to curtail the outbreak, and that was followed by the Epidemic Diseases Act, passed on 4 February 1897 by Lord Elgin, then viceroy of India. This law was applicable across the country and constituted the largest intervention by the colonial regime in the day-to-day lives of Indians until then. It enabled the inspection of people practically anywhere, disallowed public congregations, authorized destruction or confiscation of property related to the disease, and segregation and hospitalization of suspected cases with infection.

The law did not stay merely on paper but was brought to the streets of Bombay with great force. On 5 March, an army general, W.F. Gatacre, was brought in to head a plague committee in the city and lead the containment drive, emulating previous efforts of the British in Hong Kong in 1894.[32] Senior medical officers from around India were rushed to Bombay to supervise efforts in ten districts carved within the city and equipped with makeshift hospitals. They were assisted by lower-rung medical officers, over 500 soldiers tasked with 'plague duty' and even medical students. Nurses from the Daughters of the Cross at Bandora, the All Saints' Sisters at Mazagaon and other charitable institutions chipped in, and at least one of them, Sister Elizabeth, died due to the plague while on duty at the Mahim Causeway Hospital, which was in operation temporarily between 26 March and 18 May 1897.[33] Medical researchers from Russia, Austria, Germany, France, Egypt and Italy were also permitted into Bombay to work and uncover the mystery of the plague, as Kitasato and Yersin had done in Hong Kong in 1894.

This massive response was triggered because the plague in Bombay city had sent shockwaves throughout the British Empire, not least because the disease, till then confined to Hong Kong, threatened trading ties with India's leading textile centre. At the hurriedly convened tenth International Sanitary Conference in Venice in 1897, a trading embargo was proposed against India if

containment actions were not taken.[34] The memory of the plague
was still vivid in Europe, with widespread tales of horror from the
fourteenth century, the devastation of London in 1665 (especially
for the British) and more recent experiences of the Mediterranean
world in the nineteenth century.

As part of the plague prevention measures, thousands of
buildings were cleared out citing unsanitary living conditions,
property was destroyed and burnt, and drains were regularly cleaned.
Tiles were removed from the roofs of houses, and dwellings with
reported infections were marked with signs outside them and treated
'as if they were on fire'.[35] They were flushed with water from fire
engines and flushing pumps (as seen on the cover of this book)
mixed with disinfectants such as cresol or phenyl-based potassium
permanganate. Houses were also lime-washed and sulphur was
burnt inside, for which a large staff was employed. Disinfectants
were freely distributed to the public. Good ventilation and lighting
were seen to be critical in the list of sanitary measures and health
officials lamented the 'filthy, insanitary houses and chawls in which
the poorer natives live'.[36]

Street watering was stopped to reduce dampness. Warehouses
with a significant number of infections were shut for twenty days
and shops for two days. Dead rats were burnt and unclaimed
human corpses were cremated by the municipality. A year later, the
municipality patted itself on the back, claiming success in containing
the plague within 'moderate bounds'.[37]

But the measures unleashed to counter plague created panic
among the local population, which was unaware of the disease
or the rationale behind the containment measures. Above all, the
ruthlessness hurt popular sentiments around caste, religion and
gender norms. The body searches conducted at railway stations were
considered to be humiliating, especially when women were searched
by male officials, and the lack of observation of caste and religious

rules and taboos in hospitals hurt the elite.[38] The Parsis, Jains and other communities responded by setting up temporary hospitals for their own kind.[39] For instance, a Dharavi hospital was created for a while 'for the employees on the waste land between the Dharavi tanneries and Mahim Railway Station' and a Telugu hospital was set up in Kamatipura.[40] Nurses offered critical support and in one remarkable case, a small girl being carried to the 'dead-house', on the mistaken notion that she was dead, was revived by a nurse, after which she made a rapid recovery in the hospital.[41] Doctors displayed great courage in doing their duties in the hospitals despite minimal knowledge of the disease. When Dr Manser, senior doctor at the Jamsetji Hospital and president of the scientific committee appointed by the government to study the disease, succumbed to the plague in January 1897, it was described as a 'public calamity'.[42]

The poor panicked about both the disease, because it crushed them disproportionately, and about the government's measures, which targeted their dwellings and often left them homeless in the city.[43] In such an environment, there were strident protests in the local press and on the streets. Ambulances were attacked; the Arthur Road Hospital was besieged twice in October 1896 by textile mill workers who wanted the release of suspected cases.[44] Much later, in March 1898, violence would break out over the government's decision to inspect all corpses, angering Muslims in particular; cries of 'Mar dalo goreku, Mar dalo goreku (kill the white man)' filled the air.[45] Rumours abounded about cruel hospital practices; one such story was that the British were collecting Indian bodies to extract momiai, a fluid, to save themselves.[46] Strict segregation in hospitals was also dreaded as it meant that family members would be separated from each other. As per one chronicler from that time, 'every sanitary measure was opposed', and some, like the compulsory removal of the infected to the hospital, were soon rolled back.[47]

While the mode of disease transmission was still unknown, the cases in Hong Kong and Bombay were slowly shifting the opinion of the medical community away from the widely held view of human-based contagion. The example given was that of Worli, a fishing village in Bombay, that refused entry to outsiders, but contracted the plague nevertheless.[48] After seeing many dead rats, the villagers then evacuated and camped in a field outside as a precautionary measure, which was in line with the age-old practice observed in Indian history. The villagers would go to their houses to take essential supplies but stay outside for the most part, and in this manner evaded the disease to a considerable extent.

For the colonial authorities, the Worli incident tilted the scales in favour of an evacuation strategy that would be widely used later, though this should be recognized first and foremost as part of India's traditional knowledge. The British noted that the exact opposite of this had been recommended in London during the 1665 plague outbreak, when, suspecting human-to-human transmission, people were told to shut themselves indoors, with fatal results.[49]

It was also observed that there was something about the house of the infected person that was significant in explaining death by the plague. Residents of the house who left for a while avoided the disease but were often struck down by it on their return. This was attributed to 'poison', either in the soil below or in a gaseous form, that killed rats and humans simultaneously.[50] The 'poison-based' theory held sway for nearly a decade after 1896 and was finally discarded only when clear proof of the rat-flea-human transmission mechanism was presented. In the interim, much attention was paid to disinfecting houses using various substances on a trial-and-error basis.

None of these measures worked; the plague would ravage Bombay over and over in later years, with case fatality rates in excess of 70 per cent.[51] Plague-related deaths started picking up from December 1896 onwards, peaked in February 1897 and lost steam after June, with the onset of the monsoon, only to rise again later in the year. This seasonal cycle of deaths peaking in the first half of the year would be repeated time and again. All along, richer folk experienced lower mortality. Plague-related death rates between 1897 and 1900 constituted 2 per 1,000 among Europeans, around 10 per 1,000 among Parsis, Jews and Eurasians, and 15 per 1,000 among Hindu 'Brahmans'.[52] Plague death rates exceeded 20 per 1,000 for other Hindu castes, with similar rates for categories assigned as 'Ordinary Hindus' and 'Low Caste Hindus'.[53]

The plague committee report documented higher plague mortality rates among women than men, attributing it 'to the number of pregnant females who aborted'.[54] High fever, headaches, vomiting and lethargy were significant symptoms but painful buboes were the classic symptom of the plague, occurring on the bodies of almost all those affected. Cases with buboes closer to the neck and head saw greater fatalities.[55] It was also noted that the chances of survival after getting the plague were low but increased with 'early and good nursing', and especially if the patient lay down for four days until the temperature of the body was back to normal.[56]

One way out of mortality in any epidemic is to develop immunity against the disease, which was a possibility in the 1890s with successful templates of inoculation and vaccination for cholera and smallpox, respectively. Yersin himself moved to Bombay and experimented with an inoculation method he developed at Sahebs' Servants' Hospital.[57] Haffkine, then based in Bombay, got to work on anti-plague solutions and immediately came up with a fluid serum of plague bacilli destroyed by a particular method, which proved to be very promising.[58] This inoculation would not have an effect on people already diagnosed with the plague and had only short-term utility, but tests did show that to a large extent, it worked as a preventive device, if not a curative one. News spread far and wide and Haffkine was hailed in a Calcutta health journal, *Swasthya*, in 1898 as a 'great benefactor of our country'.[59] Soon, thousands were being inoculated to safeguard against the plague, though past cultural hesitations persisted.

Another way to escape mortality was migration. Unsurprisingly, therefore, it was very much in the news during the initial outbreak (as also in 2020 CE), but first the migration of rats and only then that of humans. Rat migration from one place to another was closely observed and documented. The municipal commissioner of Bombay, P.C.H. Snow, charted the migration path of rats within the city from the east to the west and then to the north, and emphasized that rat migration and mortality impeded local efforts to contain the plague among humans in newer regions.[60] The ensuing panic in Bombay led to a mass exodus from the city, such that by February 1897, half the population, nearly 400,000 people, had left, bringing economic activities to a standstill.[61] A cry heard at the time was, 'Look brother, if die we must, let us die at home.'[62] Government officials had to intervene so that the sanitation staff and the 'scavengers' of the city did not leave, else, as noted then, 'Bombay would be converted into a vast dunghill of putrescent ordure'.[63] The owners of the cotton mills worried about the loss of labour; and at least one such concern, Petit Mills, promised to take care of their workers by building a plague hospital, after which few workers left.[64] But the majority of mill labour did leave, only to return later in the year because famine conditions in the countryside were not conducive for livelihoods either.

The transmission of the disease over long distances was poorly understood at the time; officials pointed fingers at the 'banias' and 'marwadis' or traders as the primary spreaders of the disease 'because the Bania is the chief traveller'.[65] Later research suggested that transmission occurred because of the migration of infected rats in means of transport or through rat fleas embedded in grain husks or in the clothing and luggage of infected people. During the first outbreak, officials in Calcutta had telegraphed Bombay in October 1896 to enquire if inspection on the railway stations was necessary, but action was delayed until February, by when most of the exodus from Bombay had taken place.[66]

After February, under a new legislative framework, check-ups were ramped up across India, and in Bombay, officials had to worry about infection returning from the smaller towns and villages with a new wave of return migration to the city. Inspections were initiated at various stations in and around Bombay, for instance, at Santa Cruz on 17 April, where scores of detected cases were referred to a hospital in Khar.[67] Similar checks took place at points where sea traffic docked since a large part of the migratory labour to Bombay came from the Konkan region and they travelled by sea.

Inevitably, whether it was because of travel by sea or by land, plague cases slowly started appearing in other towns of India, in Karachi and in Poona in December 1896, and taking root in Calcutta much later, in 1898.[68] The plague in Poona claimed the life of Savitribai Phule (1831–1897), distinguished social reformer, on 10 March 1897, as she went out of her way to help plague-affected patients.[69] She had opened a clinic with her son, a doctor, and contracted the disease while performing her duties. Another distinguished woman who observed the plague closely in Poona was Pandita Ramabai (1858–1922), a Sanskrit scholar and social activist who penned a piece in May 1897 'to warn patients and friends of young women against the moral evils of the plague hospital and segregation camps'.[70] She documented the woeful facilities at the government's plague hospital, including the 'indescribable' filthiness of the 'only bathroom assigned for women'.[71]

But tensions in Poona were running high even without bathroom-related issues. The plague outbreak coincided with an ongoing tussle between Sandhurst, governor of the Bombay Presidency between 1895 and 1900, and Bal Gangadhar Tilak (1856–1920), a leader of the Indian National Congress.[72] Walter Charles Rand, a young officer, was appointed the chairman of the plague committee in February 1897, with sweeping powers to curtail the rapidly spreading epidemic and to overrule the relatively autonomous municipal body that comprised several Indian leaders. Rand went in for the harshest containment measures anywhere in the country, with intensive house searches conducted by European troops to identify sick people and transfer them to the hospital.[73] In the event, accusations of forced examination and misconduct, especially with women, flew thick and fast. Rand was shot on 22 June 1897 by brothers from an outraged family with the surname 'Chapekar'.[74] Rand succumbed to his injuries a few weeks later. Another British official who was mistakenly shot before him in the same encounter had died on the spot.

The sensational killings led the government to arrest Tilak for sedition and imprison him for over a year, with the allegation of instigating violence. Tilak had bitterly contested the manner in which containment measures were carried out in Poona but at the same time, had advocated the adoption of modern sanitation measures to combat the plague.[75] Further, under the plague restrictions, the Ganapati festival, popularized by Tilak, was banned in 1897, presumably not because the god had a mouse on his side, but to avoid public congregations.[76] Either way, upon his release from jail, Tilak emerged as a national hero.

The events that took place in western India because of the plague between 1896 and 1898 were quite dramatic. In the face of strong opposition, government intervention through containment measures began to slowly recede thereafter, even as the plague pandemic intensified its reach and grip. That was because in the long run, the plague pandemic in India, contrary to popular perception today, had little to do with Bombay city or with urban India. Around 200,000 people would eventually die of the plague in Bombay city over several decades, but that would turn out to be less than 2 per cent of the overall plague mortality in India. The third plague pandemic of the world claimed most of its victims in villages rather than in cities, far away from Bombay.[77]

Plague in the Hinterlands

The plague pandemic claimed over 12 million lives in the Indian subcontinent between 1896 and 1918, peaking with over 1 million deaths in 1907.[78] Maximum mortality occurred in three provinces—Punjab and the United Provinces in the north, and Bombay Presidency in the west—bypassing the eastern and southern ends of the subcontinent almost completely. Among the princely states, Hyderabad and Mysore witnessed considerable mortality. This regional variation was a bit of a mystery. Some put it down to better sanitation, as this letter, titled 'Plague in Belgaum', to a newspaper's editor in the Bombay Presidency in 1920 attests:

> The sanitation of the city is in the most unsatisfactory way. The side gutters are like the old Augean stable and are seldom cleaned. The present most unsatisfactory state of sanitation is a standing disgrace to any civilized municipality. I seldom meet a Sanitary Inspector in the streets of Belgaum. For nearly a quarter of a century I lived in Madras, where I found the sanitary staff working all day.[79]

But better sanitation could not possibly have been a reason in eastern India, where officials had lamented for decades about sanitary problems in relation with cholera. Another possible explanation offered for the regional variation was that plague spread along the migration corridors that connected Bombay to the districts that sent labour to work in the city. But the major source regions, such as the Konkan and the lower Gangetic plains, barely saw any plague during the pandemic.

Later research would show that the likeliest explanation for the sharp regional variation in plague outbreaks was the behaviour of rodents and fleas, rather than that of humans. Dr S.C. Seal, who spent his entire life studying the plague, mentioned the following in his book *Plague: Conquest and Eradication in India* which he wrote towards the end of his career in 1987:

> It would be wrong to regard squalor, poverty and absence of sanitary safeguards as the determining cause of pandemic rise because neither are these confined only to plague epochs nor are they peculiar to plague infected countries . . . What we have found is that whenever the proportion of black rat as also of *X. cheopis* was reduced or lessened due to better housing and sanitary conditions, the incidence of plague had also come down or been greatly reduced, giving a clue to its control and eradication.[80]

The house rat, *R. rattus*, was the most important source of human infection, and regions that had a higher number of these mammals were more susceptible to human plague.[81] High rat mortality in a particular year would reduce the intensity of the plague for a year or two in a region, but it would return with a vengeance if the rat population re-stabilized, keeping everyone guessing in the interim.

In rural Uttar Pradesh (earlier the United Provinces), in addition to the rat, the gerbil *Tatera indica* was also found to be spreading the plague. Its complex burrowing patterns helped explain why the disease did not necessarily spread across villages along roads.[82]

Irrigated tracks were found to increase rodent populations, perhaps accounting for the plague's grip on Punjab in the early twentieth century, by when an extensive canal network had emerged in that region.[83] The *X. cheopis* flea was less widespread in southern and eastern India and thus those regions saw relatively fewer plague outbreaks. Further, the strong seasonality of the plague—it appeared least often during the monsoon months of June–September—was later shown to be due to the high humidity levels, which affected the survival of the rat flea and its ability to transmit plague.[84]

Almost all of this was unknown during the peak of the plague pandemic in the first decade of the twentieth century. All that people and officials could see was that the plague ripped apart the villages and towns of particular regions of India: the eastern side of the Western Ghats, from Bellary in the south to Ahmedabad in the west, and from the Jhelum river in Punjab in the north to roughly northern Bihar (see map on next page).

Bombay Presidency

Over 2 million people died in the Bombay Presidency between 1896 and 1918 due to the plague.[85] Annual deaths rose quickly after 1896 and peaked in 1903 with over 300,000 deaths, which was around 2 per cent of the province's population and around a third of all deaths that year.[86] Thereafter, death rates fell and it ceased to be the province most affected by the plague, with only brief outbreaks in 1911 and 1917. The bulk of the mortality occurred in the southern regions. Plague in Dharwar, Belgaum, Satara and few other districts wiped out 10 per cent of their respective populations between 1901 and 1910.[87] Skirmishes with the local governments over plague prevention measures were often noted in the initial years, especially in Hubli–Dharwar.[88] The coastal Konkan region, however, barely saw any incidence of plague, which some attributed to the nature of its rural organization of

Regions with high plague-related mortality in India

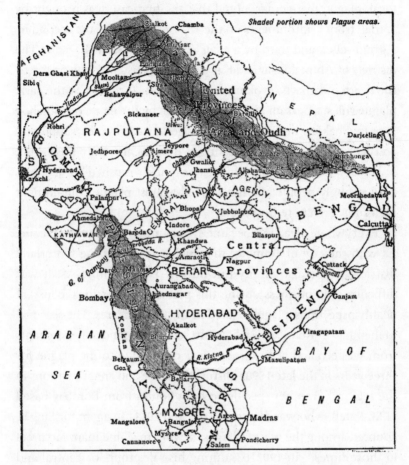

After 1905, the plague also extended to parts of central India and Hyderabad state.

Source: Charles Creighton, 'Plague in India', *Journal of the Society of Arts*, 53 (2743) (1905), p. 811.

scattered hamlets in villages compared to the compact, fortified settlements across the Western Ghats in Satara.[89]

Each district had its unique tale of how the plague arrived there, but the local bazaar or the cantonment was invariably the key suspect, hosting the movement of goods and grains, traders and soldiers, mostly by rail. In Ahmednagar district, in 1897, a local 'plague mamlatdar' noted that the first case was brought by 'a mali from Cantonments on the 10th of November, the second by a grain-seller, and third by a *Dhangar*, all from Sadar Bazar'.[90] The districts of Ahmednagar and Kaira would persistently stay on top of the death-toll charts, evoking fear and panic. Incensed by the early plague rules, a peasant and medicine man by the name of Ranchod Vira in Chaklasi in Kaira brought together a group of supporters and declared himself to be the king of the area, free from the British, in January 1898.[91] His movement was quickly crushed but it shows how strongly people felt and reacted against plague containment measures, even in remote areas.

Everywhere, dead rats became synonymous with human plague. As with the city of Bombay, the smaller towns of the hinterland districts would also empty out during plague outbreaks. It was difficult to do business during this period of desertions, constant health inspections, plague-related deaths and closures. The seasonal Maheji fair in Khandesh, which attracted thousands of merchants from western and central India, was closed due to the plague for three years in the late 1890s, disturbing trade and credit relations in the region.[92] Another specific account comes from Bombay-based N.M. Patell, who was, between 1875 and 1911, an agent for Singer, counted among the world's largest sewing-machine manufacturers in those times.[93] In 1902–03, during his sales tours of central and western India, he noted the dearth of tailors to sell his machines to since many had died of the plague or were working in famine relief centres.[94] Tailors were at a high risk of infection because the plague-causing fleas could be tucked among the clothes they were collecting and working with. Patell's tours were interrupted by sanitary cordons and regular health certifications; he even lost one of his salespersons to the plague. He wrote to the New York office, lamenting the dire situation and the difficulty of conducting business in disease-ridden India.

One place that remained relatively unaffected by the plague in the first decade of the twentieth century was the city of Ahmedabad, but that would change in 1917 when there was a serious outbreak, leading to a mass exodus of labour. This would provide the setting for the emergence of Vallabhbhai Patel (1875–1950) on the national front, decades before he became independent India's first home minister. Patel had only recently become a member of the Ahmedabad municipality and when the plague struck in 1917, he was the chairman of the sanitation committee.[95] While many were leaving the city, he not only stayed back but departed from prescribed norms and 'moved with the Municipality staff for taking effective preventive measures under his personal care'.[96] Much later, in the 1930s, he would again be involved in the Borsad plague outbreak, 100 kilometres south of Ahmedabad, first in relief work and then in identifying serious inadequacies in the government's handling of the outbreak.[97] As with Tilak in Poona, the plague was an important aspect of Patel's rise to the forefront of the freedom movement.

Punjab

Punjab, comprising regions in modern-day India and Pakistan, was, by far, the province worst affected by the plague, losing around 4 million people between 1896 and 1918, which constituted a third of all plague-related deaths in the Indian subcontinent.[98] Like in other parts of India, plague mortality would swing wildly from year to year, but unlike in those regions, the overall death rate in Punjab would also remain very high. The worst spells were 1902–05, 1907, 1910–11, 1915, 1918 and 1924, but after that, the plague rapidly plunged into insignificance, much faster than in other parts of India.[99]

The plague was first detected in Punjab in October 1897 in Khatkar Kalan, a village in Jullundur district, comprising mainly 'Jat Sikhs and Muhammadan Rawals'.[100] Locals speculated that a pilgrim returning from Haridwar was the cause, even though he had died several months before the rats started dying in the open in August and long before the epidemic broke out in October. The village was soon cordoned off, evacuated and disinfected, and was declared free of the plague by January 1898.[101] However, several villages in Jullundur and Hoshiarpur were soon affected and policemen were deployed to manage cordons.[102] By then, panic had set in. In February 1898, anonymous placards were placed in the busy marketplace of Chandni Chowk in Delhi (then a part of Punjab province) conveying annoyance with the newly instituted plague rules and a commitment to sacrificing lives, as was done during the '1857 Mutiny'.[103] And in April 1898, there was a riot in the Garnshankar market town of Hoshiarpur district due to a rumour that the authorities were poisoning wells, which was, incidentally, similar to a rumour heard in Europe during the fourteenth-century plague when Jews were blamed for poisoning wells.[104]

The annual number of plague-related deaths in Punjab remained low in the initial years. The number of plague mortalities crossed the 10,000 mark only in 1901, and that year, a rumour-based riot broke out in Shahzada in Sialkot district.[105] In 1902, over 200,000 lives were lost to the plague; Ludhiana, among others, was one of the worst affected districts.[106] The Punjab officials drew up an ambitious new plague policy, emphasizing the use of Haffkine's inoculations, only to find a new set of rumours spreading among the public. One such was as follows:

> The needle was a yard long; you died immediately after the operation; you survived the operation just six months and then collapsed; men lost their virility and women became sterile; the Deputy Commissioner himself underwent the operation and expired half an hour afterwards in great agony.[107]

Anti-Plague Inoculation Certificate provided in Punjab, c. 1901

Report on inoculation in the plague-infected areas of the Punjab and its dependencies from October 1900 to September 1901 by Major. E. Wilkinson (Chief Plague Medical Officer, Punjab), Lahore, 1903.
Source: National Library of Scotland.

Worse, in October 1902, nineteen people in Malkowal in the Gujrat district of Punjab, who had been inoculated, died of tetanus due to an infected needle.[108] That incident not only set the inoculation drive many years back but also brought Haffkine under the scanner for a while since the serum developed in Bombay had been changed to meet the large demand in Punjab.[109] Looking for a scapegoat, many in the administration, from Curzon, the viceroy at the very top, to people at the bottom, campaigned against Haffkine. It later emerged that the contamination had occurred outside Haffkine's laboratory.[110] Haffkine put up a good fight, garnering support from fellow scientists such as Ronald Ross, but nevertheless, had to vacate his job in Bombay and move to a small laboratory in Calcutta, the city which once praised him as a great benefactor of India, until his eventual retirement in 1915.[111] Not for the first time in history would a great scientist suffer a decline due to the bureaucracy.

In 1907, the peak year of plague mortality, over 3 per cent of Punjab's population was wiped out: over 500,000 lives.[112] The worst affected districts were Gujranwala, Gujrat, Shahpur, Sialkot and Rohtak.[113] A side effect of these deaths was that they raised the labour costs for landholders. To make matters worse, rust damaged the wheat crop earlier that year.[114] These factors added to the already widespread unrest over a newly introduced piece of legislation on land colonization in Punjab, leading to protests and riots. One of the implications of this politically volatile situation was the temporary deportation of the noted Punjabi political leader Lala Lajpat Rai (1865–1928), a key figure in the agitations.[115] Another impact of the 1907 plague was on housing designs in the newly built canal colonies of Punjab. Until then, authorities were rooting for compact settlement structures while the landholders wanted to build houses in the centre of the lands they owned for closer access to their fields. After the plague outbreak, officials conceded the beneficial aspects of isolated living as a way to escape the disease.[116]

By 1911, after more plague outbreaks and a vicious malarial epidemic in 1908, the plague was seen in Punjab to be as endemic as malaria. Every year, people would anticipate it, as a head of the plague operations would say, with 'extreme humility and patience'.[117]

United Provinces

In the United Provinces, the plague first struck fear into the hearts of the people, and only later struck their bodies. The massive state intervention of 1896–98 and daily news from Bombay had created a lot of anxiety among the public and the local press. The *Naiyar-i-Azam*, a newspaper in Moradabad, argued in March 1897 that 'the parda system is observed more strictly in the United Provinces than in Bombay, and the women in these Provinces will prefer death to removal to a segregation hospital'.[118] By April 1899, 'plague' had become such a buzzword that the *Hindustan* newspaper noted that it 'is even in the mouths of children'.[119] In May 1899, a stampede occurred at a fair in Benares over fears that a European, who was accompanied there by the police, was an inoculator.[120] Riots broke out in April 1900 in Kanpur when a segregation camp was attacked by millhands, Chamars and a Muslim butcher community because of the forceful detainment of women.[121]

In reality, the plague struck the United Provinces sporadically and did not result in death rates as high as in Punjab and the Bombay Presidency. However, the large size of the province's population meant that the disease would still claim over 3 million lives during the pandemic period. The plague struck the region in a big way in 1901, and death rates peaked in 1905, with 1907, 1910–14 and 1917–18 as other spells of high mortality. The plague would rear its head in the first four months of the year, with mortality usually peaking in March.[122] Kanpur, due its status of being 'one large granary', was identified as a major centre from which the plague spread outwards in north India. [123]

Instances of the plague had been documented in the Kumaon–Garhwal region in the nineteenth century, but that region did not suffer in the twentieth century outbreak. Instead, one cluster of districts in the extreme west of the United Provinces, comprising Saharanpur, Muzaffarnagar and Meerut, and another in the extreme east, comprising Azamgarh, Jaunpur, Ghazipur and Ballia, were regularly reported as 'high-mortality' plague districts.[124] One commentator in the 1940s, upon reviewing the evidence on the disease over the previous forty years, attributed the regional variation in plague mortality in the United Provinces to sanitation and medical facilities.[125] Another observer in 1905 blamed the dwelling structures and pointed out that Benares was relatively free from the plague despite being a major pilgrimage site because a large number of houses were well-built pakka structures made of stone and those houses rarely witnessed plague incidents.[126] In other cities more severely affected by the plague, like Lucknow, Bareilly, Allahabad, Kanpur and Agra, the relative number of mud-built kaccha houses was seen to be much higher. While this observation was probably correct, it was based on the wrong reasoning of stone blocking poisonous gases emanating from the soil better than mud, instead of an argument of rat-proofing that came into vogue much later.

Other parts of India

The princely state of Mysore lost over 300,000 lives to plague between 1896 and 1918, its death rate exceeding that of all other regions barring Punjab, Bombay Presidency and the United Provinces.[127] The plague was first detected in Bangalore in August 1898 where, as per census officials, it did 'great mischief', and soon affected the city of Mysore and neighbouring areas, including the Kolar Gold Fields.[128] The first response there to the plague was the same as in Bombay city, but this soon changed. As per the sanitary commissioner of Mysore in 1899–1900, the 'optional system' of segregation, introduced in Mysore city, was found to be superior to the 'compulsory segregation' practice in Bangalore city because 'there was no motive for a concealment of cases, or for destruction of plague corpses in houses, stealthily burying them in backyards and throwing them into streets'.[129] In 1898–99, over 6,000 people died in Bangalore city and around 15,000 left the city.[130] Hundreds of workers died even in the Kolar Gold Fields and there was a mass exodus of the population due to the disease and the containment measures.[131] The economic situation of that time was noted to be bleak in the plague-affected areas of Mysore:

> Traders have sustained considerable losses and the death of bread-winners has brought sorrow and ruin to many homes and families. Financial transactions have declined in number and house property has for the time being depreciated in value by 50 per cent.[132]

Policies were thereafter modified. Compulsory segregation ended in Bangalore and better housing facilities for workers were initiated in the Kolar Gold Fields. In those years, railway inspections and quarantines were strictly applied in the state of Mysore, so much so that even the royal family was quarantined in the Jaganmohan Palace, used earlier as a girl's school.[133] Plague hospitals were inaugurated. A decade later, inoculations were carried out by the government in a big way: tens of thousands were inoculated every season.[134]

The Nizam-ruled Hyderabad state also suffered from the plague, losing nearly 500,000 lives, with a death rate only somewhat lower than that in Mysore. In 1898, officials fretted as the disease started to creep towards the city of Hyderabad from the districts bordering the Bombay Presidency.[135] Soldiers were rushed to those districts, like Aurangabad, to contain the epidemic. Because the local villagers refused to cooperate or convey the number of plague deaths, the authorities had to 'count the fresh graves to ascertain the extent of the mortality'.[136] Wadi Junction on the railway route became a quarantine centre for people travelling to Hyderabad from Bombay. Various measures were taken to contain the epidemic over the next decade, including disinfectants, evacuation and inoculations, with varying success. But unlike other parts of India, most of the plague mortality in the state of Hyderabad occurred in the 1911–21 decade, after the plague struck the city of Hyderabad viciously in 1911. The exact reason for the sudden outbreak is unclear, but the city was submerged in the Musi river flood in 1908 which could have led to complications in sanitation. Desperate containment measures were put in place, evoking a strong reaction from the public. In September 1911, a mob of 3,000 people marched to the Nizam's residence from the plague-infected area of Nampally, 'beating drums and blowing shrill instruments' to convey their grievances against the local government and medical authorities.[137] The plague would eventually have a devastating effect on Hyderabad city, striking hard thrice in a decade and decimating its population by 20 per cent between 1911 and 1921.[138]

The plague claimed over 1 million lives in the populous province of Bihar and Orissa in the north.[139] Districts like Gaya and Shahabad in south Bihar, and others like Patna and Saran, bore the brunt of the calamity. So large was the impact there that the census operations of 1911 were affected because people had fled or were camping in huts outside the towns.[140] Since women stayed at home for longer periods, tended to the diseased, discarded the clothes of the dead and were among the last to evacuate, there was a higher risk of them getting the infection. Plague mortality was observed to be substantially higher among women than men, not just in Bihar but all across India.[141]

Central India and Rajputana in the west were less affected by the plague, and Assam and Bengal in eastern India were practically untouched, though it did create a furore in Calcutta. In October 1896 itself, within weeks of the outbreak in Bombay city, Calcutta had formed a special commission on the plague.[142] Working on its recommendations, passengers were screened on entry into the city and a massive cleaning drive was conducted. In 1898, when the plague broke out, it appeared to be a replay of what had happened in Bombay city the previous year. There was widespread panic and rumour-mongering over house inspections and forced inoculations, and an estimated quarter of the population left Calcutta.[143] 'Municipal scavengers' went on strike, tram lines were ripped apart, suspected inoculators were beaten up, ambulances were attacked and people rioted. This led to a sea change in plague policies, to the extent that people soon began getting monetary rewards for voluntary inoculation.[144] *Samkirtanas* or devotional songs sung in large gatherings were encouraged by the local health journal *Swasthya* as a way to lift the spirits and cancel out the more morbid '*Balahari-Haribol, Ram Naam Satya*' chants of people carrying corpses to the cremation grounds.[145] These songs must have held the city in good stead as the number of plague deaths in Calcutta never rose to the highs observed in Bombay city. In reality, of course, the lower mortality was because of the different nature of rats and fleas in the two cities.[146]

In the south, the Madras Presidency was left relatively unscathed by the plague, though the districts of Bellary, Coimbatore and Salem did occasionally see outbreaks, predominantly in urban areas.[147] One medical thesis in 1913 argued that the distribution of the plague in the presidency depended on the effect of climatic conditions on 'the length of life of the rat flea at the varying temperatures and humidities in different areas' and 'the length of life of the plague Bacillus in the fleas stomach at the different temperatures'.[148] The prevalence and behaviour of the rat flea, as later research confirmed, saved the bulk of south and east India from plague.

For the rest of India, inoculation would be tried, albeit with great hesitation from the people, as a means to escape the disease. A shift in attitudes did take place over the decades and by the 1930s, a medical institute's report remarked that 'where riots were liable to occur when inoculation was pressed, recently a riot was threatened because the supply of vaccine ran short'.[149] The clamour for better sanitation also increased, especially the demand for greater public expenditure towards eradicating the plague. *The Modern Review*, an Indian journal, published an article in 1911 called 'The Plague in India and the Duty of the State', lambasting the colonial government for showing more interest in curtailing the disease in Manchuria in China, which at that time was suffering from a pneumonic plague outbreak, than in India.[150] It argued that 'the question of plague prevention is more political, social and economical than medical' and that 'self-government is an essential condition precedent to the total examination of the plague in India'.[151] However, there is little evidence that such pleas ever met with success. During the peak of the plague pandemic in India, more than inoculation or sanitation, it would be quarantine and evacuation that would become the norm.

Quarantine and Evacuation Camps

The government appointed a plague commission in August 1898, which came out with several volumes of evidence of outbreaks but to little effect, as the plague continued to spread rapidly. The first phase of plague prevention strategies emphasized the use of disinfectants, and large sums were poured into the endeavour, but gradually, it fell out of favour. Evacuation, the traditional Indian system of withstanding the plague, was the only option left to reduce mortality. It had its downsides, as the chances of crime and theft would go up in deserted villages and towns, but it was proven to be an effective measure. It would not be an exaggeration to state that nearly 10 per cent of the population of the Indian subcontinent, or over 30 million people, moved temporarily into camps at some point or the other during the high noon of the plague pandemic.[152]

The quarantine camp was one of the most important types of camps that emerged, where the sick were brought after they tested positive for the plague. A first-person account of the horrors of quarantine camps was published in the classic memoirs of the Marathi writer Lakshmibai Tilak (1868–1936), titled *Smritichitre*, translated recently by Shanta Gokhale into English.[153] Lakshmibai was based in Ahmednagar in the Bombay Presidency with her family around the year 1899–1900, when the plague struck. She describes wittily how her god, Ganapati, arranged for her eviction by ordering his vehicle, the rat, to appear at their house one day. She had heard the popular tale of rats spinning and dying but she got to see it for herself for the first time, after which the bodies were sent for testing as per protocol and the tests confirmed that they were plague rats. The family shifted elsewhere for a while and Lakshmibai learnt about plague prevention techniques, such as airing clothes and filling rat holes, by word-of-mouth. Some doctors in the vicinity scurried for 'plague duty'.[154] The local doctor suggested that the family should inoculate, but Lakshmibai's husband, Rev. Narayan Vaman Tilak, who was busy touring for work, conveyed that he was against inoculations and that their children should be untouched, but that she was free to do it if she wanted to. Lakshmibai got herself inoculated and witnessed the instant reaction of fever and swelling in the injected arm.[155]

Unfortunately, her daughter Tara contracted the plague, and her 'screams reached fever pitch' in the house.[156] The family began preparations for living in the quarantine camp and sent a cartload of luggage there, only to have it sent back because it exceeded the prescribed limit. They set off on a bullock cart to the camp on a wintry night with less luggage, after lying to the cartman that none of them had the plague, or he would not go otherwise. Lakshmibai then described the camp in these words:

> The cottages were ventilated by openings about a span-long, running along the top and bottom of the walls. The walls were made of tin. They got so cold at night that we felt we would freeze over. We were surrounded by the sick. They screamed and beat on the tin walls. At times, a patient would climb on to a wall and jump with a loud thud into the neighbouring room. The floors of the cottage had not been levelled. When you walked, pebbles bit into the soles of your feet. There was no food in our stomachs and no sleep in our eyes. Tara's screams were heart-rending. I thought if Yama [the god of death] had a kingdom anywhere, it had to be here. The place was terrifying, the night was terrifying, the surroundings were terrifying and the state of my heart was terrifying.[157]

The relatives of patients would quarrel among themselves over patients screaming and not letting others sleep. The doctors were clueless about this aspect of the centre because they never stayed on the premises at night and when Lakshmibai pointed this out to them, they started prescribing medication for sleep to enable more peaceful nights. The standard prescription for the patients was 'belladonna' (literally 'beautiful lady'), a herbal solution administered to everyone from the same glass. The thermometers used were also the same for all, but Lakshmibai had her own set for Tara, which would show 105 degrees Fahrenheit during the worst phases. She would cradle Tara in her lap and cover her with a warm cloth, despite the high body temperature, to help her survive the cold nights.

At the quarantine centre, they had been allotted three cottages: one for cooking, one for Tara and one for Rev. Tilak to write in. The reverend continued to pray for his daughter. At the camp, he was forced by the doctors to inoculate, generating a strong bodily reaction. Lakshmibai noted that 90 per cent of those infected died after they arrived at the poorly run camp. After fourteen days at the camp, the doctors had lost hope of Tara's recovery and her family was devastated. Rev. Tilak had wanted Tara to become like Anandibai Joshi (1865–1887), the first Indian woman to graduate in medicine in the US, and wondered why God was taking the life of their only daughter.

As a last throw of the dice, Lakshmibai lit the stove, cooked flaxseed flour and plastered Tara's body with it, gave her a brew of castor oil, sugar and milk to drink and wrapped her up in a blanket. She then went deep into the neighbouring jungle and cried out for divine mercy, promising that if Tara's life were saved, she would stay at the camp to look after the other patients. Miraculously, Tara survived the plague, and both Lakshmibai and her husband moved to a nearby hut outside the camp to help the other patients. Discovering corruption in the administration of supplies, they reorganized the relief effort, squashed a sweeper's strike over pay, and even lifted corpses themselves, winning the admiration of people in the camp and outside. Lakshmibai also recounted with pride how they managed to get the case fatality rates in the camp down to 10 per cent. When they left, they got a certificate of appreciation from the colonial authorities and a prized group photograph.

In contrast to quarantine camps, evacuation camps were much larger spaces where entire populations would gravitate to avoid the plague. Some observations of these camps were made by Dr Charles Creighton in 1905, based on his three-month tour of villages and towns in western and northern India.[158] On Bijapur, he noted:

The strange spectacle every evening about sunset, in the city of Bijapur, of the whole population, save the inmates of half-a-dozen bungalows, to the number of some 20,000, quitting the

bazaars, workshops and offices, and making their way outside the
walls to a large camp on the downs around the railway station.
This phenomenon is the [sic] more suggestive at Bijapur, as the
city was deserted once before, 200 years ago, and most probably
for the same reason as now, namely, plague.[159]

In the villages around Bijapur, he noticed a similar phenomenon. He
walked in an empty fortified village that usually had 3,000 residents,
where 'the streets were deserted, and the doors of all the houses
padlocked, the whole of the inhabitants being in camp near their
fields about a quarter of a mile away'.[160] The camps in Poona were
in the city's maidans or along suburban roads and in Bombay along
the sea-facing side of the city stretching to Mahim. Near Navsari,
people built huts outside their villages, close to the fields and wells.
In Dharwar, the temporary camp was turned into a permanent site
with the government auctioning land plots at low rates. Building
outdoor camps was a tougher option in north India as it got very
cold in the winter and people were inclined to stay indoors, though
evacuation was still preferred over inoculation as a plague prevention
strategy.[161]

Remarkably, Dr Creighton's medical beliefs were steeped in
the anti-bacteriology philosophy and he described the 'scientific
theory of evacuation' as a means to evade 'soil poisons' or harmful
gases oozing out from the soil and entering the houses.[162] This
was of course not true, as we now know, but the implication that
mud houses were more susceptible to catching the plague from
underneath than well-built pakka dwellings had merit, because
kaccha houses allowed more rat holes to be formed. Creighton's
assessment that the 'miserable structure' of dwellings was the 'real
reason why the Indian plains' were 'cursed with plague' had an
element of truth, even if it was based on wrong science. The plague
rarely troubled Europeans in general or even Indians in the army, in
regions otherwise susceptible to outbreaks, presumably because of

better dwelling structures. In 1907, the peak year of plague mortality, which claimed over 1 million lives, there were only 85 cases and 56 deaths among Indian soldiers.[163]

The quarantine and evacuation camps were a routine affair across India, mitigating the impact of the plague somewhat, but officials and scientists were baffled by the irregularity in outbreaks over time and space. The unsuccessful attempt to curb the spread of the plague using massive state intervention in the 1890s paved the way for greater collaboration with Indian medical practitioners, hakims and vaids, and a push for better public education on sanitation.[164] In 1909, the 'Punjab Plague Manual', reflecting this change, started with the following words:

> The cardinal principle of all plague administration must be that no pressure or compulsion, in any shape or form, is to be brought to bear on the people. Encouragement, persuasion and the provision of facilities for carrying out the measures advocated are the only legitimate means of influencing and guiding public opinion in the direction desired.[165]

Health officials in Punjab lamented the 'apathy' towards the plague among the public as people seem to have surrendered to their fates in regions where it became endemic.[166] Top officials rued that all the efforts to prevent the plague over a decade had 'produced practically no results'.[167] The only silver lining was a slowly emerging understanding about the role of rats and fleas in the transmission of the disease, which gave a new direction to plague-control measures.

Rat Catching and Cat Calling

In 1901, the Calcutta municipal administration observed that there was 'a great difference of opinion as regards the influence of rats as to whether they spread the disease or merely suffer from it in common with human beings'.[168] This reflected the confusion in administrative and medical circles over the exact mechanism of plague transmission for a decade after the outbreak in Hong Kong in 1894. And then, in a remarkable piece of research, the mystery of the plague, scourge of humankind and destroyer of civilizations for millennia, suddenly lay deciphered.

In a simple seven-page paper with no statistical tables, titled 'Plague, Rats, and Fleas', published in February 1905 in the *Indian Medical Gazette*, Secunderabad-born William Glen Liston (1872– 1950), for the first time, laid out a coherent argument explaining the transmission of the plague from rats to humans.[169] Liston, son of an army chaplain, had joined the Indian Medical Service in 1898 after studying in Edinburgh and Glasgow, and his findings were a testimony to his persistence; earlier piecemeal discoveries by other researchers had been repeatedly dismissed by leading medical authorities.[170] Several scientists had previously pointed out the possible role of rats in transmitting the disease, and the French scientist P.L. Simond, working in Bombay in 1898, had argued that the flea could be a vector based on his observation that buboes appeared close to flea bites. However, the plague commission had dismissed these findings as being inconclusive and doubts remained as to how flea-infested plague hospitals did not see doctors and nurses being infected during an outbreak. Additionally, the soil-based poison gas theory sounded like a better explanation to many at that time.

Liston had observed these debates closely when he was posted to the Plague Research Laboratory in Bombay and was struck by Simond's insight on the possible role of fleas in transmitting the plague. He had to wait for a while before he could work on this hypothesis as he was briefly posted in Berar in central India to work on famine relief, during when he got to closely study malarial mosquitoes. He was then sent to England for additional training in medicine, where he spent a lot of time understanding the nature of rats and fleas. Back on duty at the Plague Research Laboratory in 1903, he finally had the opportunity to pursue the flea hypothesis, although that came amid considerable friction between him and Haffkine, the director at that time, who saw little merit in the idea.

From his observations, Liston concluded that the seasonality of plague deaths coincided with the high incidence of rat fleas, but the real breakthrough came in March 1903, when he got to examine the cause of death of guinea pigs in Victoria Gardens, the zoo near his office in Parel.[171] It turned out that the guinea pigs had started to fall sick a few days after dead rats were discovered around their cages. Liston found that the guinea pigs had died of the plague, and that the sick ones at Victoria Gardens were covered with rat fleas of the *X. cheopis* variety. He was bothered by the arbitrariness of rat fleas attacking guinea pigs until he hit upon the notion that starvation had driven them to do so. He argued that rats, like humans, quickly migrated out of their homes upon their intuitive detection of the plague (after seeing many deaths) and this abandonment by their natural hosts led rat fleas to scurry and bite other hosts nearby, which were often humans, or as in the case of the Victoria Gardens, guinea pigs. The plague commission's original doubt about transmission in hospitals could be explained by the fact that patients were covered in human fleas and not rat fleas. It was thus a specific flea that seemed to transmit plague.

Having reasoned this out, Liston then pointed out that the nocturnal nature of the rat flea increased the chances of plague transmission at night rather than during the day. He also argued that fewer cases of the plague had been found, then and in the past, in people working in the oil business in particular, perhaps because oil acted as a deterrent to flea bites. After Liston's research was released, a plague research commission was appointed in 1905 as an international collaboration. The team, which included Liston, was finally able to prove the rat–flea–human transmission link conclusively through a series of studies. Liston received a posthumous prize from the American Veterinary Epidemiology Society in 1971, which credited him with establishing 'the epidemiology of the first Zooanthroponosis transmitted by an arthropod' and enabling plague control measures, 'thus saving countless millions from this dread disease'.[172]

The millions saved would be humans, not rats, for one of those newer plague control policies adopted soon after Liston's work was rat extermination. Rat-poisoning, rat-baiting and, to a small extent, cat-keeping, came into greater force. It is pertinent to note that all three measures were hinted at in Kautilya's *Arthashastra*, the ancient text mentioned earlier in the chapter, raising the possibility that it was indeed the plague that prompted the measures back then as well.

Rats began to be studied in great detail from a variety of perspectives in the second decade of the twentieth century. On fertility, it was observed that rats, with a lifespan of one-two years, had a terrific breeding record: one female rat capable of giving birth to forty-eight rats in year.[173] On plague deaths, it was noted that most died after developing buboes around their necks.[174] On migration, it was documented that rats could reach far-off places via ships and trains, nestled among 'grains and rags' along with their fleas, though fleas on their own without hosts could barely move beyond thirty yards.[175] It was also estimated, without jest, that there were as many rats as humans in England and Wales, that is about 40 million, and using a similar ratio, 1 million rats were estimated to live in the city of Bombay.[176] The economic loss in India caused by their gnawing of various materials was pegged at Rs 60 crore or Rs 600 million every year.[177] Rat extermination, then, was that rare issue on which both epidemiologists and economists concurred.

Once the rat campaigns began in Bombay city, the mortality rate among rats went up from 25 per cent per year on account of natural causes to around 50 per cent:[178] around 500,000 rats were estimated

to be dying every year. The campaigns revolved around an elaborate
system of rat trapping, collection and examination. The wire cage
trap or French pattern trap, known as the 'Wonder', was the most
widely used trap and dough made with locally produced flour was
recommended as the ideal bait.[179] Rat-catchers would lay out the bait
in the evening between 5 and 7 p.m. and inspect the traps the next
morning between 6 and 8 a.m. Then the process, as described in a
sanitation manual of those times, was as follows:

> Dead rats are collected and the house, place and locality noted
> down on a card attached to the rat with the name of the collector.
> Each rat thus collected is put in a tin box and labelled and sent
> to the Bombay Bacteriological Laboratory for examination ...
> Every rat-catcher must bring 7 rats per day free and he is paid
> at anna ½ each only for those rats over and above this original
> seven per day.[180]

Rat-catching caught on as an occupation across municipalities in
India. Like the legendary story of the pied piper of Hamelin, which
itself may have started with the plagues of the past, rats, dead or
alive, were lured into examination centres for the 'unsavoury process'
of computing a rat index to monitor the plague.[181] In Bombay city,
around 2,000 rats were collected daily in the 1910s using 7,000 traps.
Not everyone agreed with the practice, as it hurt the sentiments of
'certain castes of Indians, who refuse to allow rats to be killed or
caught in their houses' and who had notices put up saying, 'No rat-
catchers allowed here'.[182] But despite these objections, the practice
spread far and wide and by 1930, around 50,000 rats were being
killed annually in places as far from Bombay as the Kolar Gold
Fields in south India.[183] In the small towns of Bihar, it was tried out
for a while by employing professional rat-killers, usually Musahars.
The small town of Jagdishpur once had a haul of 1.5 million dead

rats over two years, but the practice diminished on account of its high expense.[184] Where the expenses were justified, the practice continued, all the way to the present times. In 2018, the going rate for killing a rat in Mumbai was Rs 18, paid by the Brihanmumbai Municipal Corporation.[185]

In addition to rat extermination in the 1910s, there were calls for preventive measures like cutting off rats' access to food supplies, building rat-proof structures, and educating people to 'consider the rat as one of their greatest enemies'.[186] Among the more fascinating recommendations was regular house cleaning and moving around furniture because 'their breeding appears to be a very delicate process and the slightest disturbance is quite enough to upset them'.[187] Formal legislation for rat destruction never came about in India in a major way though there were calls to copy the one passed in England in 1919, which was known as the Rat and Mice (Destruction) Act.[188]

Rat fleas were also the target of direct destruction but through fumigation rather than disinfection, which had been tried earlier, when the focus had been to wipe out the plague bacilli from surfaces.[189] Even the mode of disinfection was changed to using 'pesterine', a new substance adapted from France for Indian conditions, as it was much more effective at killing fleas than previously used chemicals.[190]

Amidst the focus on rats and rat fleas, one member of the Indian Medical Service, Lt Col. Andrew Buchanan, who was based in Amravati in central India, set forth on a remarkable mission.[191] Intrigued by a newspaper letter in 1906 that detailed how a village called Airla near Nagpur had staved off the disease in a plague-affected region by keeping cats and reducing the number of rats, he decided to learn more about this phenomenon. What happened over the next decade was nothing short of an obsession with the theme of 'cats as plague preventers', publicized by Buchanan in India and abroad, which introduced a novel form of 'animal technology', as argued by the historian Projit Mukharji, in the world of public health. Three decades before *Tom and Jerry* was unleashed to enthral audiences, a real-life version of cat-and-mouse games, or to be more specific, cat-and-rat games, was let loose in India (the plague research commission had shown that rats were more dangerous than mice in plague transmission).[192]

Buchanan first conducted a cat census in Amravati district, covering over 1,000 villages with the help of the local police, medical staff and other members of the district administration. He then matched the results of the cat census with the plague statistics collected by the health department at the village level. In 357 villages where less than 20 per cent of the households kept cats, there were 3,258 registered plague cases in total.[193] In contrast, in 146 villages where over 50 per cent of the households kept cats, there were only 14 registered incidents. He began publishing these and other results in the *Indian Medical Gazette* and *British Medical Journal* to draw attention to the significance of cats in keeping rats away from localities. He also tried to understand the various religious sentiments about cats and rats in India, to sharpen his arguments and publicity efforts in what he called a 'people's remedy'.[194] He observed that Muslims were the most cat-friendly, Hindus were uncomfortable with killing rats because it was the vehicle of Ganapati, and that merchant castes, Parsis and Jains objected to keeping cats as pets.[195]

In 1910, he staged demonstrations in a room with glass doors of how cats killed rats to create visual awareness. His enthusiasm was supported by luminaries such as Robert Koch and S. Kitasato. However, he found few takers for his proposals in India, and stringent opposition from a few scientists abroad who argued that cats themselves could harbour the plague. Some even argued that non-venomous snakes were a better option since they did not attract rat fleas.

In the middle of this fascinating mammalian and reptilian debate, cats were introduced in plague prevention policies in British-ruled Hong Kong and in German-ruled Togoland and Japan. A small business of cat-rearing and trade also developed on the side. In 1909, Japan imported 4,000 cats from the USA and still noted a shortfall of 10,000 felines.[196] Cat breeds were compared on their efficiency in killing rats; in Japan, Kitasato praised the cats sent to him by Buchanan as 'exquisite rat-catchers' and 'of a better race' than the ones found there.[197]

After 1918, as the plague pandemic began to recede, the cat solution fell out of favour. This was fortunate since later research has shown the possibility of plague transmission to humans via cats, however rare the case may be.[198] While the medical establishment forgot about cats and continued with rat extermination, religious people did not. Jains, who had long objected to both killing rats and keeping cats, appeared to have changed their stance a little when, in one municipal debate on rat-trapping in Ahmedabad in 1936, a member 'catcalled', in more than a literal sense, by saying, 'God has created cats to kill rats, so we should not kill rats.'[199]

Legacies of the Plague in India

The plague pandemic left its mark on India in many ways, of which at least four are clearly discernible in the realms of law, politics, labour and urban governance. During the pandemic, plague-related mortality was so high and sudden in some districts that it resulted in there being several claimants on property, especially when there was little time to draw up wills, inviting substantial litigation.[200] In one court case in 1910, when the plague was presented as the cause of death, it was challenged because the 'firm and strong' signature on a will allegedly signed in the deceased's final hours was not expected of a plague patient.[201] But the more important legacy was a piece of legislation, hurriedly passed on 4 February 1897 to combat the plague, that would survive all the way to the present and be used in curtailing COVID-19 in 2020. The Epidemic Diseases Act 1897 was ill-defined in many ways, but gave sweeping powers to authorities to act and punish, and has been amended a few times in the interim, most recently to penalize people who attack doctors. Its ambiguity then, as now, means that nearly anyone can be arrested under its provisions. Concerned about the misuse of state power during an epidemic, the writer O.M. Vijayan (1930–2005) set his short story 'The Examination' in Palghat in Kerala in 1946, where a plague officer, Ananthan Pillai, ruthlessly supresses a plague outbreak, raising questions about the validity of his methods and their after-effects.[202]

The plague played a crucial role in the political movements in India of that time by throwing the spotlight on new leaders, by building organizational skills during the mass evacuation campaigns and by bringing about a sense of solidarity through volunteering services. Plague politics in Poona was, as we have seen, instrumental in creating an aura around Tilak, but it was even more important for his rival, the more moderate Gopal Krishna Gokhale (1866–1915). Gokhale was initially quite strident in his opposition to the harsh plague measures implemented in Poona but apologized soon after when challenged by the government to provide concrete evidence.[203] He then worked astutely with the government and aided a volunteer service on plague relief, culminating in the creation of the Servants of India Society in 1905. He also became president of the Poona municipality in 1902 and became the government's 'unfailing ally in plague matters'.[204]

The plague would come back into the picture in 1907, when it peaked with over 1 million deaths and formed an undercurrent to the famous Surat Congress session held that year in December, where the Congress split between the so-called Moderates (including

Gokhale) and Extremists (including Tilak).[205] The political impact was not limited to western India; between 1903 and 1907, Punjab and the United Provinces, both ravaged by the plague, played an important role in reviving the fortunes of the Indian National Congress.[206] Similarly, according to the historian Ian J. Catanach (1935–2009), the plague 'cannot be ignored in the history of the Congress in the decade before the Surat "split"'.[207] As we have seen earlier, the disease was also instrumental in the rise of Vallabhbhai Patel in later years.

The varied regional impact of the plague had little overall effect on economic activity except in 1907, the year of peak mortality. In that year, the real Gross Domestic Product (GDP) fell by 5 per cent, owing to a contraction in agriculture and manufacturing activities.[208] Notably, while rice production held up, wheat production, concentrated in plague-hit Punjab and United Provinces, crashed as yields fell by 30 per cent in 1907–08 and acreage of fallow land increased.[209] In other years, regular evacuations and quarantines in plague-affected areas slammed the brakes on livelihoods. The outbreak of the plague in Bombay city and the exodus of migrant labour in 1896–97 led to 'truly enormous' losses, according to the local industrial association.[210] The plague, in conjunction with the famines of the countryside, hit annual cotton yarn production in Bombay in 1896–97 and 1900–01 by 5 per cent and 35 per cent respectively.[211] Total yarn exports, which had grown briskly in the decade before, halved in 1900–01 'because of the plague in Bombay' and because no new cotton mills were set up in Bombay city between 1900 and 1904.[212] The 1900–01 impact was particularly severe, with even south India–based retailing firms like Spencer's telling their shareholders how they had to 'cope with the restrictions to business caused by famine and plague'.[213]

If the plague forced corporations into losses, it also gave a fillip to cooperatives. The cooperative movement in the first decade of the twentieth century, in its formative years in western India, was closely linked to the plague as some of the prominent people who headed cooperative societies in their early years were those who were involved with plague-related relief work.[214] A clearer impact of the plague can be established in the nascent world of labour movements, when the exodus of migrant workers from the mills of Bombay city mandated changes in employment relationships to win back the workers.[215] Industrialist J.N. Tata lamented in May 1897 that 'the present moment placed the employers of labour in the unenviable position of employees'.[216]

Workers had greater bargaining power and so wages were raised, a system of keeping arrears gave way to wages being paid daily, and bonuses were also paid out. Over the next two decades, the plague would strike repeatedly but with smaller exoduses and the labour market would remain in a state of flux. Plague outbreaks after 1915 in many cities in western India, especially in Ahmedabad, led to textile mill workers fleeing to their villages at a time when labour was desperately needed to run the factories to meet the high wartime demand.[217] Mill owners had to give considerable concessions to draw the workers back to the mills.

Since the plague was seen fundamentally as a problem of filth and bad sanitation, urban housing and planning received perhaps the greatest attention from the colonial authorities. In the immediate aftermath of the 1896 outbreak, British officials blamed the limited local autonomy granted earlier to urban governments for the sorry state of affairs, and in some cases, they worked to revoke it.[218] Nevertheless, the plague only intensified over the next decade. Its lasting legacy then was the creation of Improvement Trusts, first in Bombay in December 1898 and then in numerous cities: Mysore (1903), Calcutta (1911), Hyderabad (1912), Lucknow (1919), Kanpur (1919), Allahabad (1920), Delhi (1936), Nagpur (1937), Bangalore (1945) and Madras (1946), among others.[219] These trusts were the forerunners of today's urban 'Development Authorities'.

The Bombay Improvement Trust worked for thirty-five years, during which it achieved mixed results. On the one hand it upgraded residential layouts and brought in a semblance of urban planning, but on the other, it displaced a large number of poor people in the name of 'improvement'.[220] Since good ventilation was a key theme in preventing plague in the initial years, new roads were opened and existing ones cleared up so that more of the sea breeze could pass through the city. The Dadar–Matunga suburbs were developed and the famous Shivaji Park, where Sachin Tendulkar practised cricket, where the writer Shanta Gokhale wrote her books and where, less consequentially, this author was born, arose in the immediate aftermath and context of the plague.[221]

Hyderabad's City Improvement Trust Board was set up within months of the plague erupting in the city in December 1911. It had a significant impact on the city's development: new roads were built, drainage systems were installed, slums were cleared and plans for new suburbs drawn up.[222] In parts of the Deccan and in Gujarat, it was observed in 1905 that 'new suburbs' were 'actually springing up for the richer class, to avoid the infection'.[223] The plague, thus, set in motion a process of urban planning and suburbanization, either through Improvement Trusts or otherwise, in many towns and cities of India.

While the plague led to changes in policymaking in the urban sphere, its impact was also felt in rural India, where it left its mark in literature. The great plague accounts and novels of the past were urban in nature, like Giovanni Boccaccio's *The Decameron*, set in the area around Florence in the fourteenth century, or Daniel Defoe's *A Journal of the Plague Year*, set in seventeenth-century London, or Albert Camus's *The Plague*, set in the city of Oran in Algeria in the twentieth century. In contrast, the literary masterpiece from India would focus on the villages of south India in the twentieth century. *Samskara: A Rite for a Dead Man*, written in Kannada by U.R. Ananthamurthy in 1965 and translated into English by A.K. Ramanujan in 1976, looks at the dilemmas faced by a Brahmin hutment in the second quarter of the twentieth century as it deals with the death from plague of a heretic among them. 'Alive, Naranappa was an enemy; dead, a preventer of meals; as a corpse, a problem, a nuisance,' proclaims one sentence from the book, which is scathing in its observations on the plague, caste, gender and religion.[224] The 'one-syllable name' plague is so dreaded that people utter the words 'Shiva, Shiva' for divine blessings instead of the actual word itself.[225] In the middle of a vivid sexual encounter in the rural wilderness, a female character in the book worriedly mentions the following to her partner, after her village had just set ablaze a hut containing the bodies of two people who died of the plague:

> I want to tell you something. I've never seen such a thing before. Why should rats and mice come to our poor huts? Nothing there to eat. Our huts aren't like brahmin houses. Now the rats come like relatives looking for a place to stay. They fall pattering from the roof, run round and round, and die. Like folks running for life from a hut on fire, they run into the forest. I've never seen the likes of it. We must get the shaman possessed with the demon and ask him about it. Why do rats come to pariah huts and pop off? Snap! Like that! Like breaking a twig. We must ask the demon.[226]

Children, meanwhile, are momentarily delighted to see delirious rats pouring out of holes, likened to a 'wedding procession'.[227] The store room of the hutment, filled with rice and lentils, is littered with rat droppings and vultures descend on to the roofs of huts, eyeing the dead rats.[228] The plague also claims the wife of the book's protagonist, Praneshacharya, who then sets off on a reflective tour that brings him to a *mari* temple and a nearby town where plague-related safety measures are announced on the road by a town crier exhorting people to inoculate.[229] Throughout, Ananthamurthy subtly conveys a story of personal transformation against the backdrop of pain and the horror of the plague sweeping through the region.

Beyond *Samskara,* the visual memory of the plague pandemic survives today in a few places, especially in western India. Less than 50 kilometres from Pune, a mural series depicting Savitribai Phule's exemplary work countering the plague in 1897 stands in Naigaon, next to the memorial building erected in her honour.[230] A movie on the Chapekar brothers' assassination of Walter Rand in Poona was made in 1979 and titled *June 22 1897.*[231] The names of places can also evoke the era of the plague. In Bangalore, maps still show a Plague Maramma Temple in Thyagaraja Nagar. In Mumbai, Four Bungalows and Seven Bungalows, well-known localities around Andheri, refer to bungalows set up by elite families, mostly Parsi, who sailed to Versova Island from Marine Drive to escape the plague in the late 1890s.[232] Burial grounds are another reminder of the pandemic; in Mumbai, the Seaside Cemetery in Bandra was set up at that time to be at a considerable distance from residential hamlets so as to keep any contamination away. However, the high salinity of the soil there slows down the decomposition process. If people die in quick succession, their families are warned not to open the family graves too soon or else they might catch a glimpse of the previous occupant.[233]

Fittingly, the two people most closely associated with the beginning of the plague pandemic in India, Viegas and Haffkine, are memorialized in Mumbai, even if they are less known today. The Haffkine Institute (earlier known as Government House, then as Plague Research Laboratory, and then as Bombay Bacteriology Laboratory), along with its museum, stands in a fine building in Parel. And if you walk by Metro Cinema in south Mumbai, the statue of Dr Acacio Viegas stands in full glory, covered thoroughly and ironically with the droppings of pigeons, known to some as 'flying rats.'

The Plague Pandemic outside India

The third plague pandemic of the world was unusual in that around 95 per cent of deaths occurred in one place, the Indian subcontinent. The remaining 5 per cent, numbering less than 1 million people, was scattered around the world. Between 1894 and 1938, an estimated 250,000 people died of the plague in China and Taiwan, and around 200,000 in Indonesia and Burma.[234] Mortality was much lower in other regions such as Europe (1,000 deaths), North America (1,000) and South America (24,000). Madagascar in Africa lost over 30,000 lives and continues to be afflicted by the plague even today. Outside Madagascar, the plague claimed around 120,000 lives in Africa, with Uganda (60,000) and Egypt (10,000) being the harder hit regions.[235] These figures do not include the large number of plague-related deaths that took place in southern China in the decades preceding 1894, as they were less thoroughly documented and belonged to a period in which the disease was not yet a pandemic.[236]

The plague pandemic contributed to the sluggish growth of China and India, the two worst affected regions. Between 1870 and 1913, the population growth rate in China and India was half that of the global average of 0.8 per cent per annum.[237] For the same period, while the global economy grew annually at 2 per cent on average, China and India again registered the slowest growth rates of under 1 per cent.[238] Though other circumstances such as famines undoubtedly played bigger roles in dampening population and economic growth rates in this period, the plague pandemic should also be factored in, especially for the late 1890s and the 1900s.

The global mortality figures cited previously are approximate and cannot convey the sense of fear and panic that swept the world in the

decade following 1894, irrespective of whether regions were hit by
the plague or not. Much of Europe and the Americas were revelling
in a period of high economic growth and an era of mass migration
across the Atlantic Ocean. The plague threatened this prosperity
and port towns in particular were put on high alert. European
imperial powers, scarred by the memory of past pandemics, went
into overdrive.

The plague appeared in Hong Kong in 1894, in Macao and
Fuzhou in 1895, and in Bombay and Singapore in 1896. That year,
it also killed two Portuguese seamen who had sailed from Bombay
to London, which was at that time the world's largest city. Since
many of the affected territories were British-ruled, the French
authorities used this opportunity to blame the British.[239] Adrien
Proust (1834–1903), father of the writer Marcel Proust and a leading
French physician, cholera expert and 'arch-quarantinist', criticized
the British, who were seen to be hesitant with quarantines.[240] While
the French had a grouse against the British since the earlier debates
on cholera and quarantines, it would be Austria–Hungary that
would take the initiative to assemble the tenth International Sanitary
Conference in Venice in February–March 1897, fearful that their
Muslim subjects returning from Mecca may contract the plague
from Indian pilgrims.[241] The conference was convened to see whether
earlier defences against cholera could work in containing 'the rising
tide of Asiatic plague'.[242] The advisory for ships that emerged from
the conference was the following:

> The transmission of plague appears to take place by the
> excretions of patients (sputum, dejections), morbid products
> (suppuration of bubos, of boils, etc.) and consequently by
> contaminated linen, clothing and hands.[243]

In hindsight, with knowledge of the transmission mechanism, this
advisory seems bizarre. But as the plague was added to the list of

globally notifiable diseases, it led to rigorous inspection at centres on the Suez Canal following this advisory and quarantines in many places, especially Bombay city. However, ports had a vested interest in not reporting cases of the plague as they would otherwise lose business due to quarantines, and so they did not necessarily follow the advisory to the letter. As it turned out, the plague would spread to all continents of the world by 1901.

French-ruled Madagascar and British-ruled Mauritius were both affected by the plague in November 1898, the disease most likely brought by ships with rice and people from India.[244] Within a decade, Mauritius, with a large Indian emigrant population, would be counted along with India and China as the three regions worst affected by the plague.[245] In Africa, an independent epidemic of the plague was discovered in Uganda in 1897, which seemed to have been in existence for several years before that.[246]

In May 1899, the pandemic reached Alexandria in Egypt, a region ravaged by the plague earlier in the century. Because the knowledge of the disease and local engagement around it were not altogether new, European medical authorities were mindful of local religious practices while carrying out plague control measures, unlike the roughshod forays in India.[247] A more aggressive approach was used in South Africa, where the plague broke out among dock workers in Cape Town in February 1901. The mayor of the city lamented, 'The dreaded Bubonic Plague—the scourge of India—had at length made its appearance in our midst,' and soon restrictions were placed on immigration from India.[248]

Indians in South Africa were harassed by local officials in various ways, as they were considered unsanitary and carriers of the disease. It was in this context that a young Mohandas Gandhi (1869–1948), who had aided in plague relief in Rajkot in India in 1896, joined relief efforts in South Africa and educated Indians on the significance of the phrase 'cleanliness is next to godliness'.[249] More significantly for the masses, the white-skinned ruling class, who anyway favoured strong segregationist policies, used the plague to further their cause and Ndabeni, a separate township for black-skinned residents, was created in Cape Town.[250] The plague would thus contribute towards laying the foundations for the apartheid system practised there in the twentieth century.

Around 1900, the plague started appearing in South America, in cities such as Buenos Aires (Argentina) and Rio de Janeiro (Brazil). In contrast to the sluggish response in Buenos Aires, the Brazilian government was quick to rope in the services of a young Paris-trained Brazilian scientist, Oswaldo Cruz (1872–1917), who oversaw plague control measures and ushered in modern public health systems.[251] Overall, the pandemic did not claim many human lives in South America, but it created a new reservoir of plague foci among the rodents in the region, which later affected Peru and Ecuador.[252] This was similar to what happened in North America when the plague appeared in San Francisco and some other places around 1900, causing a few human casualties. In the US, the incident also led to the scapegoating of the Chinese community as carriers of the disease.[253]

The disease even reached the distant shores of Honolulu in Hawaii, where the attempt to burn an infected house in an Asian neighbourhood in January 1900 went awry and caused a great fire, displacing thousands of Chinese and Japanese immigrants.[254] Anti-Chinese prejudice would recur as a theme in Sydney in Australia, where the plague appeared in 1900, claiming few lives but creating substantial panic as the public was fed sensational news by the media.[255] Large numbers of dead rats were found by the wharf and just as Liston would observe in his celebrated paper, a doctor in Sydney commented that 'the fleas there were so numerous that the labourers tied string around the bottom of their trousers to protect themselves against the onslaughts of the vermin'.[256] Strict isolation and quarantines were enforced for a while but the health officer, J. Ashburton Thompson, convinced about the role of rats in disease transmission, embarked on one of the first rat-proofing and rat-catching campaigns of the world, which may have had some salutary effect.[257]

The British Empire was clearly the most rattled of all imperial powers, with the plague raging in India and several of its port cities around the world. So when it claimed a few lives in Glasgow in Scotland in 1900, it created a furore among the medical community. The blame was passed on to the hygiene practices of the 'Roman Catholics' and the response was an overhaul of the sanitation system.[258] Panic also ensued when Oporto, or Porto, in Portugal was struck by the plague in 1899, evoking a stringent military response, a backlash and eventually the flight of the local medical officer to Lisbon.[259] Europe was successful in keeping out the plague for the most part, but this could well have to do with the nature of rats and fleas, as in the Americas. As plague expert L.F. Hirst noted in 1953, 'the world distribution of *X. Cheopis* corresponds very closely with that of bubonic plague among man and rat'.[260]

In Asia, Burma, which was a part of British India until the 1930s, witnessed some plague mortality, not least because it was a key site of the rice trade in the region and hence conducive for sheltering rats, and also because it received hundreds of thousands of labour migrants from mainland India by ships across the Bay of Bengal. From Rangoon in Burma, the plague is suspected to have then travelled, in 1905, to a rice godown in coastal Sumatra in Dutch-ruled Indonesia.[261] Native houses made of bamboo were excellent sites for rat breeding and the high prevalence of *X. cheopis* fleas meant that a plague epidemic was soon on its way. It broke out with great ferocity in 1911 in Java and raged till 1939, claiming over 200,000 lives, peaking in 1914, 1925 and 1934 in different parts of the island.[262] Chinese and Europeans who lived in houses made of different materials escaped death, prompting locals to promote new non-bamboo-based dwelling structures. Remarkably, the 'improved' houses with better ventilation for smoke generated in the kitchens began to attract more mosquitoes, and overall mortality increased due to malaria deaths, even as deaths due to the plague reduced.[263] More effective perhaps was a 'living plague vaccine' campaign that was eventually introduced, to the benefit of several million people.[264]

The plague troubled Japan briefly after it appeared in Kobe in 1898 and also in the Philippines in 1900, but had a larger impact on Formosa or Taiwan, where it claimed over 20,000 lives from 1896 to 1917.[265] In Hong Kong, from where the pandemic is likely to have originated in 1894, deaths, though few in number, occurred regularly until 1929.

The third plague pandemic was for the most part bubonic in nature, though the deadlier pneumonic plague, based on human transmission, was also seen from time to time in a few cases. In India, a few instances of pneumonic plague were noted in Calcutta and south Bihar, but the larger outbreak was documented in Manchuria in north-east China, in 1910–11, where it claimed over 50,000 lives.[266] A noteworthy incident in this outbreak was that the railways disallowed third-class and fourth-class passengers, mostly migrant workers, to travel back home in January 1911, the usual time for the winter vacations, in order to curtail disease transmission.[267] But migrants, desperate to go home during the crisis, travelled by carts or walked home, and many died due to hunger and the cold—similar scenes were observed in India in April–May 2020 when the railways were shut down amid the COVID-19 crisis.

The pneumonic plague outbreak, whose source was uncertain, led to an international medical conference in Mukden, China, in April 1911, where many Chinese officials argued that adopting western medicine, like the railways, was essential for China to make its way forward.[268] As it happened, a few months later, the Qing dynasty that had ruled the country since the seventeenth century was overthrown in events unrelated to the conference, and a key figure in this movement was a physician inspired by Western medicine, Dr Sun Yat-sen (1866–1925).

On the whole, the third plague pandemic had a much greater impact on Asia and Africa than on Europe and the Americas, but this was not because of a sanitary, economic or even imperial disadvantage. It was first and foremost about rats and X. cheopis, as the low mortality in Bengal in eastern India shows. What the pandemic undoubtedly created was a much wider base of plague foci reservoirs in the world, even if it did not trouble humans everywhere. Where plague outbreaks occurred, it was indeed the case that rat-proofed homes withstood the onslaught much better. However, in the decade following 1894, the limited knowledge of transmission led to a confused response and a clash between the various medical systems of the world. Within the British imperial system, this was a clash between the older 'miasma' theories and newer ideas coming from the field of bacteriology. In places like India and China, it was a clash between traditional and Western medical systems, though in this case, the latter system did not offer any real advantage for a long time, and when it intruded into people's personal lives, it made matters worse. The pandemic, therefore, created sharp divisions between the medical authorities, politicians and business houses.

One business that definitely prospered because of the third plague pandemic, right up until World War I, was that of disinfectants and fumigants. For instance, the fumigation device patented by the engineer Thomas Clayton in the US in the late nineteenth century led to its rapid adoption around the world, especially in maritime networks, to kill insects and rats by blasting them with sulphuric acid gas.[269] 'Clayton's apparatus' was in use at the port of Bombay by 1903 as part of its plague control kit to disinfect ships' holds.[270] Clearly, somebody was profiting from the pandemic.

The third plague pandemic, thus, left its mark on the world in intriguing ways. According to the historian Myron Echenberg, it contributed to 'the rise of nationalism in India, the Great Fire in Honolulu, the persistence of anti-Asian prejudice in the United States and Australia, the rise of apartheid in South Africa, and the growth of public health services in Brazil.'[271] At the most basic level, though, it killed millions of humans, and many more rodents.

End of the Pandemic

The plague started declining in India, the worst affected region of the pandemic, by the 1920s. Around that time, the sanitation manual on plague control in India encompassed ten points:

> Compulsory notification and registration of cause of death; Rat prevention, killing, collection and examination; Evacuation; Disinfection; Inoculation; Improvement of insanitary areas; Complete system of scavengering; Free medical relief; Circulation of knowledge by lectures, leaflets and diagrams; Rat proof dwellings.[272]

It is difficult to state the effect any of these measures had in bringing down the number of plague cases and deaths because plague death rates began to gradually decline across India, even in areas where little of the above was done. At best, the measures made people aware of the importance of sanitation, and inoculations may have reduced case fatality rates. It was only in the 1940s that antibiotics and the DDT spray finally found use as a means to 'cure' the plague and efficiently kill rats and fleas, respectively.

The most likely cause for the recession of the pandemic by the 1920s was the growing immunity of rodents to the plague, an explanation which could be applied to the phasing away of all the great plague outbreaks of the past.[273] If rats did not die due to the plague, rat fleas would not have to bite humans, or so goes the argument. In 1954, R. Pollitzer, scientist and expert on the plague, in a document for the WHO, noted that while appreciating plague control measures, 'one should be careful not to ascribe the freedom from plague in any country to the measures taken but as an outcome of the periodicity of infection'.[274] Unlike cholera, where human ingenuity played a decisive role in reducing its prevalence, the third plague pandemic in global history appears to have behaved just like the first two, coming and going away on the whim of *Yersinia pestis*.

In India, the total plague deaths fell consistently from nearly 5 million in the decade preceding 1918 to 2 million in the 1919–28 decade, to 500,000 in 1929–38 and to 300,000 in the 1939–48 decade.[275] Plague-related deaths briefly shot up in 1947, the year of Independence and the Partition. They then rose to 700,000 in the 1949–58 decade, before plummeting to only 1,000 deaths in the next decade, until finally 1969 came to be seen as the year of eradication in India.

The plague momentarily raised its head again in September 1994 in Surat in western India, suspected to be of the pneumonic variety, and generated a massive state response similar to the one in 1896–98, leading again to public fear and a migrant exodus from one of India's fastest growing major cities at the time.[276] DDT was sprayed in the city, masks appeared on faces in leading cities and a partial lockdown was imposed in some places. At least one boarding school decided to send their students back by air, rather than train, much to the delight of the students, as this author can personally attest to.

The reappearance of the plague received major international attention and some countries even stopped air traffic to and from India. Exports were hit and tourist footfall fell by nearly half across the country. Overall, there were over 6,000 suspected cases of plague, only 288 clinically confirmed, and 55 deaths (52 in Surat and 3 in Delhi).[277] However, the outbreak seems to have been nipped in the bud and, thankfully, led to a makeover of Surat city's sanitation system. That strain of plague was later found to be a mutation of the original one that had affected India decades earlier, contributing to new medical knowledge about the possibilities of mutation in *Yersinia pestis*.[278]

The plague, as of today, has been virtually eradicated from the human species. Between 2010 and 2015, fewer than 4,000 cases and 600 deaths related to the plague were reported from around the world, and it appears to be endemic only in Madagascar, Peru and the Democratic Republic of Congo.[279] The resistance to antibiotics of newer plague strains is one lingering worry for epidemiologists.

I have had the opportunity to live in three cities of the world that were ravaged at one time or the other by the plague: Mumbai, London and Florence. If there is anything we learn from their histories, it is that the plague returns, sometimes after many centuries. If you ever see rats emerging out of their holes, delirious, spinning around and collapsing dead, this piece of age-old Indian advice may just help: evacuate. But you don't need to be scared, since a cure for plague is now available. The same, however, cannot be said about another pandemic disease, less glamorous than the plague, but equally, if not more, potent, that came close on the heels of the peak period of the third plague pandemic, and with much more devastating effect.

4

Influenza

'The hospitals were choked so that it was impossible to remove the dead quickly enough to make room for the dying; the streets and lanes of the cities were littered with dead and dying people; the postal and telegraph services were completely disorganized; the train service continued, but at all the principal stations dead and dying people were being removed from the trains; the burning ghats and burial grounds were literally swamped with corpses, whilst an even greater number awaited removal; the depleted medical service, itself sorely stricken by the epidemic, was incapable of dealing with more than a minute fraction of the sickness requiring attention; nearly every household was lamenting a death, and everywhere terror and confusion reigned.'

– A Preliminary Report on the
Influenza Pandemic of 1918 in India[1]

What happened around the year 1918? For many, that period is reminiscent of the end of World War I, which had raged since 1914. For those who admire Lenin, it brings to mind the euphoria immediately following the Russian Revolution of 1917.

In India, there is still vivid public remembrance of the Jallianwala Bagh tragedy of April 1919, when hundreds of Indians were shot down in Amritsar on General Reginald Dyer's orders. And for that rare Indian student who has diligently studied for school-level history examinations, the 'Rowlatt Act' imposed by the British and the opposition to it the same year, would perhaps ring a bell.

However, if there is anything 1918 should be known for, it is the great influenza pandemic that wiped out over 40 million human beings in the matter of a few months. Based on my estimates, around 20 million of them died in the Indian subcontinent alone.[2] These figures amounted to 2 per cent of the global population and 6.4 per cent of the Indian population at the time.[3] To put this in perspective, more people died from the influenza pandemic in India than the global death count attributed to battle casualties in World War I.[4] More Indians died in the influenza pandemic in a few months than the global death toll of the third plague pandemic.

This influenza pandemic ranks as the most catastrophic pandemic in modern history and as India's worst recorded demographic disaster till date. The pandemic's magnitude is as striking as its disappearance from public memory. What happened in 1918 and why did we forget it?

And Then Came Influenza

One person who never forgot 1918 was Norman White. On the evening of 15 October 1953, White gave a presidential address to the Royal Society of Tropical Medicine at Manson House in London, titled 'Retrospect', outlining his career.[5] Between 1920 and 1953, he had held a number of positions in leading international health efforts that preceded the formation of the WHO. Before 1920, he had spent seventeen years with the Indian Medical Service, most of them in great 'stress and anxiety', for he witnessed the medical efforts during the Great War (1914–18) and was the sanitary commissioner of India during India's pandemic nightmare.

In the first quarter of 1919, he penned *A Preliminary Report on the Influenza Pandemic in India*, noteworthy for its title which used the word 'pandemic' in Indian official records probably for the first time, and also for 'preliminary', indicating a potential follow-up report. The report estimated 6 million deaths based on data on registered deaths, which very quickly became the number highlighted by the media and political leaders of the time, though we now know that the actual number was around three times that figure. The final report on the influenza pandemic never materialized. Writer's fatigue, perhaps.

Norman White's recollection of the event is interesting because of the close attention paid to the details of the months leading up to the catastrophe. In his words,

During the latter half of the first World War, I was entrusted with the work of the Sanitary Commissioner of the Government of India. They were years of great stress and anxiety. The, at best, meagre health and medical services had been depleted by the war effort and were only just sufficient for routine work, if all went well. Things went persistently badly. In the autumn of 1917 malaria was epidemic in parts of Northern India: the plague epidemic of 1917-18 was the most severe that India had suffered for eleven years: failure of the monsoon in 1918 resulted in food scarcity and high prices: there was considerable anxiety regarding the importation of various infections, and fresh strains of infection, with troops returning from overseas: and then came influenza.[6]

In fact, 1918 in India was no ordinary year at all. Nor was 1917. Both years were climatically abnormal. A look at India's meteorological history from 1870 to 2000 shows that 1917 was on the extreme end of 'surplus rainfall', with the highest ever recorded precipitation at the all-India level.[7] And 1918 was the third worst year of 'deficient rainfall', the other two being 1877 and 1899, both of which were associated with devastating famines. India went from being abnormally wet in 1917, suitable conditions for malaria and plague, to being abnormally dry in 1918, a classic condition for famine. While the word 'famine' was used in some provinces, accounts of widespread starvation-related deaths were rare and hence 1918 was not recorded as a major famine year in Indian history. However, water scarcity did have a connection with influenza-related mortality, as we shall see in this chapter. But before that, we have to cover substantial ground to understand the mysterious properties of the disease, how it came to India in the first place and how various regions experienced it.

One Flu over the Scientist's Test

Unlike cholera and the plague, influenza usually does not evoke fear in the minds of the public. Better known by its shorter name, 'flu', it is seen to be a harmless disease that is virulent but not deadly. In Arnold Bennett's novel *The Card*, written in 1911, Mrs Machin snaps at her son's suggestion to see a doctor to check if she has influenza: 'Ye can call it influenza if ye like ... There was no influenza in my young days. We called a cold a cold.'[8]

The flu is more severe than a cold, involving fevers, chills, debilitating body aches and weakness, and does not necessarily leave a stuffy nose. While rhinoviruses are the major causes of common colds, influenza is caused by a different virus with particular types such as Type A, which circulates among humans and animals (an example being swine flu) or birds (avian flu), and Type B, which circulates only among humans. The proteins that enable entry into human cells are letter-coded as H and N, and so the virus can get a particular name like A/H1N1, the virus that caused the 'swine flu' outbreak in 2009. The flu virus is a tricky opponent because of its ability to evade pre-existing immunity by changing its coat frequently through what immunologists call 'drift and shift'.[9] Drifts refer to frequent but small changes in the coat of the virus, and shifts refer to less periodic but big changes. As a result, the flu changes across seasons and years and makes the process of developing vaccines for it that much harder.

Influenza has been hard to spot in history because its symptoms are not spectacular, like those of the plague or smallpox. An eighteenth-century reference from Italy suggests that the word 'influenza' came from the disease being acknowledged as the 'influence' of heavenly bodies.[10] Researchers have pointed out that influenza pandemics are very common historically and only a few of them have turned out to be severe in terms of fatality. Before the twentieth century, flu outbreaks were noted in several years, with large geographical spreads, as in 1580, 1729–30, 1732–33, 1781–82, 1830–31 and 1833.[11] The 1889–90 pandemic, known as the 'Russian Flu' for its supposed origin, was the first outbreak where the disease was studied systematically. In 1892, Richard Pfeiffer identified a bacillus that was believed to cause the flu. *Pfeiffer's Bacillus*, as it was called in an age when bacteriology was developing at a rapid pace, was not the real cause of the disease, as scientists discovered to their dismay during the 1918–20 pandemic.

For a long time, scientists had discounted the possibility of the flu being transmitted outside the human species, thus restricting the scope for laboratory analysis. Around 1930, Richard Shope discovered that the flu could be transmitted among pigs, and this set off a string of discoveries through animal-based experiments that revealed various properties of the virus under the emerging field of virology. During World War II, American scientists focussed on vaccination procedures to prevent a repeat of the 1918 calamity and since then, flu vaccines have helped millions across the world. But the flu virus can develop new strains and pose severe challenges, as it did in 1957–58 (the so-called Asian flu) and in 1968 (the so-called Hong Kong flu), rendering vaccines ineffective. Mortality rates in these pandemics were nowhere near the levels witnessed in 1918 and the cumulative global death count attributed to those pandemics was under 3 million. In 1976, a flu scare in the US led to a mass vaccination drive that unfortunately had a few side effects, and while the flu itself turned out to be mild, it resulted in legal suits and widespread anti-vaccination sentiment.[12]

The biggest puzzle for flu researchers in the twentieth century was the nature of the virus that caused the 1918–20 pandemic, a mystery that would only be resolved eight decades after the event. The key was to obtain body samples from the 1918 pandemic that could be analysed with the superior technology virologists had in the late twentieth century. In 1951, one young researcher, Johan Hultin, visited graves of the victims of the 1918 influenza pandemic in Alaska in order to extract samples.[13] He found corpses that had been preserved by the freezing temperatures of the region, and took samples. Unfortunately, the samples could not survive the journey to the lab. Several decades later, in 1997, he read a four-page research paper in the journal *Science* by Jefferey Taubenberger, Ann Reid and others, that marked a breakthrough in the big puzzle.[14]

That study analysed autopsy material from 1918 preserved by the US Army Medical Museum, and claimed that the 1918 flu was caused by a 'novel H1N1 influenza A virus'.[15] Hultin reached out to this study team to see if they would be interested in analysing Alaskan body samples to expand and verify the results. Taubenberger's team agreed. So Hultin, now seventy-two, once again trudged to the same graves in Alaska, dug them up after taking permission from local authorities and this time, found a body sample that could survive the journey to the lab. Hultin became a co-author with Taubenberger's team in the next research paper, which provided further results on the virus. More studies by other researchers followed and eventually, the 1918 virus was reconstructed. An experiment on mice finally confirmed what was obvious to everyone in the world in 1918: the 'unique high-virulence' property of the deadly 1918 influenza virus.[16] We now finally know what caused the lethal 1918 influenza pandemic. It is hoped that the reconstructed viruses never leave the confines of the laboratories they are currently kept in, and stay away from humans. At that time, though, there was simply no way for people to know what hit them.

Waves and Magnitudes

The locational origins of the 1918 flu are still contested, but most of the evidence points to Kansas in the American Midwest, where it appeared early in the year.[17] This was the first of two clearly discernible flu waves found around the world that year; some countries experienced a third wave in 1919 and also possibly a fourth wave in 1920.[18] The second wave, towards the end of 1918, was the deadliest of all and hence 1918 is considered to be the pivotal year of the 1918–20 pandemic. A key characteristic of the second wave, observed globally, was that it affected adults aged between twenty and forty, apart from the very young and the elderly, thus leaving a W-shaped mortality signature across age groups. Apart from the usual symptoms of fevers and body pains, cases quickly turned pneumonic, clearing a path for bacteria to attack the lungs. In serious cases, patients' faces turned blue or black.[19] The only saving grace was that unlike cholera or the plague, the flu pandemic did not stay on for decades. Populations rapidly acquired herd immunity and the virus most likely mutated into less harmful versions within months. In a sense, the virus burnt itself out by killing so many people so quickly. The first flu wave reached distant corners of the world, facilitated by passenger traffic, commerce and the movement of troops during World War I. In the middle of August 1918, the flu virus is said to have mutated and created 'three explosions' in Europe, America and Africa, in the port cities of Brest (France), Boston (USA) and Freetown (Sierra Leone), almost simultaneously.[20] On 15 August, the British naval ship *HMS Mantua* docked at Freetown with 200 sick sailors. Two weeks later, workers at the docks had been infected and then the virus began spreading to other parts of the port city and inland.[21] The wave peaked in Freetown around 6 September, and by the end of the month, two-thirds of the population of Sierra Leone was estimated to have been infected and 3 per cent had died.[22]

Brest, in France, was the landing port for nearly 800,000 American soldiers of the 2 million sent to Europe in the war.[23] The huge camps for soldiers of different nationalities were perfect sites for the rapid spread of the disease and the number of infected soldiers began to soar. Boston, a key point of transit for Americans going to the war effort in Europe and also a disembarkation point during the return journey, was the next to be affected after Brest, with the first case detected on 27 August.[24] Within two months, all of North America was affected and the final death toll there was around 675,000 Americans and 50,000 Canadians, which was less than 0.7 per cent of their respective populations.[25]

The geographical spread of the 1918 influenza pandemic was unprecedented. In 1978, the scientists Fred Hoyle and Chandra Wickramasinghe wrote an article called 'Influenza from space?', suggesting that the disease could have originated in outer space and transmitted quickly over areas through atmospheric dispersion, a theory that has consistently had few takers since it was first put forward.[26] For there were places on earth where the throw from outer space did not land perfectly, like St. Helena, an island in the Atlantic Ocean untroubled by ships, which managed to escape the flu completely.[27]

In those countries which were affected, influenza-related death rates between 1918 and 1920 were generally under 1 per cent of the population, but the pandemic still created a stir because of its high intensity in the last few months of 1918.[28] While transmission was widespread, death rates varied substantially. India (including present-day Pakistan and Bangladesh) was the worst affected country in absolute terms and deaths due to influenza accounted for over 5 per cent of its population.[29] But Iran was probably the worst affected in terms of the death rate, estimated to lie between 8 per cent to 20 per cent (1–2 million people).[30] Other countries with high influenza death rates included Kenya (5.5 per cent), South Africa (3–6 per cent), Indonesia (3 per cent), Sierra Leone (3 per cent), Mexico (2 per cent), Philippines (1.9 per cent), Russia (1.8 per cent), Portugal (1.8 per cent) and several other countries breaching the 1 per cent barrier such as Venezuela, Egypt, Hungary, Italy, Spain, Korea, Malaysia, Sri Lanka, Turkey and possibly also China.[31] Spain did not have the highest death rate, but because it was a neutral country in the war, the press at the time did not censor news of the outbreak, leading other nations to dub the disease the 'Spanish flu', a phrase widely used at the time and thereafter.[32] Globally, the pandemic wiped out over 2 per cent of the population or over 40 million lives, and in absolute terms may well have been 'the greatest single demographic shock that the human species has ever received'.[33] Considering today's global population of close to 8 billion, a 2 per cent wipeout would translate to over 150 million deaths, which is unlikely to be the end result of the COVID-19 pandemic.

The mortality statistics mentioned above for the 1918–20 influenza pandemic have been updated through various studies over the past century.[34] Death figures are collected on the basis of 'registration', which is a process that usually breaks down in a period of crisis, as observed by the health officials of those times. It leads to serious underestimation of the number of deaths, especially in poorer countries with weak data collection systems. In India, the Census of 1921 noted that due to 'the complete breakdown of the reporting staff, the registration of vital statistics was in many cases suspended during the progress of the epidemic in 1918'.[35]

The first influenza death estimates for India and the world in the 1920s were 6 million and 21 million, respectively.[36] These figures have been revised upwards, either by correcting for under-registration or by gauging the 'shortfalls' in population between two census periods. The death figures for India and the world are believed to range between 10–20 million and over 40 million, respectively.[37] Across studies, India appears as the country most affected, accounting for around 40 per cent of global deaths in the pandemic. However, the studies on India relied mainly on death statistics of districts directly ruled by the British, covering less than 75 per cent of the population of the subcontinent. This left out the princely states; two of which in particular, Rajputana (now Rajasthan) and Hyderabad, were badly affected by the pandemic.

Correcting for this, my research revised the influenza mortality estimate for the Indian subcontinent to close to or upwards of

20 million, reflecting 6.4 per cent of its population at that time.[38] This is far greater than estimates of other large disasters in India such as the famines of 1769–70 (5–10 million), 1876–78 (5 million), 1896–1901 (5 million) and 1943–44 (2 million).[39] However, for several decades after the pandemic, the figure that circulated among the public in India was 6 million, and thus, to those who had lived through the pandemic, it did not appear to be a larger toll than what the famines had taken in the past.

One major reason for the authorities not realizing the magnitude of the loss was that the bulk of mortality in India took place in rural areas, distant from the centres of news production. While urban death rates were consistently higher than rural death rates in the early twentieth century and by a fair margin, it was only in 1918 that this pattern flipped, and for that one year alone.[40] This was clear to the census officials when they went to enumerate villages in 1921, and found huge losses in population.

But how exactly did the flu spread within India? I.D. Mills in 1986 and Siddharth Chandra's research team since 2012 have empirically analysed aspects of India's tryst with the influenza pandemic of 1918. Both show that the second wave of the flu spread eastwards from the Bombay Presidency across the subcontinent in September, with death rates peaking in the Bombay Presidency in October, in most of India in November and in some parts of eastern India in December.[41]

The study by Mills also analysed prison data, which had information not only on deaths but also on those who had contracted influenza, usually unavailable for wider populations. Case fatality rates varied between 2 per cent and 12 per cent across prisons in different regions of India. Mills found that 'the prevalence of influenza was fairly constant across India, and that what varied was mortality'.[42] Broadly, western, central and northern India were hit badly while the southern and eastern parts fared much better in terms of mortality. Mills attributed this to temperature ranges being starker in a day in some parts of India, enabling easier pneumonic conditions to develop from a flu attack. Another reason could be that the virus mutated to less harmful varieties as it moved east and south. I will argue that these theories do not apply to other countries and will instead provide another explanation as to why India was affected so badly, and why some parts of the country witnessed higher mortality than others. But before that, we need to understand the experiences of different regions of the Indian subcontinent at that time and how the people described them.

The Onslaught in Western India

Influenza was well-known in Bombay city because it had experienced the 1889–90 flu pandemic, and served as the first point of entry in India before the disease spread, possibly through troop movements.[43] Called 'nayi sardi bukhar' (a new type of cold), it arrived in Bombay in January 1890, infected many and disrupted business activity in the months of February and March that year.[44]

Thus, when the next flu pandemic arrived in the middle of 1918, the medical community of Bombay was not entirely unfamiliar with the challenges that lay ahead. A ship that arrived on 29 May is said to have brought the epidemic, though the disease began attracting attention only in late June, as it spread from the docks to the city.[45] The origin of the flu was disputed as the health officer claimed that it had come from outside India while the sanitary commissioner of Bombay insisted that the flu was endemic to India, and that it was the shipping crew that caught it on arrival.[46] The dispute attracted media attention, and the press blamed the authorities for their negligence.

The Times of India, a Bombay-based newspaper, reported 'The Fever Epidemic' on 25 June, describing people falling sick, offices 'bewailing the absence of clerks' and the health department clarifying that it was only a seasonal flu.[47] The article said that symptoms included high temperature and back pains, leaving people feeling 'flat', and that the disease was mostly contracted in overcrowded, unventilated areas. It added that 'the main remedy is to go to bed and not worry'.[48] A few months later, on 19 October, it would report on 'The Spread of Influenza', the broken health system and the need to organize self-help. On 9 March 1919, its headline would say 'Six Million Deaths: Influenza's Toll in India'.[49]

Between June 1918 and March 1919, Bombay city, and the wider Bombay Presidency (including Sind) in western India, faced an unprecedented sequence of events: the first wave of a flu pandemic, the most acute drought in its recorded history, the second deadlier wave of a flu pandemic, and the declaration of famine in many regions.

A first-person account of the horrors of this time can be found in Lakshmibai's *Smritichitre,* the same memoirs that recorded the horrors of the plague quarantine camp (recounted in the earlier chapter). In 1918, Lakshmibai was based in Satara district, south of Bombay city, and she first described the onset of the drought when 'people's eyes were fixed on the clouds like the *chatak* bird, yearning for rain' but 'no rain fell and people's mouths ran dry'.[50] Prayers across religions followed and 'idols in the temples were imprisoned in water to compel them to listen to people's prayers'.[51] She observed that acute food scarcity meant that children became burdensome for their mothers. Her husband, Rev. Narayan Vaman Tilak, began eating only one meal a day and donating food to the poor. He was noted to have said that he could not eat food which others could not afford. Then she described the horror of influenza, locally known as *manmodi,* which deserves to be quoted at some length:

But disease inevitably follows drought and so it did. The disease we call manmodi, or dropneck, struck Satara first. It took away

the last shred of courage left in the people. They were too
shocked even to speak. Manmodi was almost worse than the
plague. In a family of ten, only one remained standing. The
others were flat on their backs. The animals grazing in the
forest could not be brought home and the animals at home
could not be fed or given water. Families had no food to eat, no
oil to light their lamps, no men to fetch their water. We heard
the story of a penniless man who sold his cow in exchange for
two pomegranates. Conditions were so pitiable that Mr Tilak
opened a small clinic and free kitchen. I used to brew three or
four seers of a herbal infusion every morning. Mr Tilak would
distribute this from eight to twelve in the morning along with
milk, sago, sugar, kerosene and boxes of matches to all comers:
Brahmins, Marathas, Mahars.[52]

Estimates suggest that the Bombay Presidency lost well over 6 per
cent of its population, or in absolute terms, over 1 million people.[53]
Women were struck harder than men, as also observed in other parts
of India, which was attributed at that time to the fact that 'in addition
to the ordinary tasks of the house, on them fell the duty of nursing
the others even when themselves ill'.[54] Infant mortality soared. In
Bombay city, a report showed that while Europeans and Parsis had
the lowest rates of death related to influenza (about 1 per cent of
their populations), the death rates were more than double among
Muslims and 'Caste Hindus' and more than six times as high
among 'Low Caste Hindus'.[55] Dr B.R. Ambedkar, champion of the
downtrodden, would later reflect on this episode in this observation:
'That caste can influence doctors in the ministration to the sick was
a charge made among certain doctors in Bombay in 1918 during the
influenza epidemic'.[56]

The first flu wave in June, lasting a month, claimed 1,600 lives
in the city but the second wave, whose exact origin in India is still

disputed, but was thought to be around Poona at the time, hit with great intensity between 10 September and 10 November, claiming over 15,000 lives.[57] The wave peaked on 6 October in Bombay city, with 768 people dying of influenza on just that day. So fatigued was the press in reporting that a newspaper on 10 October ran an editorial correction saying it meant 'one death every two minutes' instead of what it had printed: 'two deaths every minute'.[58]

The startling rise in mortality in September also led to conspiracy theories, chief among them being that the pandemic was caused by poison gas used by the enemy on the western front in Europe.[59] Meanwhile, the cemeteries were filling up and newspapers saw mounting obituaries of people from across professions. A student at Grant Medical College and a volunteer of the Social Service League, Krishna Natarajan (whose father edited the *Indian Social Reformer*), died while on duty, serving and nursing the poor.[60] Among the prominent people who succumbed to the flu was the chief of Manavadar, a town near Junagadh in Saurashtra, where all public life was brought to a halt for three days as a mark of respect.[61]

It is popularly believed that Mohandas Gandhi contracted the flu during the pandemic, and while it is true that he was seriously ill in the second half of 1918, spending a lot of time in Ahmedabad in his ashram, it was due to dysentery.[62] A day before his birthday, on 1 October, he sent for his sons Harilal and Devadas to look after him. Recuperation from the illness would be painfully slow for Gandhi. Influenza would not claim him but would devastate his family, claiming the lives of Harilal's wife, Gulab, and son, Shanti, who died in late October in Patharada, a village in Gujarat that they visited for a 'health-change'.[63] Gandhi's wife, Kasturba, then had Harilal's three remaining mother-less children sent over to the ashram.

In Gujarat, Kachchh and Bhavnagar were hit hard, but the worst affected was a rural tract called the Dangs, which lost over 15 per cent of its population of mostly indigenous tribes, comprising mainly Bhils. The historian David Hardiman studied aspects of the pandemic in this region and found that the memory of the 1918 flu, or *manmodi*, was preserved in local folklore as a calamity which depopulated entire villages and as a time when there were so many dead bodies that they had to be thrown off a cliff.[64] In other parts of the region, the disease was referred to as *dhani pani*. A local missionary church tried its best to help during the pandemic but had limited impact. Those who proclaimed healing powers, the *bhagats*, lost their popularity because they could not cure the disease and soon after, a new goddess, Salabai, came to be worshipped in the region.[65]

People in Gujarat suffered not only in rural and urban areas but also in transit. As in previous pandemics, return migration from big cities by trains ensued, but the intensity of the flu meant that many could not survive the journey. In the second week of October 1918, on the way from Bombay city to Gujarat, three dead bodies were found in a train at Surat, two at Ahmedabad and many more in other locations.[66]

Further south of Bombay city, in Portuguese-ruled Goa, influenza spread with 'incredible rapidity', particularly in Salsette district.[67] It claimed the lives of prominent doctors, including that of Dr Miguel Furtado, who was also the leader of the Popular Party in Salsette. Newspaper production was affected; a leading daily printed a one-page edition with print on only one side. The health officials recommended regular washing of one's mouth and nose with a solution of gomenol (a plant-based oil), boric water or thymol thrice a day. In its absence, inhalation of eucalyptus oil or camphor was recommended.

Life in western India was traumatic in the last quarter of 1918 and the historian Mridula Ramanna, who studied the response to the pandemic in detail, observed that 'confusion and inconsistency seem to have marked the response of the authorities throughout the

Presidency'.[68] Examinations were postponed in colleges and appeals to shut down schools poured in. When the Karachi municipality closed its cinema halls for three months, the owners protested, pointing out the liberty enjoyed in Bombay. Police officers fell ill and had a tough time managing the thefts and crimes committed amid high inflation.[69] The local health officer issued appeals to avoid large gatherings and crowded places but it was clear that the pandemic had overwhelmed the health services, already depleted because many were outstation for the war effort.[70] The second flu wave's penchant for adult bodies left behind a large number of orphans, and so by late November, government creches for 'influenza orphans' were announced, to be administered by district collectors and charitable organizations.[71] Scientists at the Bombay Bacteriological Laboratory scrambled to understand the disease, tried different experiments and, after a conference in Delhi in December, came out with a vaccine to be distributed free of charge, albeit with limited utility as the science about the virus was still hazy.[72] In any case, the worst of the pandemic had subsided in western India by then.

As people began to slowly recover in November, appeals were made to the Tramway Company in Bombay city to keep more open space for passengers to travel comfortably.[73] By December, the disgust with the government building memorials at a time of despair was clear when a letter to the editor demanded 'Willingdon Wells' and 'Willingdon Dispensaries' rather than a memorial in honour of Lord Willingdon, the former governor of Bombay.[74]

The government's overall response in the Bombay Presidency was tardy.[75] In January 1919, the governor wrote to his seniors about the dire conditions in the region and its potential repercussions:

> Cattle are beginning to die in considerable quantities in the Deccan and we can't get fodder enough to alleviate the trouble. Large quantities of valuable fodder are being exported from here

to Mesopotamia by the Army ... Luckily the Horniman press [*The Bombay Chronicle*] have not tumbled to the fact that fodder is being exported while the Deccan starves: if they ever do they will raise a howl and point out that Government exploit India even in famine times for their own Imperial purposes.[76]

The rural hinterlands of the Deccan plateau suffered greatly, first from the drought, then the flu, and ultimately from the declaration of famine. Districts like Sholapur, Ahmednagar, Nasik and Satara were severely affected and witnessed staggering mortality. Rev. Dr Ballantine in Ahmednagar district was quoted in the *Indian Social Reformer*, describing the dire conditions there:

> During the influenza epidemic not one family has escaped sickness and there have been many deaths. We do not know how to replace the experienced and reliable teachers who have died ... Bodies were simply taken outside, there being no one strong enough to dig a grave ... Who can feed and clothe the long procession of orphans, a line which grows longer and more pitiful every day?[77]

There were appeals in newspapers to send people from voluntary service organizations in Bombay city to affected rural areas.[78] These organizations would emerge as the saving grace of the pandemic across India. Norman White would later sarcastically quip that the outpouring of support in large numbers from the educated towards the poor in a time of distress was unprecedented 'perhaps, in the history of India'.[79]

In Bombay city, the organizations aiding in this effort were an eclectic mix of the Hindu Medical Association, the Social Service League led by N.M. Joshi and its Influenza Relief Committee, community-based hospitals for the Jains, Lohanas, Marwaris, Bohras and Parsis, St. George's Nursing Association, Young Men's Mahomedan Association, Bombay Humanitarian League, Telugu Free Library, Japanese and Shanghai Piece Goods Association and dozens of others.[80] They distributed food, medicines and often ran travelling dispensaries.

In Poona, V.R. Shinde led the relief efforts of the Depressed Classes Mission, accompanied by the Poona Volunteer Corps and Arogya Mandal.[81] Travelling dispensaries were deployed in Surat and Karachi. Everywhere, a wonderful spirit of public–private cooperation was in evidence though in reality this was forced, as people recognized that the meagre health system had been overwhelmed and it was either self-organization or death. In Ahmedabad, though, the people were furious with the government's response to the crisis; here the merchant associations and the Gujarat Sabha played an important role in relief efforts.[82] The Gujarat Sabha also aided the Salvation Army in reaching out to rural areas, though the task of relief efforts proved to be practically impossible the farther one went from the large cities, best exemplified by the tragic tale of the Dangs.

If anyone benefited at all in the mayhem of the drought and disease in western India in 1918–19, it was the few students who obtained a college degree when they may otherwise have failed. For influenza also left its mark in the softening of the hard-nosed attitudes of professors. At my mother's alma mater, Sydenham College of Commerce and Economics in Bombay, the principal blamed influenza for engendering unprecedented leniency and lamented that 'out of the least competent batch of students we have ever had, we sent out with the hallmark of our degree a far greater proportion than we have ever sent before'.[83]

Army, Posts and Delirium in Punjab

In the Punjab province of northern India, two features stood out in the transmission of influenza. The first had to do with Punjab's position as the key recruitment site for the British Indian army, especially during World War I. As recounted in the memoirs of the then Lieutenant General of Punjab, Michael O'Dwyer:

> In each of the months, August and September, 1918, over twenty-one thousand recruits were raised, surpassing all previous records, and the falling in October was due to the appalling epidemic of influenza. In a few months that epidemic carried off half a million of the Punjab population. Whereas among the half-million Punjabis who served in the War the death casualties were only some thirty thousand.[84]

In the event, few of those fresh recruits in 1918 went to the warfront but those returning were seen to bring the infection back home. The other mode of transmission that received a lot of attention in Punjab was the postal services. While the public made a link between infection spread through letters and parcels delivered by postal officials, the medical service argued that it was the postal peons who acted as a 'disseminating agency'.[85] Here is one account of a public official inspecting the Hindustan–Tibet Road for epidemic outbreaks:

> A recruit suffering from symptoms of Influenza arrived at Narkanda and stayed a night with the Khansamah [butler] of the hotel there. Three days later the Khansamah and his wife went down with Influenza. Within a few yards of the Khansamah's house lived a blacksmith and the two used to intervisit. A few days after the Khansamah was attacked all the members of the blacksmith's house were down with the disease. The postal peons used to come and sit in the Khansamah's house, with the

result that they all contracted the disease and two of them died from it.[86]

Postal employees in Bombay and Karachi were considered to be the original sources of the infection and the Railway Postal Service, the medium through which the flu arrived in Punjab.

The actual numbers 'carried off' by influenza exceeded 1 million, making it deadlier than the malarial epidemic Punjab faced in 1908. The impact varied substantially across the population and the provincial sanitation board noted that 'the case mortality in Europeans was well under 5 per cent, in Indians of the better class and those provided with qualified medical aid about 6 per cent, in the poorer classes anything from 50 per cent onwards'.[87] It also mentioned the surging food prices, especially for jowar and bajra in the last quarter of the year, and stagnant wages 'causing a reduction in the standard of living', which 'probably increased the mortality from influenza among the poorer classes'.[88] As argued earlier, the local reports of that time noted the stark variation in mortality patterns and the connection with the prevailing adverse material conditions induced by a drought and high food prices.

The first flu wave in Punjab was extremely mild; it was only towards the end of September that infections across the province began to be detected. Thomas Herriot wrote his MD thesis in 1920 on his observations of the influenza pandemic in Punjab as he was then in-charge of the military hospital in Jullundur.[89] His first-person account is a rare medical testimony of the pandemic in India and shows the harrowing time he had as his colleagues fell sick and the health services fell apart; he himself, at a later stage, battled malaria and dysentery.

Herriot had to begin by guessing the disease as information on it in the initial days was not forthcoming and lab tests showed that, with an incubation period of two to three days, it was neither malaria nor pneumonic plague. He attributed the arrival of the disease in Jullundur to 'sepoys returning from leave', and the high mortality rates among Indians to undernourishment caused by the drought.[90] The shortage of fodder for the cows and the subsequent scarcity of milk compounded the problems in nourishment. The transmission of the disease was rapid because people tended to sleep indoors in the cold winter, where there was 'over-crowding and no ventilation'.[91] In one village of 9,000 people, he observed, 3,000 had perished due to influenza. He noted that even though the plague was recurrent in the region, it was during the influenza pandemic that people actually fled their villages.[92]

Disease transmission was believed to be from 'the patient's nose, throat and lungs' and by 'sneezing and coughing'.[93] In the worst cases, pneumonic conditions quickly developed after contracting the flu and a 'peculiar colouration was observed' in the face, sometimes only lips and ears, of a 'violet lavender hue'.[94] This coloration was taken to be a sign that death was certain and, according to Herriot, even the smell of the patients turned distinctive. Patients with serious cases could also turn delirious, and some became 'excited, noisy, and in a few cases maniacal'.[95] The work of the guards in the hospital was particularly tricky, as this account describes:

> Special guards were used whose sole duty was to replace bed-clothes which had been thrown off or to put patients back to bed. Some went quietly, others fought and bit their guards. Some patients appeared to be very cunning, waiting till the guard's back was turned and leaping out of bed.[96]

Herriot recounted his frustrations with treatment, having tried various measures suggested at that time, including calomel, cinnamon and quinine, none of which seemed to work. Lab tests had to be stopped because the hospital was short-staffed and it was assumed that most patients were being reported for influenza. Due

Cholera strikes Europe: A man barricades himself in with an array of protective gear against the cholera epidemic, that is in turn portrayed as a hag. This represents an overabundance of impractical advice concerning protection against cholera. Coloured etching by J.B. Wunder, c. 1832.

'A young woman [from] Vienna who died of cholera, depicted when healthy and four hours before death. Coloured stipple engraving.'

Severe nationwide cholera outbreaks in the US occurred in 1832, 1849 and 1866. The last line of the cartoon notes: Cholera (to the exacting Owners of Tenement Houses). "You'll have to come down with your rents. I intend to occupy these premises myself!"

Source: "A Warning to Landlords", cartoon, *Harper's Weekly*, 24 March, 1866, House Divided: The Civil War Research Engine at Dickinson College.

A WARNING TO LANDLORDS.

CHOLERA (*to the exacting Owners of Tenement Houses*). "You'll have to come down with your rents. I intend to occupy these premises myself!"

'How cholera spread in Egypt—Mourners return from a funeral in the coffin,' *The Graphic*, August 1883. Egypt was one of the worst affected regions of the world in the nineteenth-century cholera pandemic.

The nineteenth century witnessed the creation of an elaborate quarantine system to guard against cholera outbreaks. This illustration shows quarantine ships during a cholera epidemic near Nijni-Novgorod, Russia, 1892.

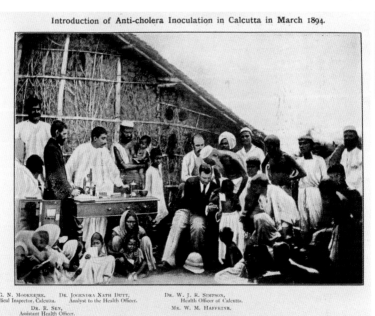

Introduction of Anti-cholera Inoculation in Calcutta in March 1894.

DR. G. N. MOOKERJEE,   DR. JOGENDRA NATH DUTT,   DR. W. J. R. SIMPSON,
Medical Inspector, Calcutta.   Analyst to the Health Officer.   Health Officer of Calcutta.
DR. R. SEN,   MR. W. M. HAFFKINE.
Assistant Health Officer.

Odessa-born Paris-trained bacteriologist Waldemar Mordechai Haffkine (1860–1930) spent an eventful two decades in India in the 1890s and 1900s, developing vaccines against cholera and plague, earning the respect of Indians and battling the bureaucracy over unfair allegations of vaccine-related malpractice.

JOHN SNOW
(1813–1858)

ROBERT KOCH
(1843–1910)

LEONARD ROGERS
(1868–1962)

SAMBHU NATH DE
(1915–1985)

Trailblazers in the fight against cholera: John Snow showed the water-borne transmission of the disease; Robert Koch systematically identified the cholera bacillus; Leonard Rogers perfected the intravenous treatment method that drastically reduced case fatality rates; and Sambhu Nath De discovered the cholera enterotoxin.

Source: Wellcome Collection; Wiki Commons

SAVITRIBAI PHULE
(1831–1897)

KITASATO SHIBASABURO
(1853–1931)

ALEXANDRE YERSIN
(1863–1943)

WILLIAM GLEN LISTON
(1872–1950)

Plague: Women played an important role in pandemic relief efforts, placing their lives in grave danger, best exemplified by the social reformer Savitribai Phule in India, who opened a clinic for plague victims but also succumbed to the disease in 1897. The scientists, Kitasato and Yersin, independently identified the plague bacillus in Hong Kong in 1894 and a decade later, Liston clarified the mechanism of disease transmission from rats to humans via rat fleas.

Source: Wellcome Collection; Portrait of Savitribai Phule for illustrative purpose

Karanja. Incantations by Women
against the Plague.

When the plague broke out in Bombay in 1896, the disease and the harsh containment measures generated mass panic and fear. The photograph shows incantations against the plague by women in Karanja, near Bombay. The Plague Visitation (album), Bombay, 1896–97. Photo by Captain C. Moss.

Hospital staff disinfecting patients during the outbreak of
bubonic plague in Karachi in 1897.

Interior of Plague Hospital, Bombay

Temporary hospitals were set up to cater to the surge in plague-related cases. The photograph shows the interior of one such plague hospital in Bombay during the outbreak of 1896–97.

VII.

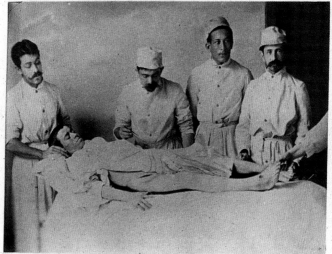

Obs. Nº 298 - A case of simple femoral-inguinal and iliac buboes with plague ulcer on the instep.

The plague pandemic swept across the world and reached as far as Brazil. This photograph shows a plague patient being treated by a medical team at the Seamen's Hospital for infectious diseases in Jurujuba, Rio de Janeiro, c. 1904/11.

'Doctors' protective costume used during an outbreak of pneumonic plague, Manchuria [China], 1910-1911.'

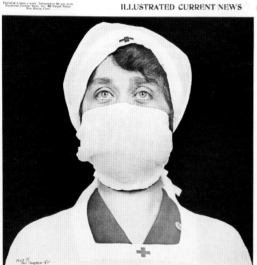

The influenza pandemic broke out in two distinct waves in 1918. The second wave was deadlier and invoked the use of masks in many parts of the world. This picture shows a Red Cross nurse with a gauze mask over her mouth and nose, and tips to prevent influenza. *Illustrated Current News*, New Haven, US, 18 October 1918.

'A monster representing an influenza virus hitting a man over the head as he sits in his armchair. Pen and ink drawing by E. Noble, c. 1918.' The 1918–20 influenza pandemic killed over 40 million people, of whom 20 million were in India.

FREE! FREE!!

INFLUENZA IS CURED IN ONE DAY.

Treatise on Influenza is sent free.

Medicine for Influenza—It cures Influenza in a very short time—Millions are saved. Highly spoken of all the world over. Price Rs. 2-8—Small phials Re. 1-4. Postage As. 10.

RAJVAID SRI BAMANDASJI KAVIRAJ.

152, Harrison Road, Calcutta.

Telegrams :—"RAJVAID" Calcutta.

An advertisement on influenza cure in India. The 1918–19 flu remained a mystery and virologists began to understand its characteristics only eight decades after the pandemic.

to the large number of the sick the hospital shifted many patients to covered verandas.[97] Herriot's assessment was that the best way to prevent getting the disease was through public education so that people kept fit, ate nutritious food and clothed themselves properly. This also seemed to increase the chances of recovery, if one caught the infection. Neglecting early symptoms and going to work was discouraged, gargling and nasal douching were encouraged, handkerchiefs were to be used, and overcrowded places like tramcars, halls and trains were to be avoided. On masks, he observed the following:

> The wearing of face masks may lessen the possibility of becoming infected. It should always be worn in the room occupied by the patient. A good mask can be made of four or six layers of fine muslin. It should be made so as to cover the mouth and nose completely.[98]

On lockdown, Herriot explained that there were two prevailing theories.[99] One argued for a shutting down of schools, theatres and places of high congregation to reduce the spread of infection. The other claimed that lockdown should be judiciously done otherwise it would induce depression and increase the risks of catching the flu. Interestingly, given the wide spread of the disease, Herriot also advised that patients should report to the hospitals only when conditions became pneumonic, rather than at the initial stage, so as to reduce the pressure on the health system. Isolation and quarantine of infected patients was strictly called for.

The anticipation around vaccination was high and Herriot indicated that it would be available 'in the near future'.[100] In reality, the development of flu vaccines would begin only in the 1940s. Among the 200-odd cases Herriot treated, around 10 per cent of the infected patients died.[101] Herriot attached the pulse reports of some of those who died at the end of his thesis, making them

some of the few medical reports on India from that time to have
survived till date.

Medical report during the influenza pandemic in Punjab

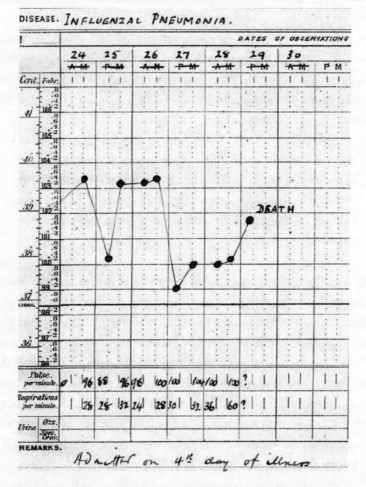

A rare medical report recording death by 'influenzal pneumonia' in
1918 of a twenty-five-year old man residing in Hoshiarpur, preserved in
Dr Herriot's thesis on Punjab, India.
Source: Thomas P. Herriot, 'The Influenza Pandemic, 1918, as Observed in
the Punjab, India' (MD thesis, University of Edinburgh, 1920), p. 55.

The influenza pandemic of 1918 ravaged Punjab with 'diabolical malignancy', with a large fraction of deaths occurring in a twenty-five-day period between 15 October and 10 November.[102] Districts closer to Delhi such as Gurgaon and Rohtak were also afflicted, losing over 10 per cent of their populations in the mayhem; rural areas were noted to have suffered much more than urban centres. Mortality rates dipped further west near Rawalpindi, and the hilly district of Simla in the north registered the lowest death rate of around 2 per cent. A cluster of districts in the middle, such as Lahore and Amritsar, were also greatly distressed. Voluntary relief efforts were in full force and, in particular, as the census officials would recollect, the 'medical students throughout the province rendered every assistance within their power'.[103]

Although the pandemic had subsided by December 1918, it had sown the seeds for mass despair and discontent. The many resentments in Punjab in 1918–19 have been attributed to the pandemic, the overburdened railway system, drought, food shortages and army recruitment drives.[104] The passing of the Rowlatt Act in March 1919 was the final nail in the proverbial coffin (scarce as they were in a pandemic). The new law drastically curtailed the civil liberties of Indians and prompted Mohandas Gandhi to call for a nationwide protest in February 1919 when the law was still being deliberated.[105] A non-violent satyagraha was to be launched on 6 April but a series of violent demonstrations broke out, especially in Punjab. On 13 April, a large crowd gathered at Jallianwala Bagh, many of whom were visiting Amritsar for the Baisakhi celebrations. This was the backdrop against which the massacre took place in Amritsar, which then fired up India's freedom movement. It would also lead to the eventual assassination of Michael O'Dwyer (not Reginald Dyer, who died in 1927) in London in 1940 by Udham Singh.

The clearly identifiable perpetrators in these events have ensured their continued remembrance in the collective memories of Indians, rather than the influenza pandemic that had killed millions only a few months earlier.

November Nightmare in the North

In other parts of north India outside Punjab, the experience of devastation in 1918 was even worse. The princely states of Rajputana were the worst hit, losing perhaps over 10 per cent of their population, as they faced their most terrible drought in 1918, unprecedented till then and unsurpassed since. The census officials observed that 'it shook the entire Province and wrought havoc surpassing all previous records'.[106] The impact, particularly during October and November, was severe in the western tracts of Jaisalmer and Marwar, where influenza was known to occur in epidemic form even in the 1890s with a quick conversion to lung complications, bronchitis and pneumonia for the 'old and feeble', as noted by one physician in those times.[107] In Jaisalmer, about a fifth of the population may have perished.[108] The effect was only somewhat lower in the northern and eastern belts of the state, including Jaipur, though the southern region fared much better. Like elsewhere in India, the voluntary relief work was immense and in Ajmer–Merwara, a voluntary organization called Sewa Samiti helped in disposing of the dead bodies and also assisted patients.[109] Colleges and schools were shut, a travelling dispensary was deployed, a camp was set up by the municipality for patients, and free medicines and milk were distributed to the sick.[110]

Further north, in Jammu and Kashmir, the two waves of the flu arrived late—in August and October, respectively—the second one wreaking 'havoc among the population regardless of climate, locality, profession, sex or age'.[111] The first death was recorded in

Jammu city on 17 October. From there, the 'War-Fever', as it was being called, spread to the surrounding villages rapidly within a few days.[112] Jammu bore the brunt of the pandemic which had reached Srinagar by November and was 'raging with full force' in places as far as Ladakh and Kargil.[113]

Delhi suffered as well, and Norman White, who was based there, had 'an intimate personal experience of the outbreak' which peaked on 26 October with 418 deaths reported in the city on that day.[114] He also observed that malnutrition did not influence infection rates but was important for the following reason:

> Malnutrition did appear to be a factor of importance in determining a fatal issue. No drugs appear to have any specific curative value but given nourishing food in a readily assimilable form, care and attention, it was surprising what apparently desperate cases ultimately recovered.[115]

Such care and attention were in short supply in India's largest province, the United Provinces (now Uttar Pradesh), a place with poor medical infrastructure in 1918. The United Provinces also suffered a massive drought that year, which eased up only a little in its eastern-most parts, and an estimated 50–70 per cent of the population eventually contracted the flu.[116] Among the worst affected areas were the districts of Agra, Hamirpur, Meerut, Bijnor, Jhansi, Bulandshahr, Unnao, Lucknow, Farrukhabad, Banda and Muzzaffarnagar, all losing 10–20 per cent of their respective populations to the pandemic.[117] Death rates not only rose enormously in cities such as Agra, Lucknow, Varanasi, Kanpur and Allahabad, but also in the cantonment areas of some of these cities. Registered influenza-related mortality in the province exceeded 2 million, while the actual number was likely to be nearly double, in a province with over 45 million people.[118] The pandemic overwhelmed the death registration system because the dead bodies had to be disposed of in unique ways.

Norman White had pointed out that in Delhi 'the disposal of the dead was a matter which tried the resources of all concerned'.[119] But in the United Provinces, the problem took on a different dimension altogether. The first mild flu wave lasted from August to mid-September but the second flu wave, beginning in October, ripped through the province and peaked in the middle of November; a large number of dead bodies accumulated in a very short time. In the hilly areas of Kumaon, corpses were thrown into the jungle and, according to the writer Jim Corbett (1875–1955), led to leopards developing a taste for human flesh and thus being labelled 'man-eaters'.[120] Down in the plains, 'numberless bodies were thrown into the rivers of the province' since there was insufficient firewood for the cremation of Hindus.[121] The Ganga, lifeline of major civilizations, flowed with death in its midst. So great was the problem that, along with managing the flu, medical authorities had to ensure that water purification systems of cities along the clogged rivers worked well and that no harm was done 'by this most objectionable practice'.[122]

In Dalmau, a town by the Ganga in Rae Bareli, Suryakant Tripathi (1896–1961), the writer better known by his pen name 'Nirala', was twenty-two when he visited the riverbank in 1918 and observed the river 'swollen with dead bodies'.[123] He lost his wife and other members of his family to the flu that year. As he later recounted about the 'strangest time' of his life in his memoirs:

My family disappeared in the blink of an eye. All our sharecroppers and labourers died, the four who worked for my cousin as well as the two who worked for me. My cousin's eldest son was fifteen years old, my young daughter a year old. In whichever direction I turned, I saw darkness.[124]

Mari in Central India

When COVID-19 broke out in India in 2020, Dr Yogesh Kalkonde was part of a team disseminating information about the pandemic in the Gadchiroli district of the Vidarbha region of central India. When he asked if people were aware of past outbreaks, one elderly person from the Gond tribe stepped up and said the following:

> My father told me when he was very young, must be more than 100 years ago, so many people died in the village because of *mari* that there was nobody to bury them ... they gave a pint of alcohol to a bullock cart driver who placed all the dead bodies in a cart and dumped them in the jungle.[125]

In this specific memory, *mari*, the generic word for epidemics, almost certainly referred to the influenza pandemic of 1918. Central India, which used to be afflicted with high death rates even in non-crisis years, was severely distressed during the pandemic. The vast region covers much of the present-day states of Madhya Pradesh, Chhattisgarh, western Odisha, Telangana, eastern Maharashtra and northern Karnataka, and was at that time under the British-ruled Central Provinces and Berar or the Nizam-ruled Hyderabad state or the many princely states that made up the Central India Agency. Large parts of this territory are rural and remote and have a high share of indigenous people or adivasis, belonging to Gond, Bhil, Baiga, Kolam and other tribes.

The Census of 1921 for the Central Provinces and Berar noted that 'in times of stress the aborigines and other backward tribes are the first to suffer'.[126] Suffer they did, as the oral history shows, and the statistics reveal that the province lost around 10 per cent of its total population of roughly 14 million people in the 1918 pandemic.[127] Damoh, Sagar, Betul, Mandla, Hoshangabad, Seoni, Yavatmal, Akola,

Amravati and Chanda districts (which included Gadchiroli) were some of the worst affected.[128] The drought in 1918 was unprecedented for most parts of the province and the kharif crops 'yielded less than half the normal crop'.[129] This alone would not have caused so much despair but unfortunately, the situation was exacerbated by a depletion of food stocks through 'large export of grain in the previous years' and the influenza pandemic, leading to famine in some regions.[130] In the words of the census officials of that time:

> The combination of high prices, influenza and failure of crops, aggravated as it was by heavy railway traffic in connection with the war and inadequate supply of waggons, produced a crisis which the Province weathered with a wonderful power of resistance. Famine was declared in an area of 12,841 square miles with a population of 1.5 millions [sic], and scarcity in 38,333 square miles inhabited by five million persons.[131]

The first flu wave in the region was barely noticed but the second, which started in late September, devastated the region for two months and continued to linger into the first few months of 1919, 'leaving behind it a melancholy wake of decimated villages and destitute orphans'.[132]

The forest department of the Central Provinces was short-staffed as deaths in the department in 1918–19 rose seven-fold over the previous year. It was also impaired by the shortage of railway wagons for moving timber and other forest produce.[133] Influenza also wreaked havoc on the education system in central India. The deputy commissioner of Nimar pointed out the adverse impact of influenza on primary education thus:

> The effect of the influenza was that a certain number of fathers and mothers died and the guardians who succeeded them did not trouble to hustle the boys off to school. Also the supply of

agricultural labour was so much reduced by the influenza that many people could not find field servants or could not pay the enhanced wages demanded, and kept their children away from school to work in the fields.[134]

The education system was paralysed and examinations were postponed by two months, from December to February, in some cases, such as the European School Certificate Board.[135] Teachers and students themselves rose to the occasion and the education department praised the 'professors and masters and the students or pupils whom they organised and stimulated' in relief works.[136] In Nerbudda, the inspector of schools praised the work of the League of Honour for its relief work during the pandemic and awarded Mr Hoyland of Hoshangabad the Kaiser-i-Hind medal.[137]

In Nizam-ruled Hyderabad state, the devastation left no area untouched. Aurangabad, Beed, Raichur, Gulbarga and the city of Hyderabad bore the brunt with the heaviest toll. In Hyderabad city, flu-related daily deaths peaked at 464 on 27 October before going down to zero by the end of November.[138] Afflicted by the plague in the preceding decade, the population of the city of Hyderabad fell to around 110,000 in 1921, even lower than what it was thirty years ago.[139]

In the princely states of the Central India Agency, the picture was no different; it was observed that because of its remoteness, with 'few railways and roads and many jungle tracts, the impossibility of reaching the sick was greatly accentuated'.[140] The flu, however, found its way to remote places because it was so virulent that even the barest human contact enabled its rapid transmission. Bagelkhand was the worst affected region and the princely state of Rewa was in the news because the pandemic flu killed its maharaja, Venkat Raman Singh. If there was anyone who benefited from the flu in this region, it was perhaps the tigers, because the maharaja was known to have killed 111 tigers in his short life spanning four decades.[141]

A Different Death Curve in South and East India

While west, central and north India were devastated by the pandemic, the situation was slightly improved in south India; the eastern parts, though, fared much better. In the deep south, in the princely state of Travancore, which covers much of modern-day Kerala, the influenza's touch was so light that the census officials in 1921 did not bother to mention it much in their records. But population growth rates did dip in that decade, suggesting that some toll had been extracted. In the remote Andaman and Nicobar Islands, where plague was unknown, the few instances of smallpox were quickly stamped out and cholera was imported with the 'Forest Coolies', measles and influenza were known to be dangerous.[142] However, during the pandemic, influenza seems to have been fatal later, only in 1920, when it claimed nearly 500 lives in June and July, out of a population of 6,000 people, in Car Nicobar.[143]

In the vast Madras Presidency, stretching coast to coast, with over 40 million people, the flu's impact was harshest in the Deccan districts of Bellary and Anantapur, followed by a few coastal districts but again, nowhere as severe as in north India. The city of Madras would not face the ravages that Bombay and Delhi would.

Most parts of south India also experienced a failed monsoon but because those regions did not depend on the monsoon rain (June–September) for all their water needs, the extent of distress in agriculture was somewhat less. Nevertheless, wartime disruptions and speculative trade affected foodgrain movement, sparking severe grain riots from May to October. The Madras Presidency in 1918 was, in fact, hit by the 'twin epidemics' of influenza and grain riots.[144] The diversion of railways and steamers along the coast for the war effort curtailed the usual imports from Burma and pushed up rice prices, causing widespread distress and panic that culminated in the looting of grain shops and ultimately, even railway warehouses.

Traders bore the brunt of the ire of the labouring classes, since they were seen to be profiting from war-related scarcities in a range of commodities. The pressure caused by the riots could be one reason why the government began to focus on food supply early on and possibly averted a major crisis during the pandemic.

The neighbouring princely state of Mysore also witnessed the price pangs of the Madras Presidency, leading to stern warnings to traders by its renowned diwan, Sir M. Visvesvaraya, on 17 October 1918:

> The strong hand of Government must always be in evidence and continue to interfere whenever any section of the community tries to take advantage of the difficulties of the public.[145]

Price distortions coincided with the second flu wave, beginning in mid-September, which, as per government sources, infected close to a million people and killed nearly 200,000.[146] The flu impaired the festive spirit of Dasara and the then maharaja of Mysore, Krishnaraja Wadiyar, admitted as much. The administration swung into action with the cooperation of the private medical fraternity, hakims and vaids, and collected daily reports and messages from the ground staff. The sanitary commissioner of Mysore released a list of cures and treatments available for influenza that included 'points for observance by the sick' such as rest, food consisting of milk or conji (rice porridge), warm coverings for the body, open windows and doors in the bedroom and 'five drops of thymol solution mixed with one ounce of water' three times a day.[147] The 'points for observance by the healthy' included staying in 'open air night and day as much as possible', self-isolation of all people who were coughing, avoiding overcrowded places, keeping the bowels free, and that same tip—using thymol—but twice a day, not thrice.[148]

Some people in the medical authority shirked their duty to avoid the epidemic as in the case of one *amildar* in Holalkere taluk who repeatedly took leave, only to be found perfectly hale and hearty after a series of complaints were lodged against him. Local observations in Mysore city on families not having lit the oven for several days on end, suffering from hunger, led to cries that the 'authorities should be held morally responsible'. An old lament heard in the Indian subcontinent was that there was 'something very rotten with regard to Government social and economic activities in the State'.[149]

Tumkur and Shimoga were the worst affected districts, and in the mining belt of the Kolar Gold Fields, 960 out of 13,600 influenza-infected people died, reflecting a case fatality ratio of 7 per cent.[150] In Bangalore city, the chief officer, R. Subba Rao, coordinated the relief efforts with a detailed plan of action to distribute medicine and food to the sick at their homes.[151] The city was compartmentalized into blocks with a door-to-door survey to identify the sick. Conji was to be prepared at a central station and made ready for distribution at 9 a.m. every day and notes had to be entered into a book on patient names, age, medicine issued and quantity of food given. A central *anna chattram* (charitable home distributing food) was designated to be the place where various parties doing relief work could access material. A temporary influenza hospital was also set up.

As many as fifty-five relief parties were working along with the government, and the Depressed Classes Mission is said to have provided relief to over 1,000 people in the weeks when the pandemic was raging.[152] The diwan of Mysore praised these efforts, especially those of students and young people who wholeheartedly participated in relief work. Overall, Bangalore's administration appeared to function most efficiently during the influenza pandemic in the state of Mysore. The state itself appeared to do relatively well, with close attention paid to foodgrain prices through price limits and low-cost grain shops, though rural areas suffered much more than the urban.

In eastern India, which had fared considerably better than the rest of the country, influenza took a toll on Bihar and Orissa, significantly curbing population growth rates for the 1911–21 decade. The death toll kept reducing as one moved further east to Bengal and Assam. The tea plantations in north Bengal, which were previously affected in the relatively milder influenza pandemic of 1890, also witnessed some flu-related mortality in 1918.[153] Various tea estates reported the arrival of the disease in early December through Marwari shopkeepers returning from Calcutta, coolies from Nagpur, and generally via the *bastis* and bazaars outside the tea plantations.[154] The city of Calcutta, like Madras, escaped lightly compared to Bombay but even then, disruptions were substantial. Students had to miss examinations as they fell ill during the pandemic, and administrative officials at universities had the unwelcome task of dealing with many medical certificates of influenza and make judgements on the students' progress.[155] And if in the west, Gandhi's family bemoaned the loss of their close ones, it was the house of Tagore in Bengal that despaired in the east. The Nobel Laureate Rabindranath Tagore (1861–1941) lost a member of his extended family, Sukeshi, in the pandemic and would himself be afflicted by influenza in later years.[156]

The Price of Death

There are competing explanations for why so many people died in India from influenza compared to other countries and why some parts of the country fared worse than others.

Across the world, per capita incomes appear to be the most important factor in explaining the variation in influenza-related death rates.[157] Since richer countries tend to be more literate, have better medical facilities and nutrition levels, this could suggest that those with improved material and health conditions rode out the storm with greater success. The evidence on India, as seen in earlier accounts across regions, suggests a role for nutrition; literacy rates across provinces also had a strongly negative correlation with influenza mortality.[158] As reports from around the world suggested, case fatality rates were lower when patients took adequate rest and were nursed well. Such medical facilities were in short supply in the poorer parts of the world, as well as in India, much more so in rural areas than in urban ones. This shows that even though population density may have been a factor in the spread of the disease, it did not necessarily translate into death, and that less densely populated, remote places could be worse hit due to the absence of medical support.

My research suggests that India's distress was particularly great because it had suffered its third worst drought in recorded history in the months leading up to September 1918. The resultant price surge reduced consumption of foodgrains and possibly other items like milk and blankets, such that, in sum, Indians took on the infection with seriously malnourished bodies.[159] The worst droughts of India before 1918, in 1877 and 1899, led to a rise in famine-related death rates in the following years.[160] The year 1918 was different because the drought and the deaths occurred in the same year.

Explanations based on temperature, as proposed by I.D. Mills in 1986, may hold validity for the sub-Indian context—colder places with extreme temperature ranges appeared to suffer more from influenza that turned pneumonic in October and November 1918—but it does not explain the variation in mortality rates.[161] The drought–food price rise–undernutrition argument is useful because it explains both India's uniqueness, compared to other parts of the world, as well as the variation of influenza-related mortality *within* the country.

One way to understand this is by looking at what happened to the health of the army in India, which had better access to medical facilities and food than the native population. Around 22 per cent of the European army in India was admitted with influenza in 1918, and the figure was 26 per cent in the Northern Army and 19 per cent in the Southern Army.[162] Yet, among those admitted, the proportion of those who died or the case fatality ratio was 4 per cent, and almost identical in the Northern and Southern Army (4.3 per cent and 3.6 per cent, respectively). Among Indian troops, admission rates were much lower at 14 per cent, with little regional variation between the north and the south, suggesting lower access to medical facilities rather than reduced chances of being infected.[163] Yet, case fatality rates among the native army were much higher at 11 per cent, again with little regional variation (10.6 per cent in the Northern Army and 12 per cent in the Southern Army).

Norman White, the sanitary commissioner of India in 1918, attributed this to the higher chances of Indian troops succumbing to pneumonia, even in normal years, and indicated that the medical establishment had long known that the clinical manifestations of pneumonia among Indians were very different from those among Europeans.[164] However, what is important to observe is that among troops with access to adequate food supplies, influenza-related mortality in 1918 did not vary across regions like it did for the general population.

To show just how varied the food price shock was within India, consider the price of rice, the most important foodgrain in the country's dietary basket. In the four years leading up to it, rice prices barely budged at the all-India level but then rose by 13 per cent in 1918.[165] This figure was 28 per cent for the province of Bombay and Sind, 26 per cent for Punjab, 21 per cent for the United Provinces and 25 per cent for the Central Provinces and Berar, all hit severely by the influenza pandemic in the last quarter of the year. In contrast, the figure was 17 per cent in the Madras Presidency, which was less affected by the pandemic, though it did experience rice riots, 7 per cent in Bihar and Orissa, and rice prices actually fell in Bengal and Assam, the least affected zones in the pandemic. The picture for wheat, extensively consumed in the north, was far bleaker, with inflation jumping from an average of 4 per cent in the four years preceding 1918, to 31 per cent in 1918.

It should be pointed out that nationwide foodgrain prices had converged substantially across locations over the four decades preceding 1918 due to improvements in transport, chiefly brought about by the railways, and communication.[166] Prices exhibited regional dislocation in 1918, however, because the drought reduced crop outputs in some regions and the railways, pressed into the war effort, could not adequately meet the concomitant mismatches in demand and supply. Speculation and hoarding, as noted earlier, were rife and in many places, grain riots ensued. Stocks accumulated in previous years were partly depleted because foodgrain exports had more than trebled to over 2 million tons in wartime conditions in 1917–18.[167]

India's massive mortality shock, then, was not entirely bad luck, as Norman White would posit, but at least partly attributable to inefficient food supply management. And while the colonial government was clearly found lacking, the princely states were not necessarily any better, the states of Rajputana and Hyderabad being particularly afflicted. Food supply mismanagement during a world war would return to haunt the people of India during the Bengal Famine of 1943–44, which affected, as if by karma, those districts in east Bengal that had been the least affected by influenza in 1918. It is a measure of the systematic improvements in foodgrain supply management since the early twentieth century (outside wartime conditions), particularly in independent India, that famines have all but disappeared from our consciousness. But then again, India has been fortunate so far as to not have faced the same intensity of droughts that it did in 1877, 1899 and 1918.

The Aftermath

It was not just the death toll but the sheer number of people infected with the flu that strained India's society and economy. With a case fatality ratio of 10 per cent and higher, as reports of that time indicated, it is possible that 40–60 per cent of the Indian population contracted the flu in 1918.[168] Its impact on the economy was devastating. Between 1900 and 2019, 1918–19 stands as the worst year for India in macroeconomic terms: output or real GDP contracted by 10 per cent and inflation surged to 30 per cent.[169] This was a supply side shock, felt acutely in the agricultural sector, where output plummeted by over 20 per cent. The annual report of the forestry department of the United Provinces listed a large number of staff who died in the pandemic of 1918 and noted that 'the labour supply was greatly affected, permanently by the great mortality and temporarily to a larger extent during the duration of the epidemic'.[170]

The kharif crop was curtailed by the monsoon drought but the winter or rabi crop was depressed by a lack of planting, since workers were either ill or dead. The net area sown fell by over 10 per cent and the acreage of fallow land increased by 50 per cent over the previous year.[171] Rice yield for the year fell by over 30 per cent to 24 million tons and the wheat yield fell by more than 20 per cent to 8 million tons, values not seen in over a decade. The only crop which witnessed a marginal increase in 1918–19 was tea, grown in eastern and southern India, both of which had a lighter brush with influenza.

The service sector showed some growth in 1918–19 because the railways, with or without dead bodies, was running at full capacity for most of the year. The banking sector did not appear to be particularly affected, but even there, the major presidency banks witnessed a decline in deposits in 1918, Bombay being more affected than Madras or Bengal, with a rebound in 1919.[172] Ironically, death would claim the 'lives' of insurance companies: their number in India, falling steadily since hitting its peak of 213 firms in 1913–14, shrank by nearly 25 per cent to only 96 by the end of 1918–19.[173]

Industrial output slipped by nearly 10 per cent in 1918–19, and came as a rude shock to industrial houses that had made huge profits due to the demand created by the war.[174] The Tata Iron and Steel Company had more than doubled its steel production since 1913, but was forced to cut back by 20 per cent and reduce its dividend outflow in 1918–19.[175] Interestingly, Godrej, which had begun in Bombay city in the year of the plague, 1897, with making security equipment, decided in 1918 to enter a new product line that was more than appropriate in the year of the flu: washing soap bars.

The next year, 1919–20, witnessed an economic rebound as agricultural output recovered and wholesale prices moderated, but retail prices continued to surge as foodgrains were still in short supply. The period of 1918–20 was thus economically very volatile. All of this injected a new momentum into the political forces combating colonial rule, and created the space for Gandhi to rise to the forefront of the movement.

Publications like *Young India*, published by Gandhi, questioned whether the government understood the psychological impact of the pandemic, and how 6 million people were allowed to die 'like rats without succour'.[176] The *Indian Annual Register* in 1919 noted the euphoria of political movements and how 'the sledge-hammers of a Curzon, O' Dyer or Influenza simply accelerate the process'.[177] Outside India too, the country's high influenza-death toll would strike a chord. In the US, Senator Malone made a speech on the Indian situation on 29 August 1919 in front of the Foreign Relations Committee of the American Senate:

Six million Indians died in the last three months of 1918 from devitalisation and from Influenza because of the exploitation of

India by England, not for India but for England, the drawing of resources out of India making it impossible for her to maintain an adequate food supply.[178]

The pandemic also brought renewed attention to the state of public finances and health. Heated discussions took place in 1919 in the legislative assembly in India over public finances as land revenues, a major source of government financial receipts, declined considerably in 1918–19. Indian representatives in the assembly repeatedly pointed out the devastating impact of influenza and used the word 'famine' to highlight the crisis. Indian representative K.V. Rangaswamy Ayyangar was scathing in his criticism:

> That the richest of agricultural countries should not be able to feed its own population is an irony of fate, a parallel to which would be hard to find. A slight delay in monsoon drives the people to death. And when is the Government going to save and protect the population by prohibiting the exports of food-stuffs when it is so much needed for the producers? And when is the Government going to change their existing policy in the matter of showing economy in extending the irrigation schemes? These famines do not testify to the good administration of India and honest handling of her resources.[179]

The inadequacy of medical facilities in India was also stressed to seek more budgetary allocations towards health. Kamini Kumar Chanda (1862–1935), a political leader from Silchar, Assam, and member of the Imperial Legislative Council, argued for greater public spending on sanitation and health during the budgetary discussions. He pointed out that the policy of neglecting health because it was not 'remunerative' was fallacious and had 'long been exploded in England'.[180] Another political leader, B.N. Sarma from south India, urged the government to depart from 'orthodox methods' and look at the health situation as Westerners did, that is, from the standpoint of 'national insurance', and pleaded for 'medical help'.[181] On the priority of public spending on railways because of higher productivity, Sarma remarked that the government was placing more emphasis on the railways than 'the lives of His Majesty's Indian subjects!'[182]

Not only did the pleas have little effect, in later years the abysmally low public spending on healthcare was further cut back amid efforts to reduce government expenditure and control the budgetary deficit.[183] Spending on health was offloaded to provincial governments but with limited options for funding, they were exposed to severe constraints. Nevertheless, a gradual uptick in the number of medical institutions in India was registered after the pandemic, from about 3,000 in 1918 to 5,700 by the late 1930s, at a growth rate faster than that of the population.[184] Soon after the influenza pandemic, the long-held designation of 'sanitary commissioner of India' was changed to 'public health commissioner of India'. Even as the perils of the plague were subsiding, the flu pandemic of 1918 firmly placed 'public health' as a phrase and concept in the psyche of the Indian subcontinent.

The influenza of 1918 spurred medical authorities and businesses into action. Doctors in India were baffled by the disease and at least one of them wrote a *Treatise on Influenza* soon after to document the knowledge of those times.[185] One forest ranger in the coastal district of South Canara was confident that decoctions of *Embelia ribes*, a climber found in the district's forest, had proved to be an effective medicine against influenza and saved many lives in villages 'where this dreadful disease played havoc'.[186]

During the pandemic, some European and Indian firms supplying medicines to counter influenza had a field day, ramping up their advertisements in print. Ads such as those by Calcutta-based

Rajvaid in September 1918, proclaiming 'Free ! Free !! Influenza is Cured in One Day', led to renewed doubt among European health officials in India about the efficacy of Indian medicines, though in reality, the flu exposed the limitations of even Western medicine.[187] No one knew what would work and the *Indian Medical Gazette* published several articles by doctors to that effect. In the September 1919 issue of the gazette, the commanding officer of the British Station Hospital in Calcutta emphasized the basics—eating healthily and exercising regularly—and was sceptical about masks:

> Here I would like to discuss the value of a mask in the prevention of influenza and other air-borne infections. First of all, it cannot be worn at all times. People must eat, speak and will continue to kiss. Secondly, Leonard Hill's researches show that the wearing of a mask is against the natural defensive mechanism of the mucous membrane of the respiratory tract. The breathing of cool air – cool and therefore low vapour tension – brings more arterial blood to the respiratory membrane. This increases evaporation from it and therefore the flow of lymph through it. The warm moist atmosphere generated by wearing a mask is against this natural washing and immunising defence.[188]

Nevertheless, the official response to the influenza, which came about by way of a memorandum from the government of India in 1919, recommended, among other things, the closure of public places, use of disinfecting sprays, gargling regularly and wearing masks to counter influenza.[189] Pneumonia would become a disease notified under the Indian Ports Act for early detection and the Bombay government allowed the use of the 1897 Epidemic Diseases Act for preventing flu outbreaks in the future.[190]

The medical response was not as paranoid as in the case of the plague because the flu had come to India from the Western world, which had already contracted it, unlike earlier, when the West feared that the plague, if uncontained in India, would travel westwards to European countries.[191]

But just as in the plague, the severe mortality impact on labourers tightened labour markets and improved their bargaining power in the immediate aftermath. As census officials observed in pandemic-hit Rajasthan, documenting a massive hike in wages between 1917 and 1921 in Ajmer through a survey:

> Thirty years ago a quantity of grain enough for food with a small amount in cash, a suit of some rough cloth per harvest, and an addition of Khesla (covering cloth) in winter were quite sufficient to attract a farm servant, but nothing less than from eight to ten rupees a month or a mixed payment in cash and kind equivalent thereto, will now induce a labourer to take up fixed engagement.[192]

The pandemic occurred after the Russian Revolution of 1917, which was undoubtedly a major inspiration for working-class movements in India. But newspaper records show an uncanny uptick after 1918 (and not 1917), in the use of words such as 'labour', 'union', 'strike' and 'protest'.[193] The word 'labour', for instance, occurred in over 8 per cent of articles published in the *Times of India* in the 1920s, the highest by far for any decade between 1850 and 2010. Similarly, the words 'strike' and 'protest' were used more frequently in the 1920s than in any other decade between 1850 and 1950.[194] Company-level records show similar accounts and to cite just two examples, the tea industry in both north Bengal and south India announced a labour shortage soon after the pandemic due to influenza-related mortality.[195] The report of the Royal Commission of Labour in 1931 identified the influenza pandemic as having a 'retarding influence' on industrial labour supply and the 'winter of 1918-19' as the turning point for strikes, which had rarely occurred until then, due to the education of the masses during the war and 'aggravated by the great epidemics of influenza'.[196]

The loss of lives in rural areas could also have given a boost to the cooperative movement. In 1920, there were 37,000 cooperative societies in India, of which nearly 34,000 were classified as being agricultural.[197] While growth was moderate in the four years preceding 1918, it picked up rapidly thereafter and by 1930, there were nearly 80,000 agricultural cooperatives in India.[198] Again, while the major inspiration for the cooperative movement may have lain elsewhere, the acute labour scarcity probably hastened the process of reorganizing production systems. Newspaper records show that the word 'cooperative' was used more frequently in the 1920s than in any other decade between 1850 and 1950.[199]

Another impact of the flu pandemic was on demographic behaviour. The disease killed millions of adult women in India and subsequently, birth rates plummeted in 1919, exacerbating a temporary slowdown in overall population growth. The dearth of female labour led to an increase in their participation rates in the short term, but this effect reversed by 1931.[200] Within the boundaries of present-day India, the decade of 1911–1921 was the only one of the twentieth century that registered a negative population growth rate. But precisely because the flu killed so many among the poor, who would have succumbed to other infectious diseases sooner or later, it also began to dampen death rates in its aftermath. Fertility also bounced back quickly by the mid-1920s, and India's population growth trajectory shifted to a higher plane after 1920. Compared to fertility and mortality, the third pillar of demography—migration—was relatively unaffected. As with the outbreaks of cholera and plague in the past, instant flight was observed in many cities but the short-lived duration of the influenza pandemic meant lesser reverse migration. The pandemic also had little impact on the traditional hotspots of the Great Indian Migration Wave—in coastal areas and the lower Gangetic plains—and the source regions of migration continued to be unaffected though places which had lost a lot of people emerged as new destinations.

Finally, in the longer term, the pandemic of 1918 (coupled with previous pandemics) may have altered India's trajectory of urban growth and regional development. Saved from the ravages of cholera, plague and influenza in relative terms, south India had a smoother starting position in the early twentieth century than other parts of the Indian subcontinent. Between 1881 and 1921, the average annual population growth rate of cities in the south was close to 1.5 per cent, double the national average.[201] In the regions comprising modern-day Rajasthan and Bihar in the north, this figure was negative, indicating urban decline over forty years. Post 1920, population everywhere started increasing, but south India held the edge in rapidly growing cities until the 1950s, after which fertility reduction dampened urban growth relative to the north. With its differential geographical impact, the Age of Pandemics could have had long-lasting influences on regional economic development in India.

From Iran to Alaska to Australia: The Global Impact

Iran, like India, suffered particularly from the flu in 1918, losing 1–2 million people. This occurred despite the absence of a major railway system, which was seen to be an important mechanism for disease transmission within countries elsewhere.[202] So virulent was the 1918 flu in Iran that it spread by road and reached remote areas. Like in India, rural areas were more affected than urban ones, locals were more affected than the British troops, and famine conditions, grain price surges and undernutrition were major causes of the high death toll.[203] The researcher Amir Afkhami has argued that chronic malaria, opium consumption and anaemia also contributed to the high influenza-related death rates in Iran in 1918. In addition to famine and disease, Iran also had to face war, as its territory was being used as a battlefield by the sparring armies of World War I.

The flu spread within north-eastern Iran with the movement of British and Bolshevik troops. The Russians surrendered on 28 August 1918, handing over a winner's curse to the British, as the disease quickly spread in the area in which they had made territorial gains. The second wave of the flu in Iran is said to have been brought in September by troops arriving from the Bombay Presidency, thus linking the fates of Iran and India.[204] Mass migration from cities followed and corpses piled up to saturate burial grounds. The threat of an inappropriate burial led some of the sick to crawl 'to die in the mosques'.[205] Indian soldiers in Iran were also scarred by the flu; like in India, their survival chances were much lower compared to those of the British. Case fatality rates were often well over 30 per cent.

South Africa was another place where the flu took a high toll of around 3–6 per cent of the population after it was first identified in Durban on 9 September 1918.[206] Returning troops from Europe had brought the disease with them and the ensuing pandemic's intensity altered the demographic structure of the region. In east Africa, the disease may have arrived by ships from Bombay in September 1918, after which it ripped through the interiors, leaving a familiar trail of destruction. In west Africa, according to the historian David Killingray, 'the pandemic interrupted food production, sometimes with serious social and economic consequences'.[207] For instance, the illness interrupted the rice harvesting season in Sierra Leone and output fell by more than 50 per cent, leading to inflation and ultimately riots in Freetown in July 1919.

Several other countries also suffered high influenza-related mortality rates. Similar to its experience with cholera in 1833, Mexico found itself caught again in the midst of a revolutionary struggle spanning several years, and the resultant disorder, and famine, compounded the influenza-related mortality.[208] The evidence from China in the 1918–20 pandemic is conflicting; the flu is likely to have been widespread but not as severe as in India.[209] Japan had a relatively low influenza-related death rate, but even there the total mortality exceeded that of the Great Kanto earthquake of 1923, considered its biggest peacetime disaster of the twentieth century which claimed over 100,000 lives.[210] Among the notable casualties in Asia, the crown prince of Siam died of influenza in June 1920 while travelling to Singapore.[211]

In Europe, the flu claimed the life of the distinguished German sociologist Max Weber (1864–1920) in Munich. It also killed many in war-ravaged eastern Europe. In North America, the flu had a disproportionate impact on the native populations, especially in Alaska, where entire villages were depopulated and mass burials took place. These graves would eventually be visited by the researcher Johan Hultin several decades later in his quest to uncover the mystery of the killer virus. In USA, the disease spread widely and in many states, wearing masks was made mandatory.[212] A newspaper in New Mexico observed that 'the ghost of fear walked everywhere, causing many a family circle to reunite because of the different members having nothing else to do but stay home'.[213]

A notable flu-related casualty in USA in 1918 was the German-American businessman Frederick Trump, paternal grandfather of the forty-fifth American president, Donald J. Trump. The then American president, Woodrow Wilson, contracted the flu in April 1919, in Paris, while negotiating the treaties after the war had ended with an armistice in November 1918. The historian Alfred Crosby speculated that the president's illness left little room for a moderate settlement, and the harsh terms finalized in the Treaty of Versailles had long-term consequences, one of which was World War II.[214] Another consequence of the pandemic in the US was that it pushed a number of women into nursing roles, which contributed partly to a vibrant movement for women's suffrage that had picked up over the course of World War I. In 1920, the Nineteenth Amendment to the US constitution was passed, enabling women to vote in the national elections.[215]

Of a more recent vintage are studies by economists who attempt to estimate the long-term consequences of the 1918 pandemic. One study on the US argues that cohorts exposed to the pandemic in-utero in 1918–19 'displayed reduced educational attainment, increased rates of physical disability, lower income, lower socioeconomic status' several decades later.[216] However, this does not appear to be a general result, as found by another study analysing over 100 countries.[217]

In Britain, more than 200,000 died in the flu pandemic, but the greater effect was on the working of its worldwide empire.[218] Since influenza was not an 'imperial' or 'notifiable' disease, colonies did not have to warn others of its progress. In Mauritius, for instance, where a large number of Indian emigrants lived, the pandemic struck only in May 1919, taking a heavy toll on the poor. The flu invaded the Caribbean region and seriously affected British Guyana, also home to a considerable Indian emigrant population.

New Zealand, on the other end, did not escape the flu either; the indigenous Maoris died in large numbers, while the smaller Pacific islands witnessed very high death rates. Uninformed about the pandemic, Western Samoa, with around 40,000 people, lost 25 per cent of its population whereas American Samoa, in isolation till 1920, managed to escape the clutches of the flu.[219] Australia went relatively unscathed due to a maritime quarantine in place in late 1918 which delayed the arrival of the flu. It was thus one of the few countries of the world that lost more people to World War I than to the pandemic.[220] It did get masks out in the public and as the oral history of that time describes, school-goers had to 'wear white cotton masks' before the schools were closed.[221] The 'masked disease' led people to wear masks even while dancing and in other large social gatherings.[222] But influenza was also seen in Australia by some in conjunction with another 'disease' unleashed by the Russian revolution: Bolshevism. In 1919, a book titled *The Two Plagues: Influenza and Bolshevism* was published in Melbourne, arguing that Bolshevism was a graver danger than influenza as it was a 'moral, mental and spiritual infection'.[223]

The consequence of all of this was that influenza was made a 'notifiable' disease in the British Empire, with closer cooperation between colonies in terms of reporting outbreaks. But the pandemic also renewed the promise of *global* cooperation on health, as was done with cholera in the previous century. The outbreaks of epidemic diseases such as typhus and relapsing fever in eastern Europe immediately after the war prompted the newly founded League of Nations to institute, first, an Epidemic Commission for Russia and eastern Europe in 1920, and then in 1921, the Health Organization. The person who would become a pivotal figure in both would be none other than Norman White, relieved from his Indian duties which he recollected as being filled with 'stress and anxiety'.[224]

The influenza pandemic of 1918 was the first truly intense global pandemic and earned a variety of names in various languages. The 'Spanish flu' is perhaps the most popular one, but in France it was known as 'La Grippe', in Iran as 'nakhushi-i-bad' or the 'illness of the wind', in Poland as the 'Bolshevik disease', in Penang as the 'Singapore Fever', among the Bagkatla in southern Africa as *'Dreidag'* (or three-day fever), in western Africa as 'Lululuku' and 'Ajukale-Arun', in Namibia as 'Kaapito Hanga' (meaning 'it came as fast as a bullet') and in India as the 'Fever Epidemic', *'mari'* or *'manmodi'*.[225] Irrespective of nomenclature, it would almost always be forgotten within a couple of generations.

The Disappearance of Memory

In 1919, Norman White wrote that 'the heart-rending scenes witnessed by all who took an active part in endeavouring to combat

the influenza outbreak in India in 1918 will never be forgotten'.[226]
But the reality is that the memory did quickly fade away over
generations.

I find it rather astonishing that even a century after the influenza
pandemic wiped out 20 million Indians in a matter of months in what
is arguably the country's greatest ever demographic disaster, very
little research has been done on the subject.[227] The pandemic figures
as a footnote, if at all, in accounts of India's freedom movement,
taught to all in schools. Medical colleges in India rarely teach medical
history and generations of doctors graduate without knowing about
the influenza outbreak of 1918. The few books that have appeared
on the pandemic have, ironically, focussed their attention on places
that were the least affected—Europe and North America—to cater
to their readerships.[228] Even there, historians have worked hard to dig
out the event as the title of Alfred Crosby's much-acclaimed book in
1989 suggested: *America's Forgotten Pandemic.*

What explains this apathy? If the pandemic was overshadowed
by World War I in the Western world, in India, it was eclipsed by
the freedom movement. And yet, overlooking the pandemic negates
a crucial context within which Mohandas Gandhi, a pivotal figure
in the fight for India's independence, rose to the fore in 1918–19.
Another explanation for neglecting the 1918 pandemic is that the
plague, though less destructive, lasted for a longer period and caught
the public's imagination to a larger extent than influenza.[229] In fact,
in Australia, oral histories of those who lived through that period,
when presented many decades later, revealed that people used the
word 'plague' to describe influenza.[230] Further, the documentation
on the plague and cholera run into several volumes with detailed
photographs, but records for 1918 in India fall short. Norman
White's *Preliminary Report* was the only official document published
on the subject, never to be followed up on. For a long time, '6 million
deaths' was the number circulated in public, comparable to some of
the catastrophic famines of the past, even though the Indian Census

of 1921 suggested a higher number. Visual material of the 1918 pandemic in India is hard to find in newspapers of the time, probably because the photographers themselves reported sick.

The first time I encountered the event was in 2011 during my research on migration, when I looked, aghast, at a map I had just created on district-level population growth rates between 1911 and 1921.[231] I had kept yellow as the colour for negative growth, and virtually all of India looked yellow. No other decade between 1901 and 2011 looked like this.

The brief nature of the influenza pandemic and its high intensity may have led to an unwillingness to document the event on the part of the people who lived through that time. With the agitations against colonial rule picking up pace in 1919 in India, there were other things to bother about. But I would argue that the fundamental reason why the 1918 pandemic was forgotten in India, and elsewhere, especially by later generations, was because there were no severe pandemics in the world after that. It is true that HIV-AIDS created a stir in the 1980s and 1990s, but the mode of transmission in that pandemic was entirely different and, eventually, it did not affect most people in a direct manner.

The memory of the influenza of 1918 was of course, vivid among those who had lived through that year. Four decades later, in 1957–58, another flu pandemic broke out, killing around 1 million people worldwide. India was barely affected, but during the initial phase, the medical community couldn't help but recall 1918. In May 1957, Dr B.G. Vad, a Bombay-based physician, wrote the following in a letter to the editor of a newspaper:

Having forgotten the lessons of the 1890 epidemic, we were caught unawares in the 1918 epidemic which took a catastrophic toll. Those who have witnessed the ferocity know of the ravages from which not even a village nor hamlet escaped. The 1918 pandemic claimed more than seven million lives in India … In the city at that time, long queues were awaiting their turns at the burning place and burial ground. These facts are mentioned to draw attention to the impending probable catastrophe before it is too late. Poverty, starvation and lack of security and shelter are the fifth columnists of this epidemic. It is therefore imperative and urgent that the public health authorities, medical societies, public bodies, and public-spirited individuals mobilise and pool all available resources and organise proper and adequate medical relief in urban as well as rural areas.[232]

Memory is important as it is the fundamental way in which knowledge accumulates. It was the memory of horrific plagues across centuries that prompted Europe to safeguard itself against the disease in the nineteenth and twentieth centuries. It is the memory of recent influenza outbreaks in Vietnam that pushed it to take strong preventive actions against COVID-19 in January 2020 itself, ahead of the curve compared to most countries.[233] And it is the recent memory of containing the Nipah virus outbreak in 2018 in Kerala in south India that placed the state in a superior position to tackle COVID-19 in 2020. Unfortunately, the history of pandemics, compared to wars, is mostly absent in education systems and public conversation. And thus, many parts of the world were caught thoroughly off-guard when they faced a major pandemic again in 2020.

5

COVID-19 in the Rear-view Mirror

'Any doctor who is called to a house to treat a severely wounded person or one suffering from unwholesome food or drink shall report the fact to the gopa and the sthanika. If he makes a report, he shall not be accused of any crime; if he does not, he shall be charged with the same offence (which he helped to conceal).' [1]

– Kautilya's *Arthashastra*

Policymakers in China, trained in the legacies of Sun Tzu's *The Art of War*, ought to be reading more of Kautilya's *Arthashastra*, ancient India's treatise on statecraft. Kautilya's words describe the functioning of a fairly coercive state with detailed instructions, rules and regulations not far removed from contemporary Chinese realities and yet, even within such a state, there is a clear guideline on not obstructing or criminalizing the flow of medical information from doctors in the field.

On 30 December 2019, Dr Li Wenliang (1986–2020), a young doctor in Wuhan, used a social media platform to warn his fellow doctors of a disease outbreak that resembled SARS (Severe Acute

Respiratory Syndrome).[2] He was quickly reprimanded by Wuhan's Public Security Bureau for spreading rumours and was asked to sign a statement to that effect.[3] On 7 February 2020, he succumbed to the same disease he had tried to issue a warning about. A few days before his death, he was interviewed by the *New York Times*, and he conveyed that 'there should be more openness and transparency' and that it would have been a lot better 'if the officials had disclosed information about the epidemic earlier'.[4] His death prompted outrage in China, as did the blogs of Fang Fang, a sixty-five-year old writer living in Wuhan, who pointed out the problems in the official response to the epidemic.[5] By then, the epidemic had been labelled by the WHO as COVID-19, or the coronavirus disease caused by SARS-CoV-2, first reported to it on 31 December 2019 as 'cases of pneumonia of unknown etiology'.[6] On 11 March 2020, the WHO stated that the outbreak could be characterized as a pandemic.

Just how much this bungling in China cost the world in terms of time to prepare for the pandemic can only be speculated. This is because major world leaders discounted the threat of COVID-19 for quite some time, even as late as the end of March 2020. By February, the first cases had already arrived in India and yet, in Ahmedabad, the city I live in, the public was expected and encouraged to throng the streets to welcome the American president for the widely publicized Modi–Trump meet. Only a few weeks later was the city administration tasked with the diametrically opposite objective of keeping people away from the streets as norms on social distancing began to be implemented. Soon enough, the health system began to show visible strain and Kautilya's wisdom on doctor's reports started to apply even in a democratic country like India, as controversies on COVID-19 testing broke out. Further, while most countries entered lockdowns of varying strictness to meet the COVID-19 crisis amid difficult policy trade-offs, India chose the most stringent lockdown option and, in the process, created an unprecedented migration crisis.

Can COVID-19 be better understood in light of the Age of Pandemics?

Origin Myths

The Age of Pandemics shows us that pandemics can originate anywhere and at any time. As proven by the most recent cholera pandemic, which originated in Indonesia, there was nothing truly 'Indian' about the disease. And yet, in the nineteenth century, it was a widely held belief that British India was the home of cholera or 'the factory of cholera', as described by one French delegate at the 1894 International Sanitary Conference.[7] But we now know that the *Cholerae vibrio* thrived in certain maritime ecosystems and only occasionally found its way to human bowels. Similarly, there was nothing 'Chinese' or 'Indian' about the plague, and reservoirs for plague foci existed in other parts of the world as well. It was a disease that essentially hurt rodents first, and then humans.

If the 1889–90 influenza pandemic was dubbed the 'Russian flu' on the basis of its supposed origin, the more accurate term for the 1918 pandemic would be the 'American flu', certainly not the 'Spanish' flu. In fact, at different times, influenza earned a variety of names based on its most proximate source. In Japan, it was referred to as 'American Influenza', in Ceylon as 'Bombay Fever', in Dakar (Senegal) as 'Brazilian Flu' and in Northern Rhodesia as 'White Man's Flu'.[8] Such labels may appear harmless but have, in the past, led to discrimination against migrants coming from the region where the disease is supposed to have originated.

This is why the WHO, sensibly, does not prefix a disease with a location. The phrase 'Chinese virus' for COVID-19, as used by some political leaders, is unwarranted. This is not to rule out the possibility of a country *deliberately* creating a pandemic in the future through biochemical weapons. In the infamous Unit 731 in north-eastern China in the 1930s, Japanese forces experimented with cholera, plague and other diseases and in 1949, a few of the Japanese soldiers were indicted by the Russians for using bio-weapons against the Chinese during World War II.[9] Curiously, the official name for Unit 731 was Epidemic Prevention and Water Supply Department and its overall efforts backfired spectacularly when the diseases they unleashed killed their own soldiers.[10]

If origin myth-making is the norm during pandemics, so is the idea of the 'super spreader'. The Age of Pandemics had many of them: pilgrims and soldiers for cholera, traders and tailors for the plague, and postal service officials and army personnel for influenza. The migrant labourer was also frequently abused. In the blame games, identities such as race, caste and religion would invariably crop up as attested in numerous reports littered across the nineteenth century. In the current pandemic, religious congregations came under close scrutiny, first, groups related with the Shincheonji Church of Jesus in South Korea, and then in India, with the Tablighi Jamaat. Both groups attracted outsized blame for weeks, amplified by the media, and exposed classic pandemic fears. This behaviour was reminiscent of the British colonial authorities blaming Hindu and Muslim pilgrims and merchants for spreading diseases a century ago. Fortunately, the blame game stopped in India when some political leaders pointed out that the coronavirus does not consider the religion of the person it attacks.

The long history of pandemics from ancient times till today suggests that there may be no particular pattern to the timing of pandemics. It is true that the Age of Pandemics occurred just as the world was becoming more globalized, but in the past century, with the world more connected than ever before, the real mystery is why pandemics have not affected us to as large an extent as they did in the

100 years before 1920. Mutations of bacteria and viruses are ongoing affairs and their outbreaks cannot be forecast in any meaningful sense. Pandemics can be curtailed, not eradicated.

Pandemic Politics

The Age of Pandemics tells us that the outcomes of pandemics are strongly influenced by politics. How much a state or government intervenes will be decided by the extent to which it is accountable to its citizens and the magnitude of their resistance. When to intervene will depend on the timing of the next elections or on how much attention the government wants the public to focus on the pandemic. And once the intervention has been chosen, its impact will always be benchmarked to someone doing worse than you.

In the late nineteenth century, this meant that colonial powers would invest heavily in upgrading public health infrastructure in their own backyards but provide endless excuses to avoid doing the same in their colonies. Cholera ceased to have a major impact in most of Europe and North America by the late nineteenth century but continued to ravage territories in Asia. It would be naïve to attribute the burden of pandemics on colonialism per se since the princely states of India or the few non-colonized parts of the world such as Siam or Thailand also suffered immensely during the Age of Pandemics. But colonialism's link with commerce and the compulsion to keep trade channels open did provide an excuse to look away from pandemic outbreaks. In the few instances of massive interventions, such as with the plague in India in 1896–98, the authorities found such strong resistance that they quickly backtracked and shirked their responsibilities, citing oriental fatalism rather than creating a meaningful engagement with their subjects. The strengthening of democracy over the twentieth century thus played an important role in increasing investments in the health infrastructure of many countries, making them better prepared to face pandemics.

As more countries experience democratic processes and the routine of elections, the timing of intervention in a pandemic has also come to depend on political strategies. If during the 1918 influenza pandemic, few states intervened lest it took attention away from the war effort, today's interventions can be based on whether elections are around the corner or not. A cross-country study already shows how electoral concerns appear to have influenced the response to COVID-19 in the first few months of 2020.[11] Countries with elections due soon cannot afford to showcase the economic contraction that accompanies a stringent lockdown and act accordingly. Further, pandemic management almost always involves the dispersal of crowds and some curtailment of religious freedoms and civil liberties, which is a political issue, as the British discovered in India in the nineteenth century. Winning the trust of the public while doing so is thus of paramount importance, just as it was eventually enshrined in India's plague policy after years of misadventure.

Ultimately, the politics of pandemics revolves around showcasing your success. Of lives saved. Of places doing worse than you. Of your timely actions. However, the Age of Pandemics tells us to do no such thing. Premature celebrations came back to haunt the British in India as pandemics tore through the subcontinent. And hence, honest politics, if there is such a thing, should be aware of two fallacies of pandemic management: concerning the number of deaths and regional variation. Close to 12 million deaths due to plague in India in the Age of Pandemics was a disaster, however one looks at it. But zero deaths should *not* necessarily be seen as a success. Europe escaped the most recent plague pandemic as much as eastern India, not because of differences in sanitation, but because of the nature of rats and rat fleas. Death rates in a pandemic are dependent on a wide variety of factors, of which pandemic management plays only one part. At the time of writing this book, the regional variation of COVID-19 death rates is so stark that any commentary on it would be premature. All one can say is that where it is exceptionally high, better pandemic management would have helped. But escaping lightly on COVID-19 is not a guaranteed certificate of good pandemic management. In the coming years, we will learn about various factors, as yet unforeseen, that could be important in explaining the distribution of COVID-19 fatality.

Herein lies the catch. In order to not look bad, there is a clear incentive for politicians to take measures to downplay pandemic deaths. This could be done in the form of under-reporting deaths, or reporting them under other causes. Or, more simply, by not testing. It could also mean, in the case of India's sub-national governments, a refusal to accept people back home in order to show clean slates. It is imperative, therefore, to heed Kautilya's advice on obtaining as much medical information from the field as possible, and also doing the best for your citizens, within and outside, irrespective of the numbers. In doing so, politicians face many risks. But by not acting soon and wisely, pandemics can claim several lives and careers, including those of politicians.

Economics, Epidemiology and the Environment

The Age of Pandemics demonstrates that there will always be a contest between those who want to shut down economic activities to control a pandemic and those who don't. Seen from the prisms of economics and epidemiology, it reflects different objectives, one that wishes to maximise economic growth (without rampant inflation) and the other that wishes to minimize deaths. This is a hard trade-off that policymakers around the world grapple with during a pandemic. It is a choice that should not be left to either epidemiologists or economists, as they are accountable to nobody, but to politicians taking counsel from *both*.

It is likely that both epidemiologists and economists have vested interests in exaggerating their fears. For it is better to project a million deaths and be proved wrong when only 10,000 occur, rather than the reverse. And it is better to project a 10-percentage point cutback in economic output and end up with only 5 per cent than the other way round. The politician's choice today is reasonably simple. Given a potential scenario of a million deaths without any action but a 10 per cent cutback in output with intervention, few would choose the former. Unsurprisingly, most governments opted for a lockdown in 2020.

A lot then depends on forecasting. And in this, I will argue that epidemiologists and economists will *never* get it consistently right. This is not to belittle the efforts of these fields, which have contributed to a reduction in death rates due to infectious diseases, and output-and-price volatility, respectively, over the past century. But pandemics are different and one has to admit humility in the face of extraordinary uncertainty.

As with any field, differences in views are but natural. Scientists quarrel with each other all the time but more so during pandemics, as a matter of ego and prestige. What better time to cement your place in history by providing useful advice in a life-and-death situation? The Age of Pandemics witnessed a legendary battle between the 'sanitarians' and the 'contagionists'. That debate was conclusively settled by the bacteriologists, but even those who ended up on the winning side, be it Snow, Koch or Liston, got certain things wrong. Liston, who proved the rat–flea link of the plague, excitedly ended his famous paper arguing that the regional distribution of plague death rates in India could be linked with the people's oil usage habits. Later research showed that it was the rat–flea incidence that mattered.

Today's quarrels are not about whether diseases can be contagious but about *how* contagious they really are and the *impact* of such contagions. Invariably, these debates centre on the measurement of the case fatality rate and thresholds above which a disease may be considered to be truly dangerous. The issue is, how can this statistic be accurately measured in real time, especially when there are asymptomatic cases? Should cases be measured as only those who report for testing or also include those who have never been tested and have experienced the disease lightly, the asymptomatic ones?

These quarrels aside, an even greater dilemma revolves around the epidemiologist's standard recommendation of a lockdown to contain a pandemic, because the burden of a lockdown is unevenly shared in society and, potentially, creates a new loop back towards diseases via the channel of undernutrition. Simply put, lockdowns in relatively poorer countries are different from those in richer countries. Lockdowns end up shutting down millions of livelihoods for those who cannot 'work from home'. Job losses, income losses or both could lead to a climbdown in the nutrition ladder through cutbacks on various food expenditures. This opens up susceptibility to infectious diseases, pandemic and otherwise. India's extraordinary death toll during the flu pandemic of 1918–19 was likely due to high food prices and undernutrition which the disease could act upon, than anything else. In fact, a stringent lockdown in that context would have made things much worse by driving up prices further. Better food distribution instead of a lockdown would seem, in hindsight, to have been the right thing to do.

Computer model-based simulations of the impact of lockdowns on pandemic deaths must therefore take into consideration the effect on nutrition and increased disease load. One can never really boast about lives saved in a pandemic by a complete lockdown, because one is never sure about how many lives were lost due to the lockdown itself. Undernutrition need not manifest in instant death *during* the course of the pandemic but by exposing people to diseases, it can lead to death *afterwards*. It can also linger intergenerationally if it affects pregnant mothers during a pandemic. A recommendation of a complete lockdown therefore must connect epidemiology with economics and ensure adequate levels of nutrition for all. This is particularly significant in places where a high proportion of the workforce does not work from home and is likely to be severely affected by a lockdown.

Economists also need to pay more attention to lockdowns. The Age of Pandemics witnessed the espousal of laissez-faire policies and limiting of quarantines and lockdowns to keep trade channels open and the economy moving. It is therefore useful to point out the economic costs of pandemics when lockdowns and quarantines are not enforced and death rates go out of control in such laissez-faire situations. In the nineteenth century world, these economic costs were mostly related with a reduction in farm output and higher prices due to the unavailability of farmhands. The influenza of 1918–19 in India is a classic case of high death rates disrupting the society and economy to such an extent that it led to a massive recession. In the absence of any significant intervention during the influenza pandemic of 1918–20, one study found that countries, on average, witnessed annual GDP and consumption declines of 6 and 8 per cent, respectively.[12] So the absence of a lockdown policy can very quickly lead to a situation of an *effective* lockdown when a pandemic goes out of control, as large numbers of people fall sick and few report to work. That is, with no intervention, a pandemic disaster is also an economic disaster.

The tensions between economics and epidemiology witnessed in the Age of Pandemics were reproduced in the current pandemic of 2020 too and will continue to emerge in similar situations in the future. The challenge for these disciplines is to come up with a strategy that minimizes both deaths and economic losses.

Undoubtedly, numerous 'models' will materialize in the coming years based on the experience of the current pandemic.

In this context, it is interesting to observe what the *Arthashastra* has to say about calamities. It is clearly not the best text when it comes to medical advice for countering epidemics and diseases, invoking 'purificatory and expiatory rites by ascetics, milking of cows in cremation grounds, burning of effigies, and even occult means by experts'.[13] This would, however, appear to be with the tenor of initial reactions in India even in February 2020, when one Member of Parliament arranged a small candle-lit prayer event with the memorable jingle 'Go, Corona, Go'. But when it comes to pragmatic advice on facing calamities, the *Arthashastra* offers an interesting balancing act:

> In the interests of the prosperity of the country, a king should
> be diligent in foreseeing the possibility of calamities, try to avert
> them before they arise, overcome those which happen, remove
> all obstructions to economic activity and prevent loss of revenue
> to the state.[14]

Apart from economics and epidemiology, there is now the added concern over the environment. Why, the environmentalists ask, is everyone geared up to face a pandemic and not the other global threat posed by climate change? Why should the economist's quest to maximize growth take precedence over the protection of the environment? Surely, those brief moments of refreshingly clean air experienced during a complete lockdown were worth the hardship to humans. Environmentalists argue that 'growth for the sake of growth is the ideology of the cancer cell' and that should not be the motto of humans.[15] Seen from this lens, it is not only *Cholerae vibrio*, *Yersinia pestis*, H1N1 or SARS-CoV-2 that can cause pandemics, but also *Homo sapiens*, whose activities can wipe out other species.

These, I believe, are valid points that emerge in the twenty-first century and should provoke us to think of newer ways to live, consume and interact. If the Age of Pandemics taught us to take into consideration both epidemiology and economics, the COVID-19 pandemic should press us further to think about our environment.

Pandemics and Migration

The Age of Pandemics tells us that it is a bad idea to shut down transport systems abruptly, and that many migrants will want to go back home during a time of crisis. It is well documented that pandemics are amplified by migration or the movement of humans or disease vectors and that curtailment of such movement is important to contain the pandemic. The question is not 'if' but 'when' and 'how'.

In the case of movement across national borders, the suspension of visas and flight traffic can be implemented swiftly. Most of those stranded will be able to take care of themselves for some time and governments can step in to help those in need. Ideally, students and a few other vulnerable categories should be given the option to go back home before the policy measures are announced. For internal migration, however, the scenario is different for the simple reason that it is not feasible to shut down internal mobility in the same manner as international mobility. There are a vast number of migrants and multiple ways to travel and escape checkpoints and if nothing else works out, the desperate will even attempt a long walk back home.

The flight of internal migrants is, therefore, one of the most stylized facts of pandemics in history. In the initial weeks of the plague in Bombay city in 1896, the government of India decided not to shut down the railways on the pragmatic grounds that people would anyway 'scatter over the country-side, and find an egress by ways which would render inspection and control difficult or impossible'.[16] It was further argued that it would 'cause great inconvenience and hardship'.[17] As recounted earlier in the chapter on the plague, the slogan of preferring to die in the villages of their birth rather than in the city was a major cultural factor prompting migrants to go back, apart from the real threat of the disease and harsh disease-control measures. Equally illuminating was the experience of China in 1911, when the shutdown of the railways led to the exact response that the British had anticipated in India: of people choosing to walk back home, and unfortunately weakening or dying in the process. It was obvious that the railway network could facilitate the spread of the disease, but it was not clear how its shutdown could stop the spread of the disease when people could still travel by other means.

Any policy that proposes to curtail internal mobility at the onset of a pandemic has to anticipate reverse migration and plan accordingly. In 2020, China got extremely lucky as the bulk of its migrant workforce, numbering in the *hundreds* of millions, had already gone back home for the Lunar New Year festival in what is routinely dubbed as the world's biggest human migration, before the Wuhan outbreak picked up steam.[18] The world's largest democracy, on the other hand, was caught napping.

At 8 p.m. on 24 March 2020, in a televised speech, the prime minister of India announced a complete nationwide lockdown for twenty-one days, including a sudden shutdown of the railway system midnight onwards. Significantly, the lockdown speech did not mention anything about migration or migrants even though they were going to be the worst affected by the decision. This was a case of remarkable oversight since the government's own reports in 2016 and 2017 had shown the high number of circular internal migrants in India and highlighted the absence of portable social security policies that limited their welfare.[19] Migration researchers in India argued that migrants should have been given the option to go back home before the lockdown was implemented.[20] It was clear that if migrants found economic security in cities but social security back home, then during a lockdown, with no assurance on income support, they would make the rational decision to try and get back home. In the event, since the transport networks were switched off, they would have to walk.

Over the next two months, Indians who had the comfort of staying securely in their houses and performing the tasks set out by the prime minister, to display solidarity with frontline workers, woke up every day to shocking visuals of a full-blown migration crisis. While middle-class India watched reruns of the *Ramayan* on television, the poorer classes were fleeing from the cities for survival. By the government's own admission, there were around 21,000 camps set up to house over 500,000 stranded migrants. But the numbers of those walking or hitchhiking were much more. As the lockdown kept getting extended, the migrants who decided to stay back got even more frustrated and began to protest. In their eyes, the containment was all the more hypocritical because the policy to shut down air travel had taken more time and planning and a few Indians stranded in foreign destinations were brought home through special flights. The lack of coordination between the central government and state governments and between state governments made matters worse.

Throughout, the media and civil society stepped up to highlight and address a major crisis within a crisis. A few journalists hit the ground running to track the migrants, covering more miles and districts at one point than perhaps even the coronavirus, and some good Samaritans showed that all it took was a bit of compassion and organizing of buses and transport options to ferry migrants back home. Finally, in May, the central government relented and started special Shramik trains that eventually transported over 5 million people back home, though some trains managed to get 'lost' and reached their destinations only after long delays. Many people also went home by buses. That this reverse migration finally occurred at a time when infection rates were much higher demonstrated the failure of the original policy of not letting people go back. I estimate that at least 30 million people, or 15–20 per cent of the urban workforce, went home during the two-month ordeal.

The initial idea of containing migrants to check the spread of disease to rural areas with limited health infrastructure was noble but flawed. This is because the holding capacity of urban areas for circular migrants without income support is limited and, as all past pandemics have shown, the cultural imperative to go back home during a crisis is very strong. As the British had correctly argued in the 1890s, shutting internal transport options for migrants would turn out to be counterproductive.

With the benefit of hindsight, there are two additional reasons why internal migrants should be allowed to go back (with due quarantining back home) in any future pandemic crisis. Because pandemics thrive on density, the decongestion of cities through reverse migration is advisable. And from an economic point of view, the earlier migrants go back, the earlier they can return and thus the economic recovery that is necessary after a lockdown is less handicapped by the absence of the migrant workforce, which India is facing in 2020. Ultimately, securing good health facilities in rural areas, whose lack the public lamented in 1918 during the influenza pandemic and again in 2020, would be the best way for rural areas to guard against pandemics, rather than preventing migrants from going back home in a crisis.

The Stages of a Pandemic

Epidemiologists define the stages of a pandemic by the extent of transmission of the disease. When it reaches the 'community-level outbreak' stage in any country, it is considered to be at critical level.

But the outbreak of a disease can also be seen as a 'social' event.[21] In one such account—based on a mid-nineteenth century American experience of yellow fever—it has been argued that the stages include the initial outbreak, a downturn and exodus, a challenge from below as the authority collapses, the emergence of community response, a declaration of the epidemic and, finally, the reconstitution of authority.[22] Another characterization is based on the four 'R's of revelation, randomness, response and retrospection, associated with epidemics.[23] On similar lines, but based on the experience of the Age of Pandemics, I posit four stages: denial, confusion, acceptance and erasure.

The greater the temporal distance between the previous and current pandemic, the greater the denial in admitting an impending one. East Asian countries were the best prepared for COVID-19 because they had recently been exposed to SARS and the flu pandemics of the late twentieth and early twenty-first centuries. These regions therefore were quick to act in January and February 2020. In India, in Kerala, K.K. Shailaja, popularly known as Shailaja Teacher, health minister in the state government, had successfully contained the Nipah virus outbreak in 2018 (the movie *Virus* is based on this). Thus, Kerala was better placed to manage the coronavirus crisis, even as the Union health ministry argued on 13 March 2020 that it was not a health emergency—two days after the WHO had declared its pandemic status.[24] India's escape from serious pandemic mortality for more than a century, barring some small-scale incidents, gave rise to all sorts of denials about the seriousness of the issue. In the UK and the USA, both countries which host tens of thousands of medical students from around the world, the political leadership was in denial mode for a long time. In Brazil, where the government got a leading Brazilian scientist to handle the plague outbreak a century ago, leaders actively dismissed the science behind the coronavirus.

By late March 2020, denial was over and confusion had set in. Confusion about how much to intervene and when to remove the interventions played out over a few months as new issues cropped up, such as the migration crisis in India, and the Black Lives Matter movement in the US. Confusion also reigned over the best treatment to be given to patients, the testing procedures, and the quality of the masks. Social media, absent in the Age of Pandemics, amplified misinformation. A bleak atmosphere of despair set in, invoking the word *kalyug* in India. Even a cursory reading of past pandemics would reveal that this was actually par for the course.

Once the transmission within borders had begun, the virus appeared to behave haphazardly, with fluctuations in cases and fatality rates over time. In some places, the graph dipped before rising again, and in others, where the disease appeared late, it started to grow exponentially. Governments which had prided themselves on containing the spread of the disease early on had to backtrack and those under pressure initially, such as Italy, began to show improvement. Acceptance of the situation began around June 2020: that the virus was here to stay for longer than expected, that the magic vaccine was still many months away, and that the pandemic was going to be a serious drag on the economy. It was clear that 2020 was going to be the worst economic year in living memory for most countries, even if it was going to be a demographic disaster for only a few of them. The first few deaths in each region evoked detailed media coverage about the lives of those who died, but over time, the names became blurred and were replaced by a statistical scoresheet.

The phase of 'acceptance' blends very slowly into the last stage, that is, the erasure of the collective memory of the pandemic. At one level, it means forgetting the safeguards against the pandemic, the norms of social distancing and mingling, for fatigue soon sets in after months of lockdowns. But as the cases and case fatality rates come down, there is an eagerness to step into a post-pandemic world.

Between acceptance and erasure, however, lies a spell of uncertainty, governed by the behaviour of the pandemic. Will it be like the flu of 1918, which lasted a few months? Or will it be like cholera and the plague, which lasted for decades? Either way, attention is diverted from the pandemic to other issues, and people continue to die from diseases, such as tuberculosis, that don't receive the same focus as the pandemic one. These four stages of a pandemic are then set into motion again in the future, but with less denial and confusion in precisely those places that resist erasure.

It is important to emphasize that between any two deadly outbreaks there will also be a series of false alarms. Each time a disease is declared a pandemic which does not materialize in very high mortality, there will be, as one scientist said, 'retrospective scoffing' by 'critics who have no burden of responsibility for a wrong guess'.[25] Managing the four stages of a pandemic is thus a challenge for everyone, but erasure of memory is a mistake that is the most easily rectifiable.

Remembrance

The year 2020 has been surreal for all of us, painful for most but also delightful for a few. Consider, for instance, the fate of students. The coronavirus came at an inappropriate time for graduating cohorts, who missed out on the convocation ceremonies they had long dreamed about. The switch to online modes of teaching has been stressful for students and teachers. And yet, the virus came in handy for thousands of students who were able to pass their exams, potentially annoying some instructors, just like that college principal in Bombay in 1918–19 who blamed the influenza pandemic for graduating the 'least competent' batch from his college. We have the remarkable case today of a fifty-one-year old student in Telangana in south India who reportedly cleared his Class 10 examination in his thirty-fourth attempt, not because he could finally master the English exam that had been his nemesis for over three decades, but because the state education board cancelled the exams and passed everyone in 2020.[26]

Our personal communication has also changed. Letters and emails now begin with the customary 'I hope you are keeping safe and well' and the phrase 'these difficult times' is routinely employed. In such times, it is useful to remind ourselves that *global* COVID-19 mortality is unlikely to surpass the mortality of a single large province in India during the Age of Pandemics. They had it much worse a century or more ago. For every few weeks or months that we have had to live in a state of a lockdown, we should remember that a century ago, millions of Indians were evacuating into camps every day in particular months of the year, for over a decade, to escape the plague.

A lot has changed since the Age of Pandemics. The WHO ensures a global health surveillance system that is vastly superior to the conferences and global cooperative efforts of the nineteenth century. It is not perfect, but the world is better off with its existence than in its absence. The people involved in pandemic curtailment are also different from those in the past. European men have given way to a more diverse set of people. The head of the WHO is an Ethiopian man, Tedros Ghebreyesus, and its chief scientist is an Indian woman, Soumya Swaminathan.

The state of medical science is so much better now than a century ago that many believe mass mortality of the kind witnessed back then is unthinkable today. This was also the prevailing attitude in 1917 when the revolution in medical science spearheaded by bacteriologists led to a growing belief in the power of science to avert calamities such as the cholera pandemics of the nineteenth century. But the year 1918 changed all that as the world witnessed the deadly influenza pandemic. The irony was that European imperialism, which boasted of having superior science and technology, was mostly clueless in the Age of Pandemics. Some decades later, when R. Pollitzer wrote his seminal book on cholera in 1959 for the WHO, it was supposed to be a closing chapter in the history of that disease, which had nearly disappeared. Almost on cue, the very next decade, a new cholera pandemic broke out. Science does not have all the answers; and sometimes it can find the answers only after the peak period of the pandemic has passed. Joshua Lederberg (1925–2008), the molecular biologist who won the Nobel Prize at the age of thirty-three, argued that pandemics should be seen as 'natural evolutionary phenomenon' and cautioned against hubris:

> The progress of medical science during the last century has obscured the human species' continued vulnerability to large-scale infection. We fail to acknowledge our relationship to microbes as a *continued* evolutionary process ... We have a reasonable lead on bacterial intruders; we grossly neglect the protozoan parasites that mainly afflict the third world; we are dangerously ignorant about how to cope with viruses.[27]

One way to always stay on guard is by developing collective memory. For Europe, the fourteenth-century plague lingered on in popular consciousness through various means over time and its memory shaped responses to diseases several centuries after the event. As a student in London, I would be annoyed with the numerous evacuation drills on fire alarms, but now I see the wisdom of that policy, for the city was burnt down not once, but several times in its long history.

When COVID-19 broke out in early 2020, the ignorance of the history of pandemics outside Europe, especially in India, was stunning. While writing this book, I am continually struck by the paucity of first-person accounts in the Age of Pandemics. The significance of this period should initiate archives and oral histories. If you have a story on past pandemics from your family's history to share, I would be happy to learn more about it. It should also spur creative public dissemination of such accounts in schools, especially in institutes in the medical world. If Johan Hultin in the US could dig up decades-old graves to help unearth the true nature of the virus that caused the influenza pandemic of 1918–20, what is stopping medical researchers in India, Egypt and other regions adversely affected in the Age of Pandemics from doing the same? Many questions on the outbreaks of those times have still not been satisfactorily answered and the subject deserves more research.

The remembrance of past pandemics also means that we should carefully document the ongoing one so that the mistakes we make today are not repeated in the future. The numerous medical and non-medical reports published on cholera and the plague in the Age of Pandemics, flawed as they were in many dimensions, provided incremental knowledge that ultimately led to fewer deaths by those diseases. Equally important is the formal recognition of the valiant services provided by the frontline workers today, through awards and other means, as they can serve as role models for tomorrow. The contributions of scientists and doctors are usually well acknowledged but the voices of so many others, including the police, nurses and, especially, overworked mortuary workers, remain unheard and need to be systematically documented.[28]

Despite their innate complexity and uncertainty, pandemics can be curtailed to some extent. For that to happen, governments, medical authorities and, above all, the general public need to be sensitized about the pandemics of the past. That they can occur anytime. From anywhere. That one must act sensibly in such times and in the best interests of society. That some amount of lockdown may be necessary. And that when doing so, the needs of migrants should be taken into account so that one does not create a crisis within a crisis.

Ultimately, a pandemic can run its lethal course in a few months, as with the great influenza pandemic of the past or last for many years as it did with cholera and the plague. It is a sobering thought indeed in 2020: we may have to bear this pandemic out, just as that officer in Punjab had once said about the plague, with 'humility and patience'.

Author's Note

This book is the outcome of serendipity and timeliness to address the loss of memory about past pandemics, written while we were in the middle of one. In writing it, I offer two core arguments. First, the cholera, plague and influenza pandemics between 1817 and 1920 need to be placed firmly in the global historiography of this period, currently dominated by themes such as nationalism, imperialism, capitalism or globalization. Second, I argue that the Age of Pandemics has been forgotten in the country most affected by it—India—and that there is value in remembering it as a major event just as the 'Black Death' plague pandemic of the fourteenth century is registered in European consciousness to this day. This is important because building such collective memory is useful to counter current and future pandemics.

My approach is partly inspired from the field of demographic history. My interest in this subject began by reading the pioneering work of Tim Dyson, whom I have never met, but with whom I have had the good fortune of interacting over email in recent years. I also learnt a lot from the work of researchers who have devoted large parts of their careers to understand the history of epidemics and health in India—Ira Klein, David Arnold, Mark Harrison, Ian Catanach, Mridula Ramanna and many others. I would particularly like to thank Maura Chhun for promptly sharing her doctoral research on Influenza in India and other relevant resources.

Remote research during a lockdown was possible only because of excellent digital archives maintained by the Wellcome Collection, National Library of Scotland (Medical History of British India), the Edinburgh Research Archive, the Visual Plague Project at the University of Cambridge, Archive.org, ProQuest Times of India Digital Database, South Asia Archives and Ideas of India Archive. The pictures from the Wellcome Collection are courtesy of the Creative Commons Attribution Non-Commercial license (CC BY-NC 4.0). The book also benefited from excellent research assistance provided by Aasha Eapen and Mrinal Tomar. While writing, I have used the old and new names of places interchangeably. The statistical analysis is provided in a separate document, available online, and mentioned in the Notes section.

I would like to thank Yogesh Kalkonde for sharing an important oral history he collected in Gadchiroli district in central India on the 1918 pandemic. To him and Ambarish Satwik, I owe a debt of gratitude for taking out time from their busy hospital schedules in the middle of a pandemic to provide feedback on the draft chapters. I also benefited from detailed comments by Tirthankar Roy and Maura Chhun.

Many others have contributed in different ways: Ravi Abhyankar, Sanghamitra Chatterjee, Lucy Taksa, Patrick French, Jeemol Unni, Amol Agrawal, Aparajith Ramnath, Aashish Gupta, Basav Biradar, C.J. Kuncheria, Yunus Lasania, Y.B. Satyanarayana, Aanchal Malhotra, Abhi Sanghani, Sudev Sheth, Amrita Roy, Sandeep Badole, Ankur Sarin, Jeevant Rampal and Sukanya Basu. Presentations in the CASI-UPenn and EHDR webinar series and discussions with Ed Glaeser and his Dev-Urban group prompted great feedback.

Swati Chopra encouraged and edited, motivated and manoeuvred this book with infectious enthusiasm, as did the wonderful team at Harper Collins. I thank Gavin Morris and Bonita Shimray for designing the cover, and Chandna Arora for her work on the copy edits. Friends and family chipped in from time to time with little known nuggets. During the lockdown, my father, Vasudev Tumbe, eased into retirement and reading, and my mother, Sudha Huzurbazar Tumbe, into prolific writing. Both of their newly acquired skills were valuable in improving this book. My wife, Divya, survived the lockdown with plants, wit, humour and her own wonderful writing, all of which added to this project, as did my son, Siddhartha, who prompted the first spark.

Good architecture provides a stimulus to thinking, or so I feel after writing this book in Louis Kahn's awe-inspiring red-brick campus of the Indian Institute of Management Ahmedabad. The tallest point among those red bricks is the Vikram Sarabhai Library, whose staff provided outstanding support for my research, locating rare material through their global inter-library ties. This remarkable effort was due to the leadership of Dr H. Anil Kumar, librarian, colleague and friend. His untimely death on 17 July 2020, the day he turned fifty-three, was a personal loss for many of us and brought home the painful reality of the pandemic. We miss you, Anil. This book, sitting on library shelves and elsewhere, is dedicated to you and your passion for books and libraries, both of which make this world a more beautiful place.

Select Bibliography

Afkhami, Amir. *A Modern Contagion: Imperialism and Public Health in Iran's Age of Cholera* (Johns Hopkins University Press, 2019).

Arnold, David. *Colonizing the Body: State Medicine and Epidemic Disease in Nineteenth-Century India* (University of California Press, 1993).

Benedict, Carol A. *Bubonic Plague in Nineteenth-Century China* (Stanford University Press, 1996).

Crosby, Alfred. *America's Forgotten Pandemic: The Influenza of 1918* (Cambridge University Press, 2003, Second Edition).

Dyson, Tim. *A Population History of India: From the First Modern People to the Present Day* (Oxford University Press, 2018).

Echenberg, Myron. *Plague Ports: The Global Urban Impact of Bubonic Plague, 1894–1901* (New York University Press, 2007).

———. *Africa in the Time of Cholera: A History of Pandemics from 1817 to the Present* (Cambridge University Press, 2011).

Hamlin, Christopher. *Cholera: The Biography* (Oxford University Press, 2009).

Harrison, Mark. *Public Health in British India: Anglo-Indian Preventive Medicine, 1859–1914* (Cambridge University Press, 1994).

————. *Contagion: How Commerce Has Spread Disease* (Yale University Press, 2012).

Hirst, L.F. *The Conquest of Plague: A Study of the Evolution of Epidemiology* (Oxford University Press, 1953).

Howard-Jones, Norman. *The Scientific Background of the International Sanitary Conferences, 1851-1938* (WHO, 1975).

Jaggi, O.P. *Medicine in India: Modern Period*, Volume IX, Part 1 of the History of Science, Philosophy and Culture in Indian Civilization Series (Oxford University Press, 2000).

Kiple, Kenneth F., ed. *The Cambridge World History of Human Disease* (Cambridge University Press, 1993).

Kotar, S.L. and J.E. Gessler. *Cholera: A Worldwide History* (McFarland & Company, 2014).

McNeill, William. *Plagues and Peoples* (Anchor Books, 1976).

Pati, Biswamoy and Mark Harrison, eds. *Society, Medicine and Politics in Colonial India* (Routledge, 2018).

Peckham, Robert, ed. *Empires of Panic: Epidemics and Colonial Anxieties* (Hong Kong University Press, 2015).

Phillips, Howard and David Killingray, eds. *The Spanish Influenza Pandemic of 1918-19: New Perspectives* (Routledge, 2003).

Pollitzer, Robert. *Plague* (WHO, 1954).

————. *Cholera* (WHO, 1959).

Ramanna, Mridula. *Western Medicine and Public Health in Colonial Bombay, 1845–1895* (Orient Longman, 2002).

————. *Health Care in Bombay Presidency, 1896–1930* (Primus Books, 2012).

Notes

A statistical appendix to this book along with an extended bibliography is available online as the following document, abbreviated as CT 2020 in the chapter-specific references:

Chinmay Tumbe, 'Pandemics and Historical Mortality in India', 2020, *IIMA Working Paper*, Indian Institute of Management Ahmedabad.

1: Pandemics of the Past

1. George Eliot, *Adam Bede* (John B. Alden, 1884 edition; first published in 1859), p. 95. George Eliot was the pen name of Mary Ann Evans (1819–1880).

2. On the reasons for mortality decline in India since 1920, see Sumit Guha, *Health and Population in South Asia: From Earliest Times to the Present* (Permanent Black, 2001).

3. Tim Dyson, *A Population History of India: From the First Modern People to the Present Day* (Oxford University Press, 2018), pp. 256 and 280.

4. See Section 9 in Chinmay Tumbe, 'Pandemics and Historical Mortality in India', *Indian Institute of Management Ahmedabad Working Paper*, 2020, henceforth referred to as CT 2020.

5. Ibid.

6.   Abdel R. Omran, 'The Epidemiologic Transition: A Theory of the Epidemiology of Population Change', *Milbank Memorial Fund Quarterly*, 49 (4) (1971): 731–757.

7.   For India: Census, 'Causes of Death Statistics, 2010–13'; For USA: National Vital Statistics Report 2017.

8.   Sonia Shah, *The Fever: How Malaria Has Ruled Humankind for 500,000 Years* (Picador, 2010).

9.   WHO, *World Malaria Report 2019* (WHO, 2019); Ira Klein, 'Development and Death: Reinterpreting Malaria, Economics and Ecology in British India', *Indian Economics and Social History Review*, 38 (2) (2001): 147–79.

10.   John Ash, *The New and Complete Dictionary of the English Language* (London, 1775).

11.   Mark Harrison, 'Pandemics' in *Routledge History of Disease*, ed. Mark Jackson (Routledge, 2017), pp. 129–46.

12.   J.H. Batten, *Official Reports on the Province of Kumaon with a Medical Report on the Mahamurree in Gurhwal, in 1849–50* (Secundra Orphan Press, 1851); Burton Stein, *A History of India*, ed. David Arnold (West Sussex, 2010; first edition in 1998), p. 121, provides a reference to *Mari* in an eleventh-century inscription.

13.   Benjamin Moseley, *A Treatise on Sugar with Miscellaneous Medical Observations* (John Nichols, 1800), p. 245.

14.   As cited in Heath Kelly, 'The Classical Definition of a Pandemic is not Elusive', *Bulletin of the WHO*, 89 (2011): 540–41.

15.   Ibid.

16.   Mark Harrison, 'Pandemics'.

17.   Ibid.

18.   Kautilya, *The Arthashastra*, ed. L.N. Rangarajan (Penguin, 1987), p. 128.

19.   George D. Sussman, 'Was the Black Death in India and China?', *Bulletin of the History of Medicine*, 85 (3) (2011): 319–55; Guido Alfani and Tommy E. Murphy, 'Plague and Lethal Epidemics in the Pre–Industrial World,' *Journal of Economic History*, 77 (1) (2017): 314–43.

20.   Sussman, 'Was the Black Death in India and China?', p. 324.

21. Peter Sarris, 'The Justinianic Plague: Origins and Effects', *Continuity and Change,* 17 (2) (2002): 169–82.

22. Writings of John of Ephesus, as cited in Sarris, 'The Justinianic Plague', p. 170.

23. Ibid., p. 173.

24. Ibid., p. 174.

25. Ibid., p. 177.

26. Angus Maddison, *Contours of the World Economy, 1–2030 AD* (Oxford University Press, 2007), pp. 376–78; Alfani and Murphy, 'Plague and Lethal Epidemics', p. 316.

27. Katharine Park, 'Black Death', in *Cambridge History of Human Disease,* ed. Kenneth Kiple (Cambridge University Press, 1993), pp. 612–16.

28. William McNeill, *Plagues and Peoples* (Anchor Books, 1976).

29. Sussman, 'Was the Black Death in India and China?', pp. 319–55.

30. Park, 'Black Death', p. 613.

31. Ole J. Benedictow, *The Black Death, 1346–1353: The Complete History* (Boydell Press, 2004); Maddison, *Contours of the World Economy*, pp. 376–78; Alfani and Murphy, 'Plague and Lethal Epidemics', p. 316.

32. Park, 'Black Death', p. 614.

33. Ibid., p. 615.

34. As cited in Alfani and Murphy, 'Plague and Lethal Epidemics', p. 333.

35. Alfani and Murphy, 'Plague and Lethal Epidemics', p. 331.

36. As cited in Alfani and Murphy, 'Plague and Lethal Epidemics', p. 329.

37. Alfred Crosby, *The Columbian Exchange: Biological and Cultural Consequences of 1492* (Praeger, 1972); Nathan Nunn and Nancy Qian, 'The Columbian Exchange: A History of Disease, Food and Ideas', *Journal of Economic Perspectives,* 24 (2) (2010): 163–88.

38. Alfred Crosby, 'Smallpox', in *Cambridge History of Human Disease,* ed. Kenneth Kiple (Cambridge University Press, 1993), pp. 1008–1013.

39. Ibid., p. 1009.

40. David Arnold, 'Diseases of the Modern Period in South Asia', in *Cambridge History of Human Disease,* ed. Kenneth Kiple (Cambridge University Press, 1993), p. 420.

41. Crosby, 'Smallpox', p. 1009–1010.

42. Ibid., p. 1010.

43. Alfani and Murphy, 'Plague and Lethal Epidemics', p. 317.

44. Crosby, 'Smallpox', p. 1010.

45. Arnold, 'Diseases of the Modern Period', p. 420.

46. Its impact on a monthly basis was certainly higher than the fourteenth-century plague.

47. The details on sources for all the mortality figures in this section are deliberated in CT 2020 and in the other chapters of this book.

48. Eric Hobsbawm, *The Age of Revolution, 1789–1848* (Vintage Books, 1962), *The Age of Capital, 1848–1875* (Abacus, 1975), *The Age of Empire, 1875–1914* (Vintage Books, 1987); Christopher Bayly, *The Birth of the Modern World, 1780–1914: Global Connections and Comparisons* (Blackwell, 2004).

49. Kenneth Pomeranz, *The Great Divergence: China, Europe, and the Making of the Modern World Economy* (Princeton University Press, 2000); Tirthankar Roy and Giorgio Riello, eds., *Global Economic History* (Bloomsbury, 2019).

50. Pandemics rarely appear in the Hobsbawm series, except for a page on cholera epidemics in 1830s Europe and a sentence on 1860s Spain. Bayly's work has slightly more coverage, but again, focussed on Europe. The global economic history literature has even less to say about nineteenth-century pandemics.

51. See CT 2020, Section 9.

52. Maddison, *Contours of the World Economy*, p. 381.

2: Cholera

1. Hakim Saiyad Amaldar Hussain, *Tiriyak-I-Haiza* (Lucknow: Naval Kishore, 1883), p. 4, as cited in Saurabh Mishra, 'Hakims and Haiza: Unani Medicine and Cholera in Late Colonial India', in *Society, Medicine and Politics in Colonial India*, eds. Biswamoy Pati and Mark Harrison (Routledge, 2018), p. 70.

2. BACSA, *South Park Street Cemetery, Calcutta: Register of Graves and Standing Tombs from 1767* (BACSA Putney, 1992).
    I would like to thank Sukanya Basu for pointing this out.

3. See CT 2020, Fig 2.1.

4. Angus Maddison, *Contours of the World Economy, 1–2030 AD* (Oxford University Press, 2007), Table A1, p. 376.

5. Niall Ferguson, *Empire: How Britain Made the Modern World* (Penguin, 2003), p. 44. The sailing frigate *Trincomalee* was launched in Bombay in 1817 and is now a museum ship in England.

6. Maddison, *Contours of the World Economy*, Table A1, p. 376. As per the Census of India 2011, the population of the Kolkata urban agglomeration was 14.1 million.

7. John Macpherson, *Annals of Cholera from the Earliest Periods to the Year 1817* (Ranken and Co., 1872).

8. Ibid; Nancy Gallagher, 'Islamic and Indian Medicine', in *The Cambridge World History of Human Disease*, ed. Kenneth Kiple (Cambridge University Press, 1993), p. 30; Guenter B. Risse, 'History of Western Medicine from Hippocrates to Germ Theory', in *The Cambridge World History of Human Disease*, ed. Kenneth Kiple (Cambridge University Press, 1993), p. 11.

9. Srabani Sen, 'Indian Cholera: A Myth', *Indian Journal of History of Science*, 47 (3) (2012): 348.

10. I. Zupanov, 'Drugs, Health, Bodies and Souls in the Tropics: Medical Experiments in Sixteenth-Century Portuguese India', *Indian Economic and Social History Review*, 39 (1) (2002): 1.

11. Ibid., p. 20.

12. Ibid., p. 20.

13. Kaushik Roy, *War, Culture and Society in Early Modern South Asia, 1740–1849* (Routledge, 2011), p. 103.

14. James Jameson, *Report on the Epidemick Cholera Morbus as it Visited the Territories Subject to the Presidency of Bengal in the Years 1817, 1818 and 1819* (Government Gazette Press, 1820), pp. xvi–xviii.

15. James Johnson, *The Influence of Tropical Climates* (Stockdale, 1813), pp. 396–414.

16. Ibid., p. 411. The exact details of this method, however, were not provided.

17. Ibid., p. 412.

18. David Gilmour, *The British in India: Three Centuries of Ambition and Experience* (Allen Lane, 2018), p. 484.

19. Jameson, 'Report on the Epidemick Cholera', p. xxiv.

20. David Arnold, 'Cholera and Colonialism in British India', *Past & Present,* 113 (1986): 121.

21. For instance: Government of Bombay, *Reports on the Epidemic Cholera which has raged throughout Hindostan and the Peninsula of India* (Jos. Fran. De Jesus, 1819); James Annesley, *Sketches of the most prevalent Diseases of India comprising a Treatise on the Epidemic Cholera of the East* (Thomas and George Underwood, 1825); Reginald Orton, *An Essay on the Epidemic Cholera of India* (Burgess and Hill, 1831); W.R. Cornish, *Report on Cholera in Southern India for the Year 1869* (Madras, 1870); C. Macnamara, *A Treatise on Asiatic Cholera* (John Churchill and Sons, 1870); James Bryden, *Note on the Epidemic Connection of the Cholera of Madras & Bombay with the Cholera Epidemics of the Bengal Presidency* (Calcutta, 1871); C. Macnamara, *A History of Asiatic Cholera* (Macmillan and Co., 1876); H.W. Bellew, *The History of Cholera in India from 1862 to 1881* (Trubner and Co., 1885); Edmund C. Wendt, ed., *A Treatise on Asiatic Cholera* (William Wood, 1885).

22. As cited in O.P. Jaggi, *Medicine in India: Modern Period*, Volume IX Part 1 of the History of Science, Philosophy and Culture in Indian Civilization Series (Oxford University Press, 2000), p. 109, and Macnamara, *A History of Asiatic Cholera*, p. 46.

23. Mark Harrison, 'A Dreadful Scourge: Cholera in Early Nineteenth-Century India', *Modern Asian Studies*, 54 (2) (2020): 512.

24. As cited in Macnamara, *A History of Asiatic Cholera*, p. 50.

25. Ibid., p. 53.

26. Harrison, 'A Dreadful Scourge', p. 511.

27. Ibid., p. 513.

28. Ibid., p. 513.

29. W.H. Sleeman, *Rambles and Recollections of an Indian Official*, Vol. 1 (J. Hatchard and Son, 1844), pp. 211–12; 302–03.

30. Ibid.; Dirk Kolff, *Naukar, Rajput and Sepoy* (Cambridge University Press, 1990), p. 147.

31. Sleeman, *Rambles*, pp. 215–16.

32. Ibid., p. 217.

33. Harrison, 'A Dreadful Scourge', p. 517.

34. Seema Alavi, *Islam and Healing: Loss and Recovery of an Indo–Muslim Medical Tradition* (Palgrave, 2008), pp. 112–13.

35. David Arnold, *Colonizing the Body: State Medicine and Epidemic Disease in Nineteenth-Century India* (University of California Press, 1993), p. 179.

36. Harrison, 'A Dreadful Scourge', p. 525.

37. Alavi, *Islam and Healing*, p. 171.

38. Savithri P. Nair, *Raja Serfoji II: Science, Medicine and Enlightenment in Tanjore* (Routledge, 2012), p. 63.

39. Harrison, 'A Dreadful Scourge', p. 529; Debjani Bhattacharyya, *Empire and Ecology in the Bengal Delta: The Making of Calcutta* (Cambridge University Press, 2018), p. 127; A. Mitra, 'Calcutta City', Census of India 1951, Vol. VI, Part III, 1954, p. 14, notes lottery-based funds used by a government appointed Committee until around 1814, which was then taken over by the Lottery Committee in 1817.

40. Harrison, 'A Dreadful Scourge', p. 534.

41. Macnamara, *A History of Asiatic Cholera*, p. 66.

42. Robert Pollitzer, *Cholera* (WHO, 1959), p. 18.

43. Macnamara, *A History of Asiatic Cholera*, p. 67.

44. Arnold, 'Cholera and Colonialism', p. 122.

45. Y.K. Lee, 'Cholera in Early Singapore (Part I) (1819–1849)', *Singapore Medical Journal*, 14 (1) (1973): 42.

46. Ibid., p. 44.

47. Christopher Hamlin, *Cholera: The Biography* (Oxford University Press, 2009), p. 74.

48. Pollitzer, *Cholera*, p. 19.
49. Ibid.
50. Ibid.
51. Macnamara, *A History of Asiatic Cholera*, p. 62.
52. Maddison, *Contours of the World Economy*, Tables A1 and A3, pp. 376–78.
53. See CT 2020, Table 3.5.
54. Ibid.
55. Ibid., Table 3.4.
56. Pollitzer, *Cholera*, Chapter 1.
57. Hamlin, *Cholera*, p. 268.
58. Paul A. Blake, 'Historical Perspectives on Pandemic Cholera', in *Vibrio cholerae and Cholera: Molecular to Global Perspectives*, eds. I. Kaye Wachsmuth, Paul A. Blake and Ørjan Olsvik (American Society for Microbiology Press, 1994), p. 294.
59. Leonard Rogers, 'The Forecasting and Control of Cholera Epidemics in India', *Journal of the Royal Society of Arts*, 75 (3874) (1927): 322–55.
60. Gilmour, *The British in India*, p. 490; Michael Zeheter, *Epidemics, Empire and Environments: Cholera in Madras and Quebec City, 1818–1910* (University of Pittsburgh Press, 2015).
61. Arnold, 'Cholera and Colonialism', p. 127.
62. Troy Downs, 'Host of Midian: The Chapati Circulation and the Indian Revolt of 1857–58', *Studies in History*, 16 (1) (2000): 75–107.
63. Sunasir Dutta and Hayagreeva Rao, 'Infectious Diseases, Contamination Rumors, and Ethnic Violence: Regimental Mutinies in the Bengal Native Army in 1857 India', *Organizational Behavior and Human Decisions*, 127 (2015): 36–47.
64. Sam Goodman, '"A Great Beneficial Disease": Colonial Medicine and Imperial Authority', in J.G. Farrell's *The Siege of Krishnapur*, *Journal of Medical Humanities*, 36 (2015): 141–56. Chapati circulation and epidemics are also fictionalized in Ambarish Satwik, *Perineum: Nether Parts of the Empire* (Penguin, 2007). On cholera in Indian fiction, see Ashoke Mukhopadhyay, *A Ballad of Remittent Fever*

(Aleph, 2020, originally published in Bengali in 2018; translated by Arunava Sinha).

65. See CT 2020, Table 3.5. Also, David Arnold, 'Cholera Mortality in British India, 1817–1947', in *India's Historical Demography*, ed. Tim Dyson (Curzon Press, 1989), pp. 261–84.

66. Maureen Sibbons, 'Cholera and Famine in British India, 1870–1930', *Centre for Development Studies Swansea Papers in International Development No. 14*, 1995.

67. Arnold, 'Cholera and Colonialism', p. 149; Sumit Guha, *Health and Population in South Asia: From Earliest Times to the Present* (Permanent Black, 2001); Ira Klein, 'Imperialism, Ecology and Disease: Cholera in India, 1850–1950', *Indian Economic and Social History Review*, 31 (4) (1994): 491–518.

68. Rajnarayan Chandavarkar, 'Plague Panic and Epidemic Politics in India, 1896–1914', in *Epidemics and Ideas: Essays on the Historical Perception of Pestilence*, eds. Terence Ranger and Paul Slack (Cambridge University Press, 1992), p. 211.

69. Gilmour, *The British in India*, p. 490.

70. Nandini Bhattacharya, *Contagion and Enclaves: Tropical Medicine in Colonial India* (Liverpool University Press, 2012), p. 30.

71. Chinmay Tumbe, *India Moving: A History of Migration* (Penguin Random House, 2018), Chapter 2.

72. See CT 2020, Table 3.2.

73. Pollitzer, *Cholera*, p. 81.

74. Y.B. Satyanarayana, *My Father Baliah* (HarperCollins, 2011), pp. 5 and 12.

75. Ibid., p. 12.

76. 'Unfit for Human Association', chapter 5 in *Collected Works of B.R. Ambedkar*, Vol. 5 (Government of Maharashtra, 1989; Dr. Ambedkar Foundation, 2014), p. 33.

77. Appendixes to the Third Report from the Select Committee of the House of Commons and Minutes of Evidence of the Affairs of the East-India Company, 17 February to 6 October 1831 (J.L. Cox and Sons, 1832).

78. Rosinka Chaudhuri, 'The Politics of Naming: Derozio in Two Formative Moments of Literary and Political Discourse, Calcutta, 1825–31', *Modern Asian Studies*, 44 (4) (2010): 857–85.

79. Roderick E. McGrew, 'The First Cholera Epidemic and Social History', *Bulletin of the History of Medicine*, 34 (1) (1960): pp. 61–62.

80. Pollitzer, *Cholera*, p. 22;

81. Richard J. Evans, 'Epidemics and Revolutions: Cholera in Nineteenth-Century Europe', in *Epidemics and Ideas: Essays on the Historical Perception of Pestilence*, eds. Terence Ranger and Paul Slack (Cambridge University Press, 1992), p. 160.

82. Ibid., p. 154.

83. Ibid., p. 156.

84. Ibid., pp. 157–58.

85. Ibid., pp. 42 and 60; See CT 2020, Table 3.5; S.L. Kotar and J.E. Gessler, *Cholera: A Worldwide History* (McFarland & Company, 2014), p. 37.

86. P. Kornhauser, 'The Cause of P.I. Tchaikovsky's (1840–1893) Death: Cholera, Suicide, or Both?', *Acta Medico-Historica Adriatica*, 8 (1) (2010); 145–72.

87. Kotar and Gessler, *Cholera*, pp. 36 and 69.

88. Ibid., p. 77.

89. Pollitzer, *Cholera*, p. 23.

90. 'Epidemic Cholera', *London Medico–Chirurgical Review*, 1832, as cited in McGrew, 'The First Cholera Epidemic', pp. 61–62.

91. Alavi, *Islam and Healing*, p. 336.

92. E.T. Renbourn, 'The history of the flannel binder and cholera belt', *Medical History*, 1 (3) (1957): pp. 211–25.

93. Kotar and Gessler, *Cholera*, pp. 354–55.

94. R.J. Davenport, M. Satchell, L.M.W. Shaw–Taylor, 'Cholera as a "sanitary test" of British cities, 1831–1866', *The History of the Family*, 24 (2) (2019): 404–38; See CT 2020, Table 3.5.

95. See CT 2020, Table 3.5; Kotar and Gessler, *Cholera*, p. 236.

96. Eric Hobsbawm, *The Age of Revolution, 1789–1848* (Vintage Books, 1962), pp. 183 and 203.

97. Blair Kling, *Partner in Empire: Dwarkanath Tagore and the Age of Enterprise in Eastern India* (University of California Press, 1976), p. 157.

98. Evans, 'Epidemics and Revolutions', p. 173.

99. A. Llopis and J. Halbrohr, 'Historical background of cholera in the Americas', *Epidemiological Bulletin*, 12 (1) (1991): pp. 10–12.

100. Kotar and Gessler, *Cholera*, p. 97.

101. Ibid.

102. Pollitzer, *Cholera*, p. 23.

103. Charles E. Rosenberg, *The Cholera Years: The United States in 1832, 1849 and 1866* (University of Chicago Press, 1962); John S. Chambers, *The Conquest of Cholera: America's Greatest Scourge* (Macmillan, 1938).

104. Kotar and Gessler, *Cholera*, p. 104.

105. John Wilford, 'How Epidemics Helped Shape the Modern Metropolis', *New York Times*, 15 April 2008.

106. Ibid.

107. Kotar and Gessler, *Cholera*, p. 112.

108. Kenneth Kiple, 'Cholera and Race in the Caribbean', *Journal of Latin American Studies*, 17 (1) (1985): 157–77.

109. Ibid., p. 169.

110. C.A. Hutchinson, 'The Asiatic Cholera Epidemic of 1833 in Mexico', *Bulletin of the History of Medicine*, 32 (1) (1958): 1–23.

111. Ibid., p. 5.

112. Ibid., p. 16.

113. Donald B. Cooper, 'The New "Black Death": Cholera in Brazil, 1855–1856', *Social Science History*, 10 (4) (1986): 467–88.

114. Ibid., p. 468.

115. Ibid., p. 472.

116. Ibid., p. 474.

117. Myron Echenberg, *Africa in the Time of Cholera: A History of Pandemics from 1817 to the Present* (Cambridge University Press, 2011), p. 16.

118. Justin McCarthy, 'Nineteenth-Century Egyptian Population', *Middle Eastern Studies*, 12 (3) (1976): 1–39.

119. Echenberg, *Africa in the Time of Cholera*, p. 74.

120. Ibid., p. 65.

121. Ibid., p. 57.

122. Ibid., pp. 53–57.

123. Ibid., p. 28.

124. Ahmad Seyf, 'Iran and Cholera in the Nineteenth Century', *Middle Eastern Studies*, 38 (1) (2002): 169–70. For Iran's tryst with cholera, also see Amir A. Afkhami, *A Modern Contagion: Imperialism and Public Health in Iran's Age of Cholera* (Johns Hopkins University Press, 2019).

125. William Johnston, 'Cholera and the Environment in Nineteenth-Century Japan', *Cross Currents: East Asian History and Culture Review*, 30 (2019): 22.

126. Julia Charlotte Maitland, *Letters from Madras During the Years 1836–1839 by a Lady* (John Murray, 1846), pp. 41–43. The book was published anonymously and she acquired her surname 'Maitland' only in the 1840s.

127. Hamlin, *Cholera*, pp. 153–55.

128. Ibid., p. 85.

129. John Snow, *On the Mode of Communication of Cholera* (John Churchill, 1849).

130. Ibid., p. 9.

131. Ibid.

132. Ibid., p. 11.

133. Hamlin, *Cholera*, p. 160; *London Journal of Medicine*, Vol. 1, (1849): 987.

134. Hamlin, *Cholera*, p. 160.

135. Ibid., p. 180.

136. Ibid., p. 180–81.

137. E.A. Parkes, as cited in Hamlin, *Cholera*, p. 189.

138. See CT 2020, Fig. 3.5; Ira Klein, 'Death in India, 1871–1921', *Journal of Asian Studies*, 32 (4) (1973): 650.

139. Hamlin, *Cholera*, p. 192.

140. Emma Grunberg, 'The Rationality of Inaccurate Science: Britain, Cholera, and the Pursuit of Progress in 1883', *Intersections,* 11 (1) (2010): 1–45.

141. Ibid., p. 2.

142. Hamlin, *Cholera*, p. 214.

143. Gerard Vallee, ed., *Florence Nightingale on Health in India* (Wilfrid Laurier, 2006); Jharna Gourlay, *Florence Nightingale and the Health of the Raj* (Ashgate, 2003).

144. Vallee, *Florence Nightingale*, p. 18.

145. Ibid., p. 166.

146. The phrase 'Anglo–Indian' in this book refers to British officers in India rather than its common usage today in terms of people with mixed ancestry.

147. Mark Harrison, 'The Great Shift: Cholera Theory and Sanitary Policy in British India, 1867–1879', in *Society, Medicine and Politics in Colonial India*, Pati and Harrison, p. 39.

148. Jeremy D. Isaacs, 'D D Cunningham and the Aetiology of Cholera in British India, 1869–1897', *Medical History*, 42 (1998): 279–305.

149. Ibid., p. 281.

150. M.C. Furnell, *Cholera and Water in India* (J. & A. Churchill, 1887).

151. Ibid., cover page and pp. 14–15.

152. Ibid., p. 3.

153. Ibid., pp. 17–18.

154. Ibid., p. 19.

155. Ibid., p. 9.

156. Poonam Bala, *Imperialism and Medicine in Bengal: A Socio-Historical Perspective* (Sage, 1991), p. 23.

157. Kautilya, *The Arthashastra*, ed. L.N. Rangarajan (Penguin, 1987), p. 370–71.

158. Ibid., pp. 373–74.

159. Sheldon Watts, 'From Rapid Change to Stasis: Official Responses to Cholera in British-Ruled India and Egypt: 1860 to c. 1921', *Journal of World History*, 12 (2) (2001): 372.

160. Ibid., p. 31.

161. As cited in Jaggi, *Medicine in India*, p. 88. More generally, Chapter 5 of the book provides details on 'insanitation, disease and remedial measures'.

162. Leonard Rogers, *Happy Toil* (Frederick Muller, 1950), p. 61, as cited in Jaggi, *Medicine in India*, p. 90.

163. As cited in Macnamara, *A History of Asiatic Cholera*, p. 277.

164. Ibid.

165. Ibid., p. 278.

166. Mishra, 'Hakims and Haiza', p. 67.

167. Ira Klein, 'Cholera: Theory and Treatment in Nineteenth Century India', *Journal of Indian History*, 58 (1980): 48–49.

168. Rogers, 'The Forecasting and Control'; Pollitzer, *Cholera*, pp. 78–81.

169. Amna Khalid, 'Of Cholera, Colonialism and Pilgrimage Sites: Rethinking Popular Responses to State Sanitation, c. 1867–1900', in *Society, Medicine and Politics in Colonial India*, Pati and Harrison.

170. Seyf, 'Iran and Cholera', pp. 169–170.

171. Leonard Rogers, *Cholera and its Treatment* (London, 1911), pp. 10, 15 and 27.

172. Arnold, 'Cholera and Colonialism', p. 141.

173. Norman Howard-Jones, *The Scientific Background of the International Sanitary Conferences, 1851–1938* (WHO, 1975).

174. Evans, 'Epidemics and Revolutions', pp. 166–170; Erwin H. Ackerknecht, 'Anticontagionism between 1821 and 1867', *Bulletin of the History of Medicine*, 22 (5) (1948): 562–93; 'Quarantine and Cholera', *Calcutta Review*, 48 (95) (1869): 118–66.

175. Evans, 'Epidemics and Revolutions', p. 167.

176. Harrison, 'The Great Shift', p. 37.

177. Ibid., p. 49–52.

178. Mark Harrison, 'Quarantine, Pilgrimage, and Colonial Trade: India, 1866–1900', *Indian Economic and Social History Review*, 29 (2) (1992): 143; Saurabh Mishra, *Pilgrimage, Politics and Pestilence: The Haj from the Indian Subcontinent, 1860–1920* (Oxford University Press, 2011).

179. John Slight, *The British Empire and the Hajj, 1865–1956* (Harvard University Press, 2015).

180. Valeska Huber, 'The Unification of the Globe by Disease? The International Sanitary Conferences on Cholera, 1851–1894', *The Historical Journal*, 49 (2) (2006): 453–76.

181. Howard-Jones, *The Scientific Background*, p. 11.

182. As cited in Norman Howard-Jones, 'Cholera Therapy in the Nineteenth Century', *Journal of the History of Medicine and Allied Sciences*, 27 (1972): 373.

183. Ibid.

184. Ibid., p. 376.

185. Ibid., p. 380.

186. Ibid., p. 383.

187. Ibid., p. 384.

188. Ibid., p. 373.

189. As cited by Mishra, 'Hakims and Haiza', p. 61.

190. Mishra, 'Hakims and Haiza', p. 66.

191. Ibid., p. 65.

192. Hamlin, *Cholera*, p. 237.

193. Barbara J. Hawgood, 'Waldemar Mordechai Haffkine, CIE (1860–1930): Prophylactic Vaccination against Cholera and Bubonic Plague in British India', *Journal of Medical Biography*, 15 (1) (2007): 9–19.

194. W.M. Haffkine, *Anti-Cholera Inoculation: Report to the Government of India* (Thacker Spink and Co, 1895).

195. Nikolas Gardner, 'Morale of the Indian Army in the Mesopotamia Campaign, 1914–17', in *The Indian Army in the Two World Wars*, ed. Kaushik Roy (Brill, 2012), pp. 399–400.

196. Arnold, 'Cholera Mortality', pp. 275–76.

197. Howard-Jones, 'Cholera Therapy', pp. 386.

198. Leonard, *Happy Toil*, pp. 140–44, as cited in Jaggi, *Medicine in India*, pp. 117–22.

199. Ibid.

200. Hamlin, *Cholera*, p. 73.

201. Fiona Bateman, 'An Irish Missionary in India: Thomas Gavan Duffy and the Catechist of Kil–Arni', in *Ireland and India: Colonies, Culture and Empire*, eds. Tadhg Foley and Maureen O'Connor (Irish Academic Press, 2006).

202. Sambhu Nath De, *Cholera: Its Pathology and Pathogenesis* (Oliver and Boyd, 1961).

203. Hamlin, *Cholera*, pp. 257–58.

204. Ibid., p. 268.

205. S. Almagro-Moreno and R.K. Taylor, 'Cholera: Environmental Reservoirs and Impact on Disease Transmission', *Microbiology Spectrum*, 1 (2) (2013): 1.

206. Ibid., p. 11.

207. Rogers, 'The Forecasting and Control of Cholera Epidemics in India', would be a good starting point to re–analyse the complexities of cholera outbreaks in India. Johnston, 'Cholera and the Environment', provides some clues to how this can be done.

208. As cited in Hamlin, *Cholera*, p. 72.

209. See CT 2020, Table 1.1. Based on an analysis of ProQuest Historical Newspapers: The *Times of India* Digital Database.

210. See CT 2020, Table 3.5, and the detailed notes therein.

3: Plague

1. Mu'tamad Khan's *Ikbal-nama*, as cited in W.J. Simpson, *A Treatise on Plague* (Cambridge University Press, 1905), p. 41.

2. See CT 2020, Table 5.3; L.F. Hirst, *The Conquest of Plague: A Study of the Evolution of Epidemiology* (Oxford University Press, 1953), p. 300; Myron Echenberg, 'Pestis Redux: The Initial Years of the Third Bubonic Plague Pandemic, 1894–1901', *Journal of World History*, 13 (2) (2002): 429–49.

3. Ian J. Catanach, 'The "Globalization" of Disease? India and the Plague', *Journal of World History*, 12 (1) (2001): 131–53.

4. David E. Davis, 'The Scarcity of Rats and the Black Death: An Ecological History', *Journal of Interdisciplinary History*, 16 (3) (1986): 455–70.

5. As cited in Lucy Taksa, 'The Masked Disease: Oral History, Memory and the Influenza Pandemic, 1918–19', in *Memory and History in Twentieth-Century Australia*, eds. Kate Darian–Smith and Paula Hamilton (Oxford University Press, 1994), pp. 77–91.

6. Kautilya, *The Arthashastra*, ed. L.N. Rangarajan (Penguin, 1987), pp. 130–31.

7. As cited in Simpson, *A Treatise on Plague*, p. 40.

8. Simpson, *A Treatise on Plague*, pp. 41–44. References to plague in India, using Persian or Arabic sources before the seventeenth century in Simpson's work may need revision in light of the research presented for the fourteenth century by George D. Sussman, 'Was the Black Death in India and China?', *Bulletin of the History of Medicine*, 85 (3) (2011): 319–55.

9. Simpson, *A Treatise on Plague*, pp. 41–44.

10. Ibid.

11. Aparna Nair, 'An Egyptian Infection': War, Plague and Quarantines of the English East India Company at Madras and Bombay, 1802', *Hygiea Internationlis*, 8 (1) (2009): 7–29.

12. Ibid., pp. 10–13.

13. Ibid., pp. 14–18.

14. Ibid., pp. 18–19.

15. J.E. Johnson, *An Address to the Public on the Advantages of a Steam Navigation to India* (D. Sidney & Co., 1824).

16. Simpson, *A Treatise on Plague*, p. 46.

17. Ibid., p. 46; R. Nathan, *The Plague in India, 1896, 1897, Vol II* (Simla, 1898), pp. 82–106.

18. Simpson, *A Treatise on Plague*, pp. 39 and 46.

19. Ibid., pp. 48–49.

20. Ibid., p. 54.

21. Ibid., p. 59.

22. Ibid., p. 62.

23. J.A. Turner, *Sanitation in India* (Bombay, third edition: 1922; first edition: 1914), p. 477.

24. W.G. Liston, 'Plague, Rats, and Fleas', *Indian Medical Gazette* (February 1905), pp. 43–49.

25. George Lambert, *India: The Horror-stricken Empire Containing a Full Account of the Famine, Plague and Earthquake of 1896–7* (Mennonite Publishing Co., 1898).

26. See CT 2020, Table 8.1.

27. Simpson, *A Treatise on Plague*, p. 66–67.

28. B.F. Patell, *History of the Plague in Bombay* (Caxton Works, c. 1897–99), p. 7.

29. Ian J. Catanach, 'The Globalization of Disease'.

30. Simpson, *A Treatise on Plague*, p. 67; Kalpish Ratna, *Room 000: Narratives of the Bombay Plague* (Macmillan India, 2015).

31. Patell, *History of the Plague in Bombay*, p. 9.

32. H.M. Birdwood, 'The Plague in Bombay', *Journal of the Society for Arts*, 46 (2362) (1898): 326.

33. Ibid., p. 327; W.F. Gatacre, *Report of the Bubonic Plague in Bombay* (Times of India Steam Press, 1897), p. 41.

34. David Arnold, 'Disease, Rumour, and Panic in India's Plague and Influenza Epidemics, 1896–1919', in *Empires of Panic: Epidemics and Colonial Anxieties*, ed. Robert Peckham (Hong Kong University Press, 2015), p. 113.

35. Birdwood, 'The Plague in Bombay,' p. 323.

36. Ibid., p. 321.

37. Ibid., p. 324.

38. On the plague and railways, including a list of inspection stations across India, see Ritika Prasad, *Tracks of Change: Railways and Everyday Life in Colonial India* (Cambridge University Press, 2015), pp. 181–91.

39. Gatacre, *Report of the Bubonic Plague in Bombay*, p. 4.

40. Ibid., pp. 129–32.

41. Ibid., p. 134.

42. Birdwood, 'The Plague in Bombay,' p. 323.

43. Prashant Kidambi, 'An Infection of Locality: Plague, Pythogenesis and the Poor in Bombay, c. 1896–1905', *Urban History*, 31 (2) (2004): 249–67.

44. Arnold, 'Disease, Rumour, and Panic', p. 117.

45. David Arnold, *Colonizing the Body: State Medicine and Epidemic Disease in Nineteenth-Century India*, (University of California Press, 1993), pp. 216–17; Rajnarayan Chandavarkar, 'Plague Panic and Epidemic Politics in India, 1896–1914', in *Epidemics and Ideas: Essays on the Historical Perception of Pestilence*, eds. Terence Ranger and Paul Slack (Cambridge University Press, 1992), p. 220.

46. Arnold, 'Disease, Rumour and Panic', p. 116.

47. Simpson, *A Treatise on Plague*, p. 68.

48. Birdwood, 'The Plague in Bombay', p. 312.

49. Ibid.; In sixteenth-century Italy, the evacuation remedy was offered by a physician, translated as 'run swiftly, go far, and return slowly', as cited in Echenberg, 'Pestis Redux', p. 438.

50. Ibid.

51. Birdwood, 'The Plague in Bombay', p. 317–18; Gatacre, *Report of the Bubonic Plague in Bombay*, p. 53.

52. Ira Klein, 'Plague, Policy and Popular Unrest in British India', *Modern Asian Studies*, 22 (4) (1988): 729.

53. Ibid.

54. Gatacre, *Report of the Bubonic Plague in Bombay*, pp. 52–53.

55. Ibid.

56. Ibid., p. 69.

57. Ibid., p. 114.

58. Birdwood, 'The Plague in Bombay,' p. 310; J.K. Condon, *The Bombay Plague: A History of the Progress of Plague in the Bombay Presidency from September 1896 to June 1899* (Education Society's Steam Press, 1900), p. 61, shows case mortality rates across districts in Bombay Presidency for 1896–99.

59. 'Plague and the Results of Vaccination', *Swasthya*, June–July issue, 1898, as cited in Pradip Kumar Bose, ed., *Health and Society in Bengal: A Selection from Late 19th Century Bengali Periodicals* (Sage, 2006), p. 211.

60. Birdwood, 'The Plague in Bombay', p. 313.

61. Arnold, 'Disease, Rumour, and Panic', p. 116.

62. As cited in Ian J. Catanach, 'Plague and the Indian Village, 1896–1914', in P. Robb (ed.), *Rural India Land, Power and Society under British Rule* (Curzon Press, 1983), p. 220.

63. Arnold, *Colonizing the Body*, p. 207.

64. Chandavarkar, 'Plague panic', p. 230.

65. As cited in Ibid., p. 209.

66. Gatacre, *Report of the Bubonic Plague in Bombay*, p. 153.

67. Ibid., p. 158.

68. Simpson, *A Treatise on Plague*, pp. 69–70.

69. Reeta and Vinit Raj, *First Indian Woman Teacher: Biography of Savitribai Phule* (Educreation Publishing, 2018), p. 10; Nitin Brahme, 'When Savitribai fought plague,' *Pune Mirror*, 21 Aug 2009.

70. Meera Kosambi, *Pandita Ramabai: Life and Landmark Writings* (Routledge, 2016), pp. 231–35.

71. Ibid., p. 233.

72. Arnold, *Colonizing the Body*, pp. 226–28.

73. Chandavarkar, 'Plague Panic', p. 221.

74. Ibid.; Ian J. Catanach, 'Poona Politicians and the Plague', in *Struggling and Ruling: The Indian National Congress, 1885–1985*, ed. J. Masselos (New Delhi, 1987), p. 198.

75. Arnold, *Colonizing the Body*, p. 224.

76. Ibid., p. 226.

77. S.C. Seal, *Plague: Conquest and Eradication in India* (Indian Council of Medical Research, 1987), p. 22.

78. CT 2020, Tables 5.1 and 8.1. See also, Norman White, *Twenty Years of Plague in India with Special Reference to the Outbreak of 1917–18* (Simla, 1920).

79. K.R.G. Aiyar, 'Plague in Belgaum', *Times of India*, p. 5.

80. Seal, *Plague*, p. 18.

81. Ibid., p. 23.

82. Catanach, 'The "Globalization" of Disease', p. 144.

83. Ibid., p. 146.

84. Seal, *Plague*, p. 25; Hwa-Lung Yu and George Christakos, 'Spatiotemporal Modelling and Mapping of the Bubonic Plague Epidemic in India', *International Journal of Health Geographics*, 5 (12) (2006): 1–15.

85. See CT 2020, Table 5.2.

86. See CT 2020, Figures 5.2 and 5.3.

87. Ira Klein, 'Death in India, 1871–1921', *Journal of Asian Studies*, 32 (4) (1973): 652.

88. Chandavarkar, 'Plague Panic', p. 219.

89. Charles Creighton, 'Plague in India', *Journal of the Society of Arts*, 53 (2743) (1905): 810–32.

90. Condon, "The Bombay Plague', p. 198.

91. Vinayak Chaturvedi, 'The Making of a Peasant King in Colonial Western India: The Case of Ranchod Vira', *Past & Present*, 192 (2006): 155–85.

92. Douglas Haynes, 'Market Formation in Khandesh, c. 1820–1930', *Indian Economic and Social History Review*, 36 (3) (1999): 285–89.

93. David Arnold, *Everyday Technology: Machines and the Making of India's Modernity* (University of Chicago Press, 2013), p. 71.

94. Ibid., p. 131.

95. Howard Spodek, 'Sardar Vallabhbhai Patel at 100', *Economic & Political Weekly*, 10 (50) (1975): 1933–1935.

96. P.D. Saggi, ed., *Life and Work of Sardar Vallabhbhai Patel* (Overseas Publishing House, 1953), pp. vii, 13 and 31.

97. Ibid., p. 35.

98. See CT 2020, Table 5.2.

99. See CT 2020, Figure 5.3; Seal (1987), Table 2, p. 13.

100. C.H. James, *Report on the Outbreak of Plague in the Jullundur and Hoshiarpur Districts* (Lahore, 1898), p. 1.

101. Ibid., p. 16.

102. Aanchal Malhotra, 'When the 1897 bubonic plague ravaged India', *Mint*, 26 April 2020; Sasha, *Social History of Epidemics in the Colonial Punjab* (Partridge, 2014).

103. Arnold, *Colonizing the Body*, pp. 230–31.

104. Catanach, 'Plague and the Indian Village', pp. 224–225.

105. Ibid., p. 226.

106. Ira Klein, 'Death in India, 1871–1921', *Journal of Asian Studies*, 32 (4) (1973): 653.

107. Catanach, 'Plague and the Indian Village', p. 224.

108. Arnold, *Colonizing the Body*, p. 234.

109. Ibid.

110. Mridula Ramanna, *Health Care in Bombay Presidency, 1896–1930* (Primus Books, 2012), p. 29.

111. Ian J. Catanach, 'Plague and the Tensions of Empire, 1896–1918', in *Imperial Medicine and Indigenous Societies*, ed. David Arnold (Oxford University Press 1989), pp. 160–61.

112. See CT 2020, Figure 5.3.

113. Annual Report of the Sanitary Commissioner with the Government of India for the Year 1907 (Calcutta, 1908), p. 87.

114. N. Gerald Barrier, 'The Punjab Disturbances of 1907: The Response of the British Government in India to Agrarian Unrest', *Modern Asian Studies*, 1 (4) (1967): 363.

115. Catanach, 'Plague and the Indian Village', p. 225.

116. Neeladri Bhattacharya, *The Great Agrarian Conquest: The Colonial Reshaping of a Rural World* (State University of New York Press, 2019), p. 403.

117. Ibid., p. 229.

118. Article on Plague Rules, *Naiyar-i-Azam* (Moradabad), 19 March 1897 (Selections from the Vernacular Newspapers Published in the Panjab, North-Western Provinces, Oudh, Central Provinces and Berar; South Asia Open Archives).

119. As cited in Arnold, *Colonizing the Body*, p. 223.

120. Ibid., p. 221.

121. Ibid., p. 214; Ian Catanach, 'South Asian Muslims and the Plague, 1896–c. 1914', *South Asia: Journal of South Asian Studies*, 22 (S1) (1999): 89–90.

122. A.R. Sen, *Vital Statistics in United Provinces: A Critical Analysis of Forty Years Data* (Allahabad, 1948), p. 17.

123. Catanach, 'Plague and the Indian Village', p. 218.

124. Sen, *Vital Statistics*, p. 30.

125. Ibid., p. 37.

126. Creighton, 'Plague in India', p. 822.

127. See CT 2020, Table 5.2.

128. Census of India 1951, Vol. 1, Part 1–B, Appendix IV, 'Famine and Pestilence', Government of India, 1955, p. 283.

129. 'Plague Work in Mysore', *Times of India,* 8 March 1900, p. 4.

130. Ibid.

131. Janaki Nair, 'Dangerous Labour: Crime, Work and Punishment in Kolar Gold Fields, 1890–1946', *Studies in History,* 13 (1) (1997): 44.

132. As reported in 'Plague Work in Mysore', *Times of India,* 8 March 1900, p. 4.

133. S. Narendra Prasad, 'When Plague Struck Mysore State', *Deccan Herald,* 11 Nov 2014.

134. 'Plague in Mysore: Official Report', *Times of India,* 13 April 1911.

135. 'Plague in the Nizam's Dominions', *Times of India,* 23 Feb 1898, p. 4.

136. Ibid.

137. 'Plague in Hyderabad: Mob at the Palace', *Times of India,* 19 Sep 1911, p. 8.

138. Census of India 1951, 'Famine and Pestilence', p. 285.

139. See CT 2020, Table 5.2.

140. Alok Sheel, 'Bubonic Plague in South Bihar: Gaya and Shahabad Districts, 1900–1924', *Indian Economic and Social History Review,* 35 (4) (1998): 425.

141. Ian Catanach, '"The Gendered Terrain of Disaster"?: India and the Plague, c. 1896–1918', *South Asia: Journal of South Asian Studies,* 30 (2) (2007): 253–55.

142. Mary P. Sutphen, 'Not What, but Where: Bubonic Plague and the Reception of Germ Theories in Hong Kong and Calcutta, 1894–1897', *Journal of the History of Medicine,* 52 (1997): 106.

143. Anindita Ghosh, *Claiming the City: Protest, Crime, and Scandals in Colonial Calcutta,* c. 1860–1920 (Oxford University Press, 2016), pp. 273–78.

144. Ibid.

145. 'Plague and Devotional Song', *Swasthya,* March–April issue, 1900, as cited in Pradip Kumar Bose, ed., *Health and Society,* p. 225.

146. Seal, *Plague,* p. 41–50.

147. J. Taylor, *The Epidemiology of Plague in Madras Presidency India* (Glasgow University M.D. Thesis, 1913), pp. 1–4. See also, Vempalli

Raj Mahammadh, 'Plague Mortality and Control Policies in Colonial South India, 1900–47', *South Asia Research*, 40 (3) (2020): 1–21.

148. Taylor, *The Epidemiology of Plague*, conclusion section.

149. 'Report of the Haffkine Institute for the Year 1930', *Indian Medical Gazette*, 67, pp. 476–77, as cited in Arnold, 'Disease, Rumour, and Panic', p. 117.

150. 'The Plague in India and the Duty of the State', *The Modern Review*, 9 (1) (1911): 502.

151. Ibid., pp. 507–08.

152. Based on the regions highlighted for high plague intensity in various health reports and the map provided by Creighton, 'Plague in India', p. 811.

153. Lakshmibai Tilak, *Smritichitre* (Originally published in Marathi in two volumes in 1934 and 1936; translated by Shanta Gokhale through Speaking Tiger, 2017), pp. 207–13 and 257–68.

154. Ibid., p. 208.

155. Ibid., p. 259.

156. Ibid., p. 261.

157. Ibid., p. 263.

158. Creighton, 'Plague in India', pp. 810–32.

159. Ibid., p. 823.

160. Ibid., p. 823.

161. Ibid., p. 824.

162. Ibid., p. 824.

163. Annual Report of the Sanitary Commissioner with the Government of India for 1907 (Calcutta, 1908), p. 45.

164. Arnold, 'Disease, Rumour and Panic', p. 118.

165. As cited in, Ibid.

166. As cited in, Ibid.

167. As cited in Catanach, 'Plague and the Tensions of Empire', p. 162.

168. Report on the Municipal Administration of Calcutta for the Year 1900–1901, Part I (Calcutta, 1901), p. 5.

169. W.G. Liston, 'Plague, Rats, and Fleas', *Indian Medical Gazette* (February 1905): 43–49.

170. 'Posthumous Presentation of the 1971 Karl F. Meyer Award [to Liston]', *Journal of the Royal Army Medical Corps,* 119 (1) (1973): 49–56.
171. Liston, 'Plague, Rats, and Fleas', p. 46.
172. 'Posthumous Presentation', p. 49.
173. Turner, *Sanitation in India,* p. 478.
174. Ibid., pp. 472–76.
175. Ibid., p. 486.
176. Ibid., p. 479.
177. Ibid., p. 479.
178. Ibid., p. 479.
179. Ibid., pp. 493–94.
180. Ibid., pp. 496–98.
181. Ibid., p. 497–500.
182. Ibid., p. 498.
183. Personal communication with Basav Biradar, based on his research.
184. Sheel, 'Bubonic Plague', pp. 439–40.
185. Rupsa Chakraborty, 'Now, BMC has rat killers working through the night', *Mid-day,* 18 July 2018.
186. Turner, *Sanitation in India,* p. 489.
187. Ibid., p. 490.
188. Ibid., p. 492.
189. Klein, 'Plague, Policy and Popular Unrest', p. 753.
190. Turner, *Sanitation in India,* p. 506.
191. Projit Bihari Mukharji, 'Cat and Mouse: Animal Technologies, Trans-Imperial Networks and Public Health from Below, British India, c. 1907–1918', *Social History of Medicine,* 31 (3): 510–532.
192. R. Pollitzer, *Plague* (WHO Monograph Series No. 22, Geneva, 1954), p. 300.
193. Mukharji, 'Cat and Mouse', p. 517.
194. Ibid., p. 520.
195. Ibid., p. 522.
196. Ibid., p. 529.
197. Ibid., p. 529.

198. For instance, see B.G. Weniger, A.J. Warren, V. Forseth, et. al. 'Human Bubonic Plague Transmitted by a Domestic Cat Scratch', *Journal of the American Medical Association*, 251 (1) (1984): 927–28.

199. 'Cats Should Kill Rats! Jain Argument at Ahmedabad', *Times of India*, 25 April 1936, as cited in Mukharji, 'Cat and Mouse', p. 520.

200. Based on an analysis of cases on plague in Indiakanoon.org. Bombay High Court> D.K. Shrotri vs N.V. Ashtekar on 6 September 1910.

201. (1911) 13 BOMLR 38, Bombay High Court, D.K. Shrotri vs N.V. Ashtekar on 6 September 1910.

202. O.M. Vijayan, *After the Hanging and Other Stories* (Penguin, 1989; translated from Malayalam by the author), pp. 61–76. Separately, 'The yakshi crosses the moat', *Kerala Studies*, 12 (12) 1977.

203. Catanach, 'Poona Politicians and the Plague', pp. 198–215.

204. Ibid., p. 208.

205. Ibid.

206. Chandavarkar, 'Plague Panic', p. 239. United Provinces referred to as North-West Provinces therein.

207. Catanach, 'Poona Politicians and the Plague', p. 208.

208. S. Sivasubramonian, *The National Income of India in the Twentieth Century* (Oxford University Press, 2000).

209. Statistical Abstract of British India, 1910–11.

210. Rusi Daruwala, *The Bombay Chamber Story–150 Years* (Bombay Chamber of Commerce & Industry, 1986), p. 55.

211. Statistical Abstract of British India, 1905–06.

212. Amiya Kumar Bagchi, *Private Investment in India, 1900–1939* (Cambridge University Press, 1972), p. 9 and 69.

213. S. Muthiah, *The Spencer Legend* (Eastwest Books, 1997), p. 181.

214. Catanach, 'Poona Politicians and the Plague', p. 207.

215. Aditya Sarkar, 'The Tie that Snapped: Bubonic Plague and Mill Labour in Bombay, 1896–1898,' *International Review of Social History*, 59 (2014): 181–214.

216. *Times of India*, 10 May 1897, as cited in Sarkar, 'The Tie that Snapped', p. 194.

217. Achyut Yagnik and Suchitra Sheth, *Ahmedabad: From Royal City to Megacity* (Penguin, 2001), p. 200.

218. Arnold, *Colonizing the Body*, p. 229.

219. K.N. Singh, *Urban Development in India* (Abhinav Publications, 1978), p. 34; James Heitzman, *The City in South Asia* (Routledge, 2008), p. 158.

220. Heitzman, *The City in South Asia*, pp. 158–159; Prashant Kidambi, *The Making of a Metropolis: Colonial Governance and Public Culture in Bombay, 1890–1920* (Ashgate, 2007), pp. 71–114.

221. Shanta Gokhale, *Shivaji Park – Dadar 28: History, Places, People* (Speaking Tiger, 2020).

222. Serish Nanisetti, 'Plague Passports Please', *The Hindu*, 3 July 2020; Syed Akbar, 'Plague Changed Hyderabad's Landscape', *Times of India*, 2 May 2020.

223. Creighton, 'Plague in India', pp. 826–27.

224. U.R. Ananthamurthy, *Samskara: A Rite for a Dead Man* (Oxford University Press, 1976, originally published in Kannada in 1965; translated by A. K. Ramanujan), p. 5.

225. Ibid., p. 17.

226. Ibid., p. 36.

227. Ibid., pp. 45 and 50.

228. Ibid., pp. 45 and 52.

229. Ibid., pp. 81 and 108.

230. Brahme, 'When Savitribai fought plague'.

231. Catanach, 'Poona Politicians and the Plague', p. 198.

232. Shanta Gokhale, *Crowfall* (Penguin, 2013).

233. Naresh Fernandes, *City Adrift: A Short Biography of Bombay* (Aleph, 2013), pp. 10–12.

234. Hirst, *The Conquest of Plague*, p. 300; CT 2020, Table 5.3.

235. Ibid.; Robert Pollitzer, *Plague* (WHO Monograph Series No. 22, Geneva, 1954), pp. 32 and 39.

236. On China, see Carol A. Benedict, *Bubonic Plague in Nineteenth-Century China* (Stanford University Press, 1996).

237. Angus Maddison, *Contours of the World Economy, 1–2030 AD* (Oxford University Press, 2007), Table A2, p. 377.

238. Ibid., Table A5, p. 380.

239. Myron Echenberg, *Plague Ports: The Global Urban Impact of Bubonic Plague, 1894–1901* (New York University Press, 2007), p. 79.

240. Ibid.

241. Norman Howard-Jones, *The Scientific Background of the International Sanitary Conferences, 1851–1938* (WHO, 1975), p. 78.

242. Ibid.

243. Ibid., p. 79.

244. Echenberg, *Plague Ports*, p. 80.

245. Simpson, *A Treatise on Plague*, p. 75.

246. Ibid.

247. Echenberg, 'Pestis Redux', p. 446.

248. Francis Dube, 'Public Health and Racial Segregation in South Africa: Mahatma (M.K) Gandhi Debates Colonial Authorities on Public Health Measures, 1896–1904', *Journal of the Historical Society of Nigeria*, 21 (2012): 27–28.

249. Ibid., p. 32; Rajmohan Gandhi, 'How a remark by a doctor in Wuhan evoked Gandhi's efforts, why it matters', *Indian Express*, 6 June 2020.

250. Echenberg, 'Pestis Redux', p. 447.

251. Ibid., pp. 445–46.

252. Hirst, *The Conquest of Plague*, p. 298.

253. Echenberg, 'Pestis Redux', p. 445.

254. Ibid., p. 444.

255. Lucy Taksa, 'Pandemics bring social pain, too', *Unleashed*, 30 April 2009.

256. Liston, 'Plague, Rats, and Fleas', p. 48.

257. Echenberg, 'Pestis Redux', p. 444.

258. Ibid., p. 448.

259. Ibid., p. 447.

260. Hirst, *The Conquest of Plague*, p. 302.

261. I. Snapper, 'Medical Contributions from the Netherlands Indies', in *South East Asia: Colonial History*, ed. Paul H. Kratoska (Routledge, 2001), p. 141.

262. Ibid., p. 143.

263. Ibid., p. 144.
264. Ibid., p. 145.
265. Hirst, *The Conquest of Plague*, p. 298.
266. Pollitzer, *Plague*, p. 28; Mark Gamsa, 'The Epidemic of Pneumonic Plague in Manchuria, 1910–11', *Past & Present*, 190 (2006): 147–83.
267. Gamsa, 'The Epidemic', p. 156.
268. Ibid., p. 153.
269. Lukas Engelmann and Christos Lynteris, *Sulphuric Utopias: A History of Maritime Fumigation* (MIT Press, 2020).
270. Annual Report of the Health Officer of the Port of Bombay for the Year Ending 31st December 1903 (Bombay, 1904), p. 6.
271. Echenberg, 'Pestis Redux', p. 434.
272. Turner, *Sanitation in India*, p. 488.
273. Klein, 'Plague, Policy and Popular Unrest', p. 754; Seal, *Plague*, p. 18.
274. Pollitzer, *Plague*, p. 242.
275. Figures are from Seal, *Plague*, 1987, Table 1, p. 11, scaled up by a factor of 1.2, to correct for under–registration. See CT 2020 for discussion on scaling factor.
276. Dileep Mavalankar, 'Indian "Plague" Epidemic: Unanswered Questions and Key Lessons', *Journal of the Royal Society of Medicine*, 88 (October 1995): 547–51.
277. Ibid., p. 547.
278. Catanach, '"Globalization" of Disease', p. 150.
279. WHO URL: https://www.who.int/news–room/fact–sheets/detail/plague, Accessed on 29 June 2020.

4: Influenza

1. Norman White, *A Preliminary Report on the Influenza Pandemic of 1918 in India* (Government of India Press, 1919), pp. 8–9, citing the official report from Punjab; Punjab Sanitary Board Report for 1918, 'The Influenza Epidemic of 1918 in Punjab', Lahore, p. xi.
2. See CT 2020, Tables 6.2 and 6.3 for the range of estimates on influenza mortality in India and the world respectively. See Section 6 for my method of estimating 20 million deaths, using the inter-censal

method, including data on the princely states, that had been left out
by most previous studies.

3. Robert Barro, Jose Ursua and Joanna Weng, 'The Coronavirus and
    the Great Influenza Epidemic: Lessons from the "Spanish Flu" for the
    coronavirus' potential effects on mortality and economic activity' in
    American Enterprise Institute Economics Working Paper, 2020–02 (March
    2020); See CT 2020, Section 6.

4. Stephen Broadberry and Mark Harrison, 'The Economics of World
    War I: An Overview', in *The Economics of World War I*, eds. Stephen
    Broadberry and Mark Harrison (Cambridge University Press, 2005),
    p. 27.

5. Norman White, 'Retrospect', *Transactions of the Royal Society of
    Tropical Medicine and Hygiene*, 47 (6) (1953): 441–50.

6. Ibid., p. 441.

7. See CT 2020, Figure 7.1; Refers to June–September rainfall.

8. Arnold Bennett, *The Card: A Story of Adventure in Five Towns* (Penguin,
    1975; first edition: 1911), p. 134.

9. John Rhodes, *The End of Plagues: The Global Battle Against Infectious
    Disease* (Palgrave Macmillan, 2013), p. 143.

10. Alfred Crosby, 'Influenza', in *Cambridge History of Human Disease,* ed.
    Kenneth Kiple (Cambridge University Press, 1993), p. 808.

11. Ibid., p. 809.

12. Ibid., p. 810.

13. Gina Kolata, *Flu: The Story of the Great Influenza Pandemic of 1918 and
    the Search for the Virus that Caused It* (Touchstone, 1999).

14. Jeffery K. Taubenberger, Ann Reid, Amy Krafft, Karen Bijwaard
    and Thomas Fanning, 'Initial Genetic Characterisation of the 1918
    "Spanish" Influenza Virus', *Science*, 275 (March 21) (1997): 1793–96.

15. Ibid., p. 1793.

16. T. Tumpey, C.F. Basler, P.V. Aguilar, H. Zeng, A. Solorzano, D.E.
    Swayne, N.J. Cox, J.M. Katz, J.K. Taubenberger, P. Palese, A. Garcia–
    Sastre, 'Characterisation of the Reconstructed 1918 Spanish Influenza
    Pandemic Virus', *Science*, 310 (5745) (2005): 77–80.

17. Howard Phillips and David Killingray, Introduction to *The Spanish Influenza Pandemic of 1918–19: New Perspectives*, eds. Howard Phillips and David Killingray (Routledge, 2003), p. 5; John Barry, 'The Site of Origin of the 1918 Influenza Pandemic and its Public Health Implications', *Journal of Translational Medicine*, 2 (1) (2004).

18. Barro, Ursua and Weng, 'The Coronavirus and the Great Influenza Epidemic', p. 2.

19. Phillips and Killingray, 'Introduction', p. 5.

20. Alfred Crosby, *America's Forgotten Pandemic: The Influenza of 1918* (Cambridge University Press, 2003, Second Edition), p. 37.

21. Phillips and Killingray, 'Introduction', p. 6.

22. Crosby, *America's Forgotten Pandemic*, p. 38.

23. Ibid.

24. Ibid., p. 39.

25. Phillips and Killingray, 'Introduction', p. 7; Barro, Ursua and Weng, 'The Coronavirus and the Great Influenza Epidemic', Table 1.

26. Fred Hoyle and Chandra Wickramasinghe, 'Influenza from Space?', *New Scientist*, 28 September 1978. While this first article did not mention 1918, subsequent articles did.

27. Phillips and Killingray, 'Introduction', p. 4.

28. Barro, Ursua and Weng, 'The Coronavirus and the Great Influenza Epidemic', Table 1.

29. See CT 2020, Section 6.

30. Amir Afkhami, 'Compromised Constitutions: The Iranian Experience with the 1918 Influenza Pandemic', *Bulletin of the History of Medicine*, 77 (2) (2003): 383.

31. Barro, Ursua and Weng, 'The Coronavirus and the Great Influenza Epidemic', Table 1; David Killingray, 'A New "Imperial Disease": The Influenza Pandemic of 1918–19 and its Impact on the British Empire', *Caribbean Quarterly*, 49 (4) (2003): 30–49.

32. Phillips and Killingray, 'Introduction', p. 7.

33. Barro, Ursua and Weng, 'The Coronavirus and the Great Influenza Epidemic', Table 1; Crosby, 'Influenza', p. 810.

34. See CT 2020, Tables 6.2 and 6.3 on India and the world, respectively.

35. Census of India 1951, Vol. 1, Part 1–B, Appendix IV, 'Famine and Pestilence', Government of India, 1955, p. 290.

36. Ibid.

37. See CT 2020, Section 6.

38. Ibid.

39. Census of India 1951, Vol. 1, Part 1–B, Appendix IV 'Famine and Pestilence', Government of India, 1955, p. 273, 275, 292; Tirthankar Roy, *Natural Disasters and Indian History* (Oxford University Press, 2012), p. 30. See CT 2020, Table 8.1.

40. CT 2020, Section 1.

41. I.D. Mills. 'The 1918–19 Influenza Pandemic – The Indian Experience', *Indian Economic and Social History Review*, 23 (1) (1986): 1–40; Siddharth Chandra and Eva Kassens–Noor, 'The Evolution of Pandemic Influenza: Evidence from India, 1918–19', *BMC Infectious Diseases*, 14 (510) (2014): 1–10; Olivia Reyes, Elizabeth C. Lee, Pratha Sah, Cecile Viboud, Siddharth Chandra and Shweta Bansal, 'Spatiotemporal Patterns and Diffusion of the 1918 Influenza Pandemic in British India', *American Journal of Epidemiology* 187 (12) (2018): 2550–60.

42. Mills, 'The 1918–19 Influenza Pandemic', p. 13.

43. Glen Liston, 'Influenza Epidemics: History and Experience', *Times of India,* 11 October 1918, p. 8.

44. Ibid.

45. White, 'A Preliminary Report', p. 7.

46. Mridula Ramanna, 'Coping with the Influenza Pandemic: The Bombay Experience', in *The Spanish Influenza Pandemic*, Killingray and Phillips, pp. 87–88.

47. 'The Fever Epidemic', *Times of India*, 25 June 1918.

48. Ibid.

49. 'The Spread of Influenza', *Times of India,* 19 October 1918; 'Six Million Deaths', *Times of India*, 6 March 1919.

50. Lakshmibai Tilak, *Smritichitre* (originally published in Marathi in two volumes in 1934 and 1936; translated by Shanta Gokhale; Speaking Tiger, 2017), p. 410.

51. Ibid., p. 410.
52. Ibid., pp. 410–411.
53. Mills, 'The 1918–19 Influenza Pandemic'.
54. Census of India, 1921, as cited in Mills, 'The 1918–19 Influenza Pandemic', p. 23.
55. Bombay Municipal Commissioner's Report as cited in Mills, 'The 1918–19 Influenza Pandemic', p. 33.
56. 'The Condition of the Convert', chapter 30 in *Collected Works of B.R. Ambedkar*, Vol. 5 (Government of Maharashtra, 1989; Dr. Ambedkar Foundation, 2014), p. 452.
57. White, 'A Preliminary Report', p. 8; J.T. Marten, 'The Census of India of 1921', *Journal of the Royal Society of Arts*, 71 (3672) (1923): 362.
58. 'Bombay Influenza', *Times of India*, 10 October 1918, p. 5.
59. White, 'A Preliminary Report', p. 2; 'The World Wide Epidemic', *Times of India*, 18 September 1918, p. 5.
60. Letter to the Editor, *Times of India*, 18 October 1918, p. 8.
61. 'Chief of Manavadar Dead', *Times of India*, 22 October 1918, p. 8.
62. Ramachandra Guha, *Gandhi: The Years that Changed the World, 1914–1948* (Penguin Random House, 2018), p. 73.
63. Gopalkrishna Gandhi, 'Gandhi at the time of the Spanish flu,' *Telegraph India*, 19 April 2020.
64. David Hardiman, 'The Influenza Epidemic of 1918 and the *Adivasis* of Western India', *Social History of Medicine*, 25 (3) (2012): 644–64.
65. Ibid., p. 647.
66. 'Dead in Trains', *Times of India*, 12 October 1918, p. 10.
67. 'Influenza in Goa', *Times of India*, 5 October 1918, p. 10.
68. Ramanna, 'Coping with the Influenza Pandemic', p. 90.
69. The Policy Administration Report for the Bombay Presidency, including Sind and the Railways, for the year 1918, 1919.
70. Ramanna, 'Coping with the Influenza Pandemic', p. 89.
71. 'Government Creches for Influenza Orphans', *Indian Social Reformer*, 24 November 1918: 170.
72. Ramanna, 'Coping with the Influenza Pandemic', p. 91.
73. Letter to the Editor, *Times of India*, 4 November 1918, p. 9.

74. Letter to the Editor, *Times of India*, 19 December 1918, p. 5.

75. For a fuller account, see Maura Chhun, 'Death and Disorder: The 1918–19 Influenza Pandemic in British India' (PhD diss., University of Colorado at Boulder, 2015).

76. Letter from George Llyod to Montagu, as cited in Rajnarayan Chandavarkar, *The Origins of Industrial Capitalism in India: Business Strategies and the Working Classes in Bombay, 1900–1940* (Cambridge University Press, 1994), p. 115.

77. 'A desolate picture', *Indian Social Reformer*, 2 March 1919: 341.

78. 'Influenza at Ahmednagar,' *Times of India*, 7 November 1918, p. 5.

79. White, 'A Preliminary Report', p. 12.

80. Ramanna, 'Coping with the Influenza Pandemic', pp. 93–94.

81. Ibid.

82. Ibid., p. 95.

83. Report of the Director of Public Instruction in the Bombay Presidency, 1918–19.

84. Michael O'Dwyer, *India as I Knew It, 1885–1925*, p. 226.

85. Report on the Sanitary Administration of the Punjab and Proceedings of the Sanitary Board for the year 1918 (Govt. Printing, 1919), p. xv.

86. Ibid., p. xv.

87. Ibid., p. xiii.

88. Ibid., p. 1.

89. Thomas P. Herriot, 'The Influenza Pandemic, 1918, as Observed in the Punjab, India' (MD thesis, University of Edinburgh, 1920).

90. Ibid., pp. 4–6.

91. Ibid., p. 6.

92. Ibid., p. 3.

93. Ibid., pp. 5 and 42.

94. Ibid., pp. 10–11.

95. Ibid., p. 20.

96. Ibid., p. 20.

97. Ibid., p. 36.

98. Ibid., pp. 43–44.

99. Ibid., p. 45.

100. Ibid., p. 45.

101. Ibid., p. 50.

102. Punjab Sanitary Board Report, 1918, xi; Ruby Bala, 'The Spread of Influenza Epidemic in the Punjab (1918–1919)', *Proceedings of the Indian History Congress*, 72 (Part 1) (2011): 986–96.

103. Census of India 1921, Vol. XV, Punjab and Delhi, Part I– Report, p. 60.

104. Rob Johnson, 'The Indian Army and Internal Security, 1919–1946', in *The Indian Army in the Two World Wars*, ed. Kaushik Roy (Brill, 2012), p. 363.

105. Bipin Chandra, Mridula Mukherjee, Aditya Mukherjee, Sucheta Mahajan and K.N. Panikkar, *India's Struggle for Independence, 1857–1947* (Viking, 1987), pp. 181–83.

106. Census of India 1921, Vol. XXIV, Rajputana and Ajmer–Merwara, Part I–Report (Calcutta, 1923), p. 16.

107. Archibald Adams, *The Western Rajputana States: A Medico–Topographical and General Account of Marwar, Sirohi and Jaisalmir* (Junior Army & Navy Stores, 1899), pp. 218 and 229.

108. Census of India 1921, 'Rajputana and Ajmer–Merwara,' p. 34.

109. Ibid.

110. Ibid., p. 19.

111. Census of India 1921, Vol. XXII, Kashmir, Part I–Report (Lahore, 1923), p. 13.

112. Ibid.

113. Ibid., p. 14.

114. White, 'A Preliminary Report', p. 7.

115. Ibid.

116. Census of India 1921, Vol. XVI, United Provinces of Agra and Oudh, Part I–Report (Allahabad, 1923), p. 13.

117. White, 'A Preliminary Report', p. 9.

118. Mills, 'The 1918–19 Influenza Pandemic.'

119. White, 'A Preliminary Report', p. 7.

120. As cited in David Arnold, 'Death and the Modern Empire: The 1918–19 Influenza Epidemic in India', *Transactions of the Royal Historical Society*, 29 (2019): 200.

121. White, 'A Preliminary Report', p. 9; Mills, 'The 1918–19 Influenza Pandemic', pp. 35–36.

122. White, 'A Preliminary Report', p. 9.

123. Suryakant Tripathi Nirala, *A Life Misspent* (translated by Satti Khanna, Harper Perennial, 2016), p. 53. The book also has references to the plague on pp. 5, 6 and 50.

124. Ibid., p. 54.

125. In personal conversation with Dr Yogesh Kalkonde.

126. Census of India 1921, Vol. XI, Central Provinces and Berar, Part I–Report (Nagpur, 1923), p. 4.

127. The excess mortality estimates are in the range of 7–8 per cent and correcting for under-registration, it would exceed 10 per cent. The Inspector of Schools in Berar estimated a minimum of 10 per cent of the population to have died from influenza in his circle. Report on the State and Progress of Education in the Central Provinces and Berar for the year 1918–19 (Nagpur, 1919), p. 9.

128. Kenneth Hill, 'Influenza in India 1918: Excess Mortality Reassessed', *Genus* 67 (2) (2011): 24.

129. Census of India 1921, 'Central Provinces & Berar', p. 5.

130. Ibid.

131. Ibid., p. 6.

132. Ibid., p. 5.

133. Report on the Forest Administration of the Central Provinces for the Year 1918–19, pp. 1 and 3.

134. Report on the State and Progress of Education in the Central Provinces and Berar for the year 1918–19 (Nagpur, 1919), p. 9.

135. Ibid., p. 19.

136. Ibid., p. 2.

137. Ibid., p. 26.

138. Census of India 1921, Vol. XXI, Hyderabad, Report (Hyderabad, 1923), p. 6.

139. Ibid., p. 47.

140. Census of India, 1921, Vol. XVIII, Central India Agency, Part I–Report (Calcutta, 1923), p. 5.

141. Weblink: http://www.rewacity.in/p/history.html, accessed on 22 June 2020.

142. Census of India 1921, Vol. II, The Andaman and Nicobar Islands, Part I– Report (Calcutta, 1923), p. 14.

143. Census of India 1921, Vol. II, The Andaman and Nicobar Islands, Part I– Report (Calcutta, 1923), p. 18.

144. David Arnold, 'Looting, Grain Riots and Government Policy in South India 1918', *Past & Present* 84 (1) (1979): 111–45.

145. As cited in T.V. Sekher, 'Public Health Administration in Princely Mysore: Tackling the Influenza Pandemic of 1918', in *India's Princely Sates: People, Princes and Colonialism*, eds. Waltraud Ernst and Biswamoy Pati (Primus Books, 2007), p. 194.

146. Ibid., p. 195.

147. Ibid., p. 198.

148. Ibid.

149. 'Social Work in Mysore', *Indian Social Reformer*, 22 December 1918: 221.

150. 'Mysore Gold Mining Company, Limited', *The Economist*, 12 April 1919: 624.

151. Sekher, 'Public Health Administration', p. 200.

152. Ibid., p. 201; 'Depressed Classes Mission', *The Indian Social Reformer*, 8 December 1918: 195.

153. Nandini Bhattacharya, *Contagion and Enclaves: Tropical Medicine in Colonial India* (Liverpool University Press, 2012), p. 72.

154. Ibid., pp. 125–26.

155. Minutes of the Syndicate for the Year 1919, University of Calcutta, 3 March 1919, p. 356; Also for 22 April 1919, p. 66.

156. Chitra Deb, *Women of the Tagore Household* (translated by Smita Chowdhry and Sona Roy; Penguin, 2010); Krishna Dutta and Andrew Robinson, eds., *Selected Letters of Rabindranath Tagore* (Cambridge University Press, 1997).

157. Christopher Murray, Aland D. Lopez, Brian Chin, Dennis Feehan and Kenneth H. Hill, 'Estimation of Potential Global Pandemic Influenza Mortality on the Basis of Vital Registry Data from the 1918–20

Pandemic: A Quantitative Analysis', *The Lancet*, 368 (December 23/30) (2006): 2211–18.

158. See CT 2020, Section 6.

159. See CT 2020, Section 6.

160. See CT 2020, Sections 1 and 7.

161. The cross country study of Murray et. al., 2006, doesn't find latitude to be a significant variable affecting influenza-related mortality.

162. Annual report of the Sanitary Commissioner with the Government of India for 1918, 1920, pp. 5–6.

163. Ibid., pp. 31–32.

164. White, 'A Preliminary Report,' p. 5.

165. Data from various statistical abstracts of British India.

166. Tahir Andrabi, Sheetal Bharat and Michael Kuehlwein, 'Post Offices and British Indian Grain Price Convergence', *Economic History of Developing Regions*, 35 (1) (2020): 23–49.

167. Census of India 1951, Vol. 1, Part 1–B, Part D, 'Import and Export of Food Grains in Relation to India's Foreign Trade', Government of India, 1955, pp. 311–312.

168. See Census of India 1951, 'Famine and Pestilence', p. 290, for an estimate of the all-India case fatality ratio to be 10 per cent.

169. See CT 2020, Figure 6.5.

170. Annual Progress Report of Forest Administration in United Provinces for the Forest Year, 1918–19, p. 32.

171. Statistical Abstract of British India, 1922–23.

172. Amol Agrawal, 'How India's Banks Navigated the Last Global Pandemic', *Bloomberg Quint*, 19 June 2020.

173. Statistical Abstract of British India, 1922–23.

174. S. Sivasubramonian, *The National Income of India in the Twentieth Century* (Oxford University Press, 2000), Table 6.1; Dwijendra Tripathi, *Oxford History of Indian Business* (Oxford University Press, 2004).

175. Annual Report of the Tata Iron and Steel Company, 1955–56, Appendix Table.

176. As cited in Ramanna, 'Coping with the Influenza Pandemic', p. 98.

177. 'India in 1919', *Indian Annual Register 1920* (Calcutta, 1919): 64.

178. As cited by the *Indian Annual Register 1920* (Calcutta, 1919): 224.

179. Financial Statement of the Government of India, March 1919, p. 107.

180. Samiksha Sehrawat, *Colonial Medical Care in North India: Gender, State and Society, c. 1840–1920* (Oxford University Press, 2013), p. 57.

181. Ibid., p. 59.

182. Ibid., pp. 59–60.

183. Ibid., p. 63.

184. Ibid., p. 31, Figure 2.1.

185. Rajendra Kumar Sen, *A Treatise on Influenza: With Special Reference to the Pandemic of 1918* (Assam, 1923).

186. K. Menon, 'Embelia Ribes: A Medicine for Influenza', *The Indian Forester*, April 1919: 210.

187. Advertisement in the *Times of India*, 25 September 1918; Ramanna, 'Coping with the Influenza Pandemic', p. 97.

188. Austin, 'A Plea for Simplicity in the Prevention and Cure of Bacterial Infection', *Indian Medical Gazette*, September 1919: 334.

189. Ramanna, 'Coping with the Influenza Pandemic', p. 96.

190. Ibid., p. 97.

191. David Arnold, 'Disease, Rumour, and Panic in India's Plague and Influenza Epidemics, 1896–1919', in *Empires of Panic: Epidemics and Colonial Anxieties*, ed. Robert Peckham (Hong Kong University Press, 2015), p. 123.

192. Census of India 1921, 'Rajputana and Ajmer–Merwara', p. 244.

193. Based on an analysis of ProQuest Historical Newspapers: The Times of India Digital Database.

194. See also Sumit Sarkar, *Modern India, 1885–1947* (Pearson, 2014), p. 152, on influenza as one of the factors causing popular distress.

195. Nandini Bhattacharya, *Contagion and Enclaves*, p. 126, on north Bengal; 'Seaforth Plantations', *Financial Times*, 4 March 1919.

196. Report of the Royal Commission on Labour in India, 1931, pp. 21 and 333.

197. Statistical Abstract of British India, 1924.

198. Statistical Abstract of British India for 1922–23 to 1931–32, 1935, Table No. 161.

199. Based on an analysis of ProQuest Historical Newspapers: The Times of India Digital Database.

200. James Fenske, Bishnupriya Gupta and Song Yuan, 'Demographic Shocks and Women's Labor Market Participation: Evidence from the 1918 Influenza Pandemic in India', *Warwick Economics Research Papers*, No. 1286 (2020).

201. Based on the analysis of the database constructed for this paper: Chinmay Tumbe, 'Urbanization, Demographic Transition and the Growth of Cities in India, 1870–2020', 2016, *International Growth Centre Working Paper*, C-35205-INC-1.

202. Afkhami, 'Compromised Constitutions.'

203. Ibid., pp. 367 and 372.

204. Ibid., p. 377.

205. Ibid., p. 380, as cited therein.

206. Killingray, 'A New "Imperial" Disease', p. 36; Howard Phillips, *In a Time of Plague: Memories of the 'Spanish' Flu Epidemic of 1918 in South Africa* (Van Riebeeck Society, 2018).

207. Killingray, 'A New "Imperial" Disease', p. 35.

208. Ryan M. Alexander, 'The Spanish Flu and the Sanitary Dictatorship: Mexico's Response to the 1918 Influenza Pandemic', *The Americas*, 76 (3) (2019): 443–65.

209. Christopher Langford, 'Did the 1918–19 Influenza Pandemic Originate in China?', *Population and Development Review*, 31 (3) (2005): 473–505.

210. Geoffrey W. Rice and Edwina Palmer, 'Pandemic Influenza in Japan, 1918–19: Mortality Patterns and Official Responses', *Journal of Japanese Studies*, 19 (2) (1993): 389–420.

211. 'Crown Prince of Siam', *Times of India*, 16 June 1920, p. 9.

212. Kolata, *Flu*, pp. 22–23.

213. Ibid.

214. As cited in Phillips and Killingray, 'Introduction', p. 17.

215. Alisha Gupta, 'How the Spanish Flu Almost Upended Women's Suffrage', *New York Times*, 28 April 2020.

216. Douglas Almond, 'Is the 1918 Influenza Pandemic Over? Long-Term Effects of *In Utero* Influenza Exposure in the Post-1940 U.S. Population', *Journal of Political Economy*, 114 (4) (2006): 672–712.

217. Sebastian Vollmer and Juditha Wojcik, 'The Long-Term Consequences of the Global 1918 Influenza Pandemic: A Systematic Analysis of 117 IPUMS International Census Data Sets', *CINCH Series* # 2017/08.

218. Killingray, 'A New "Imperial" Disease', pp. 30–49. See also, Niall Johnson, *Britain and the 1918–19 Influenza Pandemic: A Dark Epilogue* (Routledge, 2006).

219. Ibid., p. 40.

220. Barro, Ursua and Weng, 'The Coronavirus and the Great Influenza Epidemic', Tables 1 and 2.

221. Lucy Taksa, 'The Masked Disease: Oral History, Memory and the Influenza Pandemic, 1918–19', in *Memory and History in Twentieth-Century Australia*, eds. Kate Darian-Smith and Paula Hamilton (Oxford University Press, 1994), p. 83.

222. Ibid., p. 88.

223. Ibid., p. 87.

224. White, 'Retrospect', pp. 441–43.

225. Taksa, 'The Masked Disease', pp. 86–87; Afkhami, 'Compromised Constitutions', p. 376; Killingray, 'A New "Imperial" Disease', pp. 34–37.

226. White, 'A Preliminary Report', p. 7.

227. Valuable research work has been done by Kingsley Davis, I.D. Mills, Mridula Ramanna, T.V. Sekher, Siddharth Chandra and Chandra's many co–authors, Kenneth Hill, Wakimura, Ruby Bala, David Hardiman, David Arnold and Maura Chhun, as the references of this chapter suggest. A debate on surplus labour in India between Amartya Sen and Theodore Schultz in *The Economic Journal* in 1967 also revolves around the 1918 influenza pandemic. Almost all of this work has, however, missed out the princely states, which suffered greatly in the pandemic.

228. For instance, John Barry, *The Great Influenza: The Story of the Deadliest Pandemic in History* (Viking, 2004), pp. 364–65, has only a couple of paragraphs on India, mentioning Bombay, Delhi and Punjab.

229. David Arnold, 'Death and the Modern Empire: The 1918–19 Influenza Epidemic in India', *Transactions of the Royal Historical Society,* 29 (2019): 181–200.

230. Taksa, 'The Masked Disease', pp. 77–91.

231. Chinmay Tumbe, *Migration and Remittances in India: Historical, Regional, Social and Economic Dimensions* (PhD diss., Indian Institute of Management Bangalore, 2012) contains inter-censal population growth rate maps at the district level in the jurisdiction boundaries of 2001 for the period 1901–2011.

232. B.G. Vad, 'Flu Epidemic', *Times of India*, 22 May 1957.

233. Anna Jones, 'Coronavirus: How "overreaction" made Vietnam a virus success', *BBC News Online*, 15 May, 2020.

5: COVID-19 in the Rear-view Mirror

1. Kautilya, *The Arthashastra,* ed. L.N. Rangarajan (Penguin, 1987), p. 360.

2. Andrew Green, 'Obituary of Li Wenliang', *The Lancet,* Vol. 395, February 29, 2020: 682.

3. Ibid.

4. Ibid.

5. Fang Fang, *Wuhan Diary: Dispatches from a Quarantined City* (translated by Michael Berry; Harper Collins, 2020); Hemant Adlakha, 'Fang Fang', *The Diplomat*, 23 March 2020.

6. WHO website: https://www.who.int/csr/don/05–january–2020–pneumonia–of–unkown–cause–china/en/, last accessed on 5 August 2020.

7. As cited in Christopher Hamlin, *Cholera* (Oxford University Press, 2009), p. 137.

8. Niall Johnson, *Britain and the 1918–19 Influenza Pandemic: A Dark Epilogue* (Routledge, 2006), p. 160.

9. S.L. Kotar and J.E. Gessler, *Cholera: A Worldwide History* (McFarland & Company, 2014), p. 296.

10. Tsuneishi Keiichi, 'Unit 731 and the Japanese Imperial Army's Biological Warfare Program', in *Japan's Wartime Medical Atrocities*, eds. J.N. Nie, N. Guo, M. Selden and A. Kleinman (Routledge, 2010), pp. 23–31.

11. Massimo Pulejo and Pablo Querubin, 'Electoral Concerns Reduce Restrictive Measures During the COVID-19 Pandemic', *NBER Working Paper No. 27498*, July 2020.

12. Robert Barro, Jose Ursua and Joanna Weng, 'The Coronavirus and the Great Influenza Epidemic: Lessons from the "Spanish Flu" for the coronavirus' potential effects on mortality and economic activity', *American Enterprise Institute Economics Working Paper, 2020–02* (March 2020).

13. Kautilya, *The Arthashastra*, p. 130.

14. Ibid., p. 116.

15. The quote is credited to Edward Abbey (1927–1989).

16. R. Nathan, *The Plague in India, 1896, 1897* (Simla, 1898), p. 293.

17. Ibid.

18. Maggie Hiufu Won, '3 Billion Journeys: World's Biggest Human Migration in China', CNN Travel, 10 January 2020.

19. The Economic Survey of India, 2016–17, Chapter 12, and the 2017 Report of the Working Group on Migration by the Ministry of Housing and Urban Poverty Alleviation.

20. Chinmay Tumbe, 'In times of a lockdown, support migrant workers', *Hindustan Times*, 26 March 2020. At least in Ahmedabad, after the thirtieth of the month, the attitude shifted from 'nobody cares' to considerable compassion for the migrant.

21. Evan Stark, 'The Epidemic as a Social Event', *International Journal of Health Services*, 7 (4) (1977): 681–705.

22. Ibid.

23. Attributed to the historian Charles Rosenberg, as cited by Mark Harrison, 'A Dreadful Scourge: Cholera in Early Nineteenth-Century India', *Modern Asian Studies*, 54 (2) (2020): 505.

24. 'Covid-19 is not health emergency, no need to panic: Health Ministry', *The Hindu*, 13 March 2020.

25. Joshua Lederberg, 'Pandemic as a Natural Evolutionary Phenomenon', *Social Research*, 55 (3) (1988): 351.

26. Arnab Mitra, 'After 33 Failed Attempts, 51-year old clears SSC exams; thanks Coronavirus', *Indian Express*, 31 July 2020.

27. Lederberg, 'Pandemic as a Natural Evolutionary Phenomenon', p. 343.

28. Sohini Chattopadhyay, 'What researching cremations of the dead in colonial India taught me about life in our cities today', *Scroll*, 23 August 2020.

Index

About the Author

Chinmay Tumbe loves to laugh and learn. He is passionate about migration, cities and history, and is currently a faculty member at the Indian Institute of Management Ahmedabad. An alumnus of the London School of Economics and Political Science; the Indian Institute of Management Bangalore; Ruia College, Mumbai; and Rishi Valley School, Madanapalle, he has been a faculty member at the Tata Institute of Social Sciences, Hyderabad. He was a 2013 Jean Monnet Fellow at the European University Institute, Florence, and the 2018 Alfred D. Chandler Jr. International Visiting Scholar in Business History at Harvard Business School, Boston. His first book, *India Moving: A History of Migration*, was published in 2018.